THE UNKNOWN PATTON

Patton at the wheel of a launch on the Kammersee, Austria, May 1945.

THE UNKNOWN PATTON

Charles M. Province

BONANZA BOOKS
New York

The author gratefully acknowledges the use of material taken
from The Associated Press, United Press International and for
permission granted to use material from *The Patton Papers* and
other books published by Houghton Mifflin Company.

This 1984 edition is published by Bonanza Books, distributed
by Crown Publishers, Inc., by arrangement with Hippocrene
Books, Inc.

Manufactured in the United States of America.

Library of Congress Cataloging in Publication Data

Province, Charles M.
    The unknown Patton.

    Bibliography: p.
    1. Patton, George S. (George Smith), 1885–1945.
2. Generals—United States—Biography. 3. United States. Army—
Biography. 4. United States—History, Military—20th century.
I. Title.
E745.P3P76   1984   940.54′1′0924 [B]   84-14483
ISBN 0-517-455951

h g f e d c b a

*This book is dedicated to
Lacy Monet-Duvalier Province and Michelle Dawn Province
and my father, even though he lied to me.*

Contents

(Illustration section follows page 118.)

Introduction

Although this book contains a good deal of biographical information concerning General Patton, it is not a biography. The general scope of the work is twofold: to distinguish and assess some of the major controversies that arose in regard to Patton, and to bring to light some interesting information about that unusual man that has not been previously brought to public attention.

It will be noticed that the book contains no footnotes or formal references. The attempt has been to create a simple, readable text that could be easily absorbed without forcing the reader to halt at intervals to check a reference, and so disturb continuity and concentration. Although there are no notes, exhaustive research was undertaken for the book. The Appendix gives a list of sources consulted.

Not all source material has been reproduced literally in the form of direct quotation nor even utilized as textual content; it served primarily as background for the author's guidance, to supply a feeling for and an understanding of a situation prior to writing about it.

To add a sense of currency, and also to evoke the atmosphere of past events for the reader, each chapter is followed with a ***NEWS ITEM***. These are actual wire service stories that were carried in American newspapers during the Second World War.

The final chapter, "The Secret of Victory." was included because it was written by Patton as a succinct compilation of his views about leadership and warfare. It was written in 1926 where Patton was a Major, and it is significant in that the attitude expressed in the essay differs little, if at all, from his WWII approach to combat after a lapse of 16 years. The chapter demonstrates the consistency—and in the author's view the reliability—of Patton's judgment of military matters.

The illustrations include photographs of General Patton and of Patton memorabilia drawn from the collection of the Patton Society.

C.M.P.

THE UNKNOWN
PATTON

Early Years

Many influences in the early life of General George S. Patton, Jr., contributed to making him the great military leader that he became. Patton had a long heritage of war and military distinction. His father had lived through the Civil War and had vivid memories of the Confederacy. In the Patton home, there were many mementos of that war, ranging from steel engravings of General Lee and Stonewall Jackson to the shell fragment that was taken from the lifeless body of the first George Patton. In a recent interview, Patton's daughter, Ruth Ellen Patton Totten, recalled: "Until he was 15 years old, my father thought those steel engravings were of God and Jesus Christ."

One of the senior Patton's best friends was Colonel John Mosby, the fabled "Grey Ghost" of J.E.B. Stuart's legendary cavalry. During visits to the Patton Ranch in Southern California, Colonel Mosby would re-enact the Civil War with George, Junior; playing himself, he let George play the part of General Lee as they evoked the battles of the war, astride their horses.

Although young George was called "Junior," he was actually the third to bear the name George Smith Patton. The first Patton was killed in the Civil War at the Battle of Winchester at the age of 26. He was commanding the 22nd Virginia Regiment in the Shenandoah Valley. Walter Taswell Patton, a brother of the first George Patton, was killed at Gettysburg while leading a regiment under the command of Major General George E. Pickett.

These brothers were two of the eight sons of John Mercer Patton. Six of those sons fought for the Confederate States of America. The other two remained at home only because they were not yet in their teens.

The Patton family origins have been traced to Scotland in the 18th century. They go back to a mysterious event that forced a young man to flee his native city of Aberdeen, from which he eventually made his way to Fredericksburg, Virginia, during the Revolutionary turmoil of the 1770's. The young man's real name was lost after his departure from Scotland. He probably had reason to obscure it in order to prevent the authorities from tracking him down in the New World. He traveled under the assumed name of "Robert Patton." He became rich and respectable in the Colonies and married Anna Gordon Mercer, the only daughter of Dr. Hugh Mercer, a physician who served as an army surgeon with Colonel George Washington in the Braddock Expedition against Fort Duquesne in 1756. General Mercer was later Surgeon-General in the Revolutionary War of Independence.

Robert Patton and Anna Mercer Patton were the parents of John Mercer Patton. John Patton married Margaret French Williams. One of the sons of John and Margaret was the first George Smith Patton.

It has been claimed by some members of the Patton family that the family roots have been traced so far back in history as to include sixteen of the signers of Magna Charta. There is also a branch of the family that is related to George Washington by way of his uncle, John Washington.

The first George Patton was buried as a Brigadier General, survived by his wife, two sons, and a daughter. She was later remarried, to a Colonel George H. Smith. Colonel Smith and his newly acquired family set out for California shortly after the Civil War was ended.

In California, there was a man known as "Don Benito" Wilson. His real name was Benjamin Davis Wilson, and he was one of the earliest pioneers in the Mexican territory of Alta California.

Wilson, an ex-Tennessean, had operated his own trading post when only 15 years of age, trading with the Choctaws and Chickasaws near Vicksburg, Mississippi. Later he was a trapper for the Rocky Mountain Fur Company, and during that time, he was captured by and escaped from the Apaches in New Mexico. He survived a wound inflicted by a poison arrow in an encounter with a band of marauding California Indians; he decided to settle in California in 1841. He had originally planned to go to China, but when he arrived in the village of Los Angeles, there was no ship, so he stayed where he was.

Wilson was highly respected in California. Aside from being wealthy and a member of the "aristocracy" of the region, he was known as a savage fighter. He was not a man to cross. He once returned from a raid on some Indians carrying baskets filled with the heads of the enemy.

There is a story told about Don Benito's lending $5000 to Colonel Claus Spreckles, the "Sugar Baron" of San Diego. Wilson, a man of honor, asked only a handshake to seal the bargain, in lieu of a promissory note. When Wilson later requested payment of the loan, he was told that since he had no legal paper requiring re-payment of the debt, he would not be repaid. He then buckled his gunbelt around his waist, entered the office of Spreckles and asked Spreckles' secretary if he had ever seen a man die. When the man said, "No," Wilson said, "Young man, you have never seen death? Well, then, wait about one minute." There was no death that day, but the debt was quickly paid.

It was Wilson who was responsible for the start of the citrus industry in California. He also experimented with the farming of sugar cane, and he planted some of the first vinyards for fine wines.

He was an Indian agent who was among the first to advocate rights for the displaced Indians, feeling strongly that it was the Indian who needed protection from the white man rather than the other way.

He was Alcalde of the "Pueblo de Nuestra Señora la Reina de Los Angles de Parciuncula" when it was Mexican, and then Mayor of Los Angeles when it became United States territory; he also served three terms as a California State Senator.

Contrary to the popular belief that Mount Wilson in California was named for President Wilson, it was actually named in honor of Benjamin D. Wilson after his death. It was Wilson who made the first trek up the mountain and built a useable road around its slopes.

After Wilson had settled in California, he married Ramona Yorba, the daughter of Don Bernardo Yorba, a prominant Mexican "don" and *ranchero*.

Ramona later died, and Wilson married Margaret S. Hereford of Los Angeles.

It was a daughter of that union, Ruth Wilson, who married

George Patton, the son of the Civil War commander. George and Ruth were the parents of George Smith Patton, Jr., the future Commanding General of the Third Army. He was born on November 11, 1885.

Patton was reared on his father's ranch. He learned to hunt, fish, sail, and be a skilled horseman during the years when other children were learning to read from a "McGuffy's Reader."

Recently, there has been much discussion and speculation about the fact that Patton did not begin his formal education until the age of 11. It has been claimed that Patton's parents kept him out of school because he suffered from a disorder known today as "dyslexia," which is a motor disfunction of the eye and the brain, causing a transposition of letters when reading or writing. Such a disability makes learning to read and write much more difficult than it normally is. But there is no way of proving that claim. Although Patton was a terrible speller throughout his lifetime, he did not show any signs of a writing problem caused by dyslexia. And if the claim of dyslexia were correct, it would only add to the admiration that should be felt for Patton. To overcome such a handicap and complete the rigorous study that he accomplished, as well as to become the fluent writer and stylist that he was, would have been in itself marvelous feats of willpower. Again, at the time of his death, Patton had one of the most comprehensive military libraries in private hands. It rivaled even the collections of military institutions. And each volume had not merely been read— it was studied. Virtually all the books in his library contain notes and remarks in the margins. A volume that Patton especially liked, which was written by one of his favorite military theorists, General J.F.C. Fuller, not only had profuse marginal notes, but Patton later formalized additional observations on the book, and these amounted to seven typewritten, single-spaced pages.

There is, moreover, one view that makes the dyslexia claim particularly suspect. In his biography of General Patton, General Harry H. Semmes, a longtime friend of Patton, states: "His father's theory of education consisted almost entirely of the child's being read to by his elders. It was founded on the belief that the youthful mind should be led along a path that parallels the development of the mind of the race. The books should be read aloud to the child until his early teens, because his ability to absorb by ear is far greater than his ability to read, and the rhythm and beauty of sound adds a great deal to the pleasure. Under this theory of education, the child would find his proper channel, his true interest. Young George never cared greatly for any of this program except the legends, the epics, and heroics. He found there his true interest. At the age of seven, he could repeat whole pages of Pope's translation of The Iliad."

Further evidence is that Patton's sister was educated in the same manner as was the future general. It is doubtful that both she and her brother would suffer from the same disorder.

At any rate, it must have been an interesting situation at Stephen Cutter Clark's Classical School for Boys in Pasadena when Patton was initially enrolled for classes. Though he could neither read nor write, he could quote long passages out of works that other students had not yet read, but there his capabilities ended. He was at home in the world of great ideas, but at first he could not turn out a theme or cope with arithmetic.

From Clark's school, Patton went on to Pasadena High School, and upon being graduated, he spent a year at the Virginia Military Institute in preparation for West Point. The Senior Patton had himself been a graduate of VMI.

Patton took five years to be graduated from West Point because of having failed a French examination by a fraction of a point. By some obscure technicality, the failure in French necessitated an additional test in mathematics. He passed the French examination, his original stumbling block, but failed the second mathematics examination, again by a fraction of a point. Luckily, he had shown abilities in other areas. In addition to his exemplary military deportment he had displayed great desire. He was "allowed" to re-enter West Point, and to repeat his plebe year.

While at West Point, he fractured both his arms while playing football, but he won his coveted Army letter by breaking a record in a track event, the 220 yard low hurdles.

II

A phenomenon among historians is the ability to encapsulize a person's life. Patton has been the subject of several first-rate biographies and others which are less than good. His WWII service has been portrayed in a two-hour motion picture. His entire life and military career has been the subject of a number of thirty-minute documentaries. Even this book suffers from the disease of time and space. For that reason, quite often Patton is remembered as "the general who slapped a soldier" or a "tank general in WWII," thereby encompassing his whole life and career of sixty years in a single phrase or sentence.

Patton certainly did more than just serve in WWII or slap a soldier.

His first post was Fort Sheridan, Illinois, when the cavalry was still glamorous. He was the Army's first "Master of the Sword," a position which required him to re-write the cavalry training regulations for the Army. He redesigned the Army's cavalry saber in 1913, changing it from what he called a "curved hacking tool" into a straight-bladed attack weapon. While stationed at Fort Sheridan, Patton acquired his first nickname, "Saber George."

In 1912, Patton placed fifth in the Military Olympics at Stockholm, Sweden. Out of 5 events, he placed second in swimming; third in cross-country riding; first in fencing—having handed the French champion his only defeat; and he finished twenty-seventh in pistol shooting. Had it not been for his poor showing in the pistol competition, he probably would have finished first in the pentathlon instead of fifth as he did.

The probable reason for his poor score in pistol shooting was the weapon he used. Because the events in which he competed were a "military pentathlon," Patton insisted on using a regulation military firearm, a .38 caliber revolver. There were no requirements as to what pistol had to be used, and the other entrants chose to use .22 caliber weapons. In the previous day's practice, Patton had set a world record. On the day of the actual competition, Patton shot almost all ten's and two nine's. The problem arose when the judges called a "complete miss."

Because of the relatively large .38 caliber bullets he was

firing, Patton had almost torn out the center "bulls-eye" with his scores of 10. What must have happened was that a bullet had gone through the torn area without leaving a complete hole for the judges to witness. Even his competitors admitted this to be so, but there weren't available then the exacting measuring devices we have now, and the judges could only score the firing as they saw it—a "miss," as difficult as it was to believe that.

After WWII, Patton took a short leave and visited Sweden, where he met with some of his old competitors. During a "rematch," he scored much higher than he had in 1912.

After the 1912 Olympics, Patton returned home, waiting for a "good war." He went to Mexico in 1916 with General Pershing and, as recounted in the next chapter, ushered in the "age of motorized warfare" while killing three of Pancho Villa's followers.

He served in WWI initially on Pershing's staff and then he almost singlehandedly created the American Tank Corps. He was severely wounded in combat and almost died from loss of blood. For his performance during the Great War he received the Distinguished Service Cross, the Distinguished Service Medal, and the Purple Heart.

The years between WWI and WWII were spent in unceasing military study, polo playing, and tank study. In 1932 he commanded troops at the "Bonus War" in Washington, D.C. He taught himself navigation, then bought and sailed his own schooner, the *Arcturus*. He learned to fly, then bought and flew his own Stinson Reliant airplane.

He was injured severely in accidents at least three times, and came close to death twice because of embolisms. It was an embolism which finally killed him after he had been paralyzed because of an automobile accident in 1945.

He was awarded the Congressional Lifesaving Medal for saving the lives of three boys off Salem Bay, Massachusetts. The boys had overturned their small boat during a heavy squall, and while his wife Beatrice sailed the Pattons' sloop, tacking back and forth, George swam three times through the choppy waters, towing the boys to safety.

Patton was not just a remarkable man; he was a remarkable man who lived his life to the fullest. His was a life filled to the brim with excitement, adventure, and danger; he enjoyed it all. In the words of Kipling, he "...filled the unforgiving minute with 60 seconds worth of distance run."

★★★ NEWS ITEM ★★★

PATTON SECOND YANK GIVEN VERDUN MEDAL; PERSHING ONLY OTHER

Metz, France, Nov. 25 (AP)

General George S. Patton, former U.S. Third Army Commander, today received the Medal of Verdun, an honor accorded to only one other American, General of the Armies John J. Pershing. The award was part of the military and civil ceremonies celebrating the first anniversary of the Third Army's liberation of Metz and surrounding towns.

Patton was made an honorary citizen of Metz, Thionville, Toul, Verdun, Sarreguemines, and the city of Luxembourg. The U.S. Twentieth Corps Commander, Lt. Gen. Walton H. Walker, was made an honorary citizen of Thionville.

General Walker gave a cowboy hat to the Mayor of Metz, in the name of the City of Dallas, Texas.

Motorized Warfare in Mexico

George S. Patton and Winston Churchill had more in common than the fact that both were great men.

In the year 1898, Winston Churchill joined Sir Herbert Kitchener's Twenty-first Lancers. The Regiment was stationed in Cairo, Egypt, prior to beginning a trek up the Nile River on their way to Omdurman, the Dervish capital of the Sudan. Kitchener expected a decisive battle to be fought there. Churchill had reached the battlefront just in time to participate in what is considered to be one of the very last "classic" cavalry charges in history. With thundering hoofs, kicking up clouds of dust, he galloped at the command of "Charge Sabers" to smash headlong into a waiting line of some 3,000 Dervish troops.

Conversly, in 1916, Patton was the officer in charge of the world's first "motorized" military action.

Benedict Crowell, assistant Secretary of War in 1919, submitted an official report in which he stated: "The Punitive Expedition into Mexico in 1916 in pursuit of Francisco Villa marked the real beginning of the use of motor transportation for the Army, although for many years the motor truck had received some attention for military purposes."

Setting the stage for the future daring battle actions of a commander who blazed a Sherman-like path across Europe in WWII, a young hell-for-leather Lieutenant by the name of George S. Patton, Jr., made military history in this same punitive expedition. The following is the story of Patton's courageous attack on an enemy stronghold. It made history because it was the very first instance on record of a motorcar being used in an actual combat situation by the American Army.

Lieutenant Patton was officially assigned to the 10th Cavalry, but he had been attached to Troop H of the 11th Cavalry as an Aide de Camp to General Pershing.

During the first week of May in 1916, troops had been deployed in an attempt to locate Julio Cárdenas. Cárdenas was Captain of the "Dorados," the bodyguard of Francisco Villa. In accordance with Mexican Revolutionary decorum, he called himself "General" Cárdenas.

West of the town of Rubio, near Lake Itascate, the 16th Infantry detachment met with Patton and his troop of cavalry. Patton was informed of the existence of a small ranch nearby called San Miguelito, where the wife and mother of Cárdenas were reported to be living.

Patton led his troop to the ranch and spent a few hours there in reconnaissance. He familiarized himself with the area, the location of the hacienda, corral, fences, and gates.

The following week, on May 14th, to be exact, Pershing was made cognizant of a shortage of corn, which was the staple food for the soldiers in the expedition.

Pershing directed Patton to take three Dodge Touring cars to nearby haciendas in order in purchase the needed supplies of corn.

With Patton went one corporal, six privates, and a civilian named Lunt. Mr. Lunt was the interpreter for the group.

The first and second stops made were at Las Cayotes and Rubio. Neither place had adequate supplies of corn, so the party continued to Las Cíenegas. Patton, knowing that Cárdenas was headquartered there, surrounded the village just in case the Mexican might be there. Unfortunately, only corn was found at Las Cíenegas.

The trip to Las Cíenegas was not a total loss, however. A man to whom Patton had spoken had somehow aroused Patton's suspicions that Cárdenas might be at the San Miguelito hacienda. Patton decided to visit the rancho, which was located some six or eight miles to the north. Recent reports had indicated that Cárdenas might have as many as twenty men with him, so Patton felt he should investigate cautiously.

Lieutenant Patton halted his automobiles on the reverse slope of a hill about a mile from the hacienda. Taking the leading automobile, Lunt, one soldier, and the driver, Patton ordered the rest of the party to remain hidden.

Patton was to pass the house and stop at the northwest corner. The soldier and driver were to remain with the automobile to cover the west and north sides of the house. Patton and Lunt would go around the north side toward the front.

The second and third automobiles were to halt at the southwest corner. Six of the men were ordered to cover the west and the south sides. Two of them were to move around the south side to meet Patton in front of the east face of the hacienda.

The corporal remained with the group at the automobiles, and the order was for them to join the others in the event of any serious fighting.

Since Patton had been to the hacienda previously, he knew where he was going and he quickly left Lunt and the other soldiers behind.

Arriving at the east face, Patton saw an old man and a young boy near the fence in front of the gate, skinning a steer.

It was only a moment before Patton saw three horsemen emerge from the hacienda. They were armed with rifles and pistols. Catching sight of Patton, they wheeled their mounts and made for the southeast corner of the rancho. Upon arriving there, they encountered the other soldiers advancing from the south.

Patton held his fire. Pershing had gone into Mexico with explicit orders that his men were not to "initiate" any action, that is to say, attack the enemy. They could, however, defend themselves if they were fired upon.

The Mexican General and his two men had turned their horses again, heading north. Apparently they thought that they would have a much better chance against the lone figure of Patton. They had no way of knowing that they would be going against one of the finest marksmen in the United States Army, perhaps in the world. For Patton had, as was previously mentioned set a world's record at the Olympics at Stockholm during practice for the pistol competition in 1912.

At a distance of about twenty yards, the Mexicans opened fire on Patton. Patton returned the fire with a deliberate 5 rounds. One of the rounds hit the lead rider and broke his arm. Another round went into the belly of the horse he was riding.

By this time, the other American soldiers had made their way around the corner and had started shooting. Patton ducked back around the corner to get out of their line of fire. Patton reloaded his single-action Colt.

The other two riders galloped by him at a range of ten paces, firing at and missing both Patton and Lunt.

Patton returned the fire, hitting the nearest Mexican's horse, which fell on the rider. Patton actually waited for the man to extricate himself from underneath the animal. When he was free and he rose to fire at Patton, Patton killed him with one shot.

The third Mexican swerved his horse to the right and galloped to the east. Patton and two other soldiers opened up at the fleeing horseman.

Mr. Lunt, being a civilian, was unarmed. He could not join in the shooting, and was, indeed, happy that he was with Lieutenant Patton.

More gunfire was heard from the southeast corner where the corporal and three men were posted. The first man that Patton had wounded was running along the south wall. With all of the Americans firing at him, he returned the fire. He then stopped shooting. When he was approached, he raised his left arm, apparently in surrender.

He then drew his pistol with his right hand, fired once, and crumpled to the ground, dead.

It was found upon examination that he had been hit only once. Patton's Colt .45 had put a bullet through his left forearm and into his chest. He was the first one shot, the last to die, and he was identified as Cárdenas.

The second was named Juan Gaza. The third man was never identified.

The old "life goes on" adage was exemplified by the actions of the old man and the young boy. All through the gun battle they had quietly continued to skin the steer on which they had been working. It speaks volumes for the discipline and courage of the American soldiers that they did not fire at them, as well as the others.

After securing the roof of the hacienda, Patton entered the front door and searched the premises for any other armed enemy. No one was present except women and children.

The three dead Villistas were then strapped across the fenders of the Dodge Touring cars. As a precaution, the telephone lines into the town of Rubio were cut. Although the town was filled with Villa sympathizers, and the sight of the dead Mexicans caused much excitement, the party of Americans made it through without incident.

Patton reached camp and he interrupted Pershing in a meeting. Pershing was furious until he saw the three bodies that Patton had placed in front of Pershing's tent. From then on, Pershing referred to Patton as his "Bandit."

When the wire services picked up the story, Patton was an immediate national hero. His adventure was the only exciting action to come out of the entire Punitive Expedition.

Oddly enough, the only other interesting occurrence in the Expedition also involved Patton. He had accompanied some troopers during the capture of another Villista named Pedro Lugán. Much to Patton's disappointment there were no gunfights involved in this affair.

In a letter to Beatrice dated May 17, 1916, Patton wrote: ". . .you are probably wondering if my conscience hurts me for killing a man. It does not. I feel about it just as I did when I got my first swordfish; surprised at my luck."

Most certainly not troubled by his conscience, he carved two notches into the left "Eagle" grip of his Colt .45. He was now a blooded soldier and proud of it.

With the exception of the Cárdenas Affair and the Lugán capture, Patton was bored with the monotony of the overall expedition.

His adventures, though, were enough to make up his mind that Field Operations was the place for him. That was definitely where the action would be, if there ever was any.

To help break the monotony he did manage to exercize his keen sense of humor.

In a postscript in a letter to a friend dated August 28, 1916, Patton wrote, "There are some officers here very much interested in the Indian Ruins. They talk very learnedly about them. So yesterday I took some one-cent pieces and beat them upon a rock. Then I hid them in a ruin; they were soon found and caused great excitement. Fancy the men of the stone-age using money. You will see it in the next *Scientific American* or *National Geographic*. I enclose one of the coins which I made."

It was reported to U.S. newspapers by one correspondent that at the end of the gunfight at San Miguelito, Patton said, "The motorcar is the modern warhorse." Unless that story is wholly apochryphal, then with that pronouncement, Patton officially ushered motorization into warfare.

★★★ NEWS ITEM ★★★

MAN AT WORK

New York, July 15 (UP)

In Sicily, Messerschmitts circled a nearby hill, but Technical Sergeant Richard Redding, stringing wire atop a telephone pole and a perfect target, worked on. Someone yelled up from below, "What are you doing up that pole?"

"Working," said Redding, too engrossed to glance down.

"How long you been there?"

"About 20 minutes."

"Don't the planes bother you?"

"Hell, no—but you do!"

At the foot of the pole, Lieutenant General George S. Patton, Jr., who had been doing the yelling, kept his peace.

Beatrice

On Thursday, May 26, 1910, a lovely Spring day, Beatrice Ayer and George Patton were married at Beverly Farms Episcopal Church near Boston, Massachusetts. Both of their daughters would also be married in the same gothic church years later.

Beatrice, the daughter of Frederick Ayer of Boston, who was owner of the American Woolen Company, could have done much better than George Patton, a shavetail career soldier just two years out of West Point. At least that was the consensus among many family friends.

Luckily, "doing better" never occurred to Beatrice. She loved Lieutenant Patton and he loved her. They were devoted to each other.

Hardly anything has ever been written about Mrs. Patton or about the Patton marriage. Yet it well deserves more than just a few lines. It deserves a chapter of its own.

The Patton marriage was not like so many present-day marriages, which seem to be based negatively upon a pre-nuptial contract deciding who gets what if the marriage breaks up. The Pattons began their marriage with a foundation of love, trust, and devotion. When they vowed to love, honor, and obey, they both meant every word of it.

Beatrice and George met for the first time when they were children. Beatrice had been visiting with relatives, the Bannings, on Catalina Island. The Pattons, friends of the Bannings, were also on the island. George was a tall, slim boy of 14. Bea was still a child carrying around a doll which was almost as large as she was. Beatrice would follow George wherever he went, always at his heels. When she was 13 years old, Beatrice decided that she would either marry George or become an old maid.

About three years later, when Beatrice was noticeably more "grown up," George realized what Beatrice had known all along. They were destined to be with each other. As a member of the Patton family said later, "Neither of them ever had another sweetheart."

Even before they were married, while George was at West Point, he entered in his diary, "Should a man get married, he must be just as careful to keep his wife's love as he was to get it. He must always love her and never adopt the attitude of now that I've got you, I can take you for granted. Don't do that, ever."

After George's graduation from West Point, he visited Catalina Island again when Beatrice was at the Bannings' home. He galloped his steed up the front steps onto the porch, jumped off, bowed deeply with a sweep of his hat, and at Beatrice's feet asked her hand in marriage.

Beatrice was not just in love with George, she was wholeheartedly devoted to him. She made up her mind quickly that she would be a true "soldier's wife," dedicating her life to him and his career. Very early on she realized his desire to achieve greatness.

One of the reasons that he had to be great was because of Beatrice. He had to prove to her that he was worthy of her love since she deserved a man who could achieve the highest ambition.

Knowing full well how important her attitude was in its effect on George's career, she once remarked, "There is no career except that of a minister's wife in which a woman can be such a help, or such a detriment, to her husband as that of an Army wife. She lives practically at his place of business and sees his associates daily. Her reputation begins at her first post and sticks to her as closely as her skin until she dies. I have known several able officers to be ruined absolutely by malicious, gossipy wives.

"I joined the Army in 1910, in the piping times of peace. But the older women knew. Before my first child was born I had seen my husband's bedding roll at the front door, ready to leave if the regiment went to Mexico. Since then I have seen him off to three wars. He has led troops in battle, he has been gravely wounded, and he has been decorated for extraordinary heroism. Now I belong to the older generation of Army women who preach, 'Be happy today, who knows what tomorrow may bring.'"

A great deal is said in Beatrice's "Be happy today." One of the truths that must be faced as an Army wife is that when a husband leaves, he may never return. What did Beatrice think of the "Farewells of Wartime"?

She confided, "They are the ones that must be said bravely and cheerfully, though they're the hardest of all to say. The thing is actually not to say goodbye at all. You are just sort of casual about it. After all, the only important thing is how he feels. How you send him away. You can say, 'I love you' and 'I'll miss you,' but it's not fair to cry or to make a scene. It's too tough on the man who's going.' "

With regard to love and what it is, Beatrice's feelings were: "Of course, young people don't believe older ones can really be in love. They think love is the possession only of youth. They don't realize that love grows stronger and closer, bigger and finer, and more essential with each year that passes. Especially, if it's the only love you ever had."

It is little wonder that George loved Beatrice. When away from her, separated by war, he would write every day, and often he wrote twice a day. Though he was a professional soldier who loved his job, he loved and missed his great lady.

An excellent example of the letters that George wrote to Beatrice is one written after he had been in an accident in Mexico. A gasoline lantern had exploded in his face and he was badly burned. He wrote to her on October 7, 1916, "I love you with all my heart and would have hated worst to have been blinded because I could not have seen you."

Throughout his career, when he was away from Beatrice he often wrote such intimacies. One letter, dated March 19, 1918, reads, "Well, this is the second letter that I have written to you today. I only wish it were not necessary and that I could hold you in my arms and squeeze you. I have almost forgotten how soft you are even with corsets on, to say nothing of your softness in your wedding nighty. I love you so, Bea. . . . I am not so hellish young and it is not spring, yet still I love you just as much as if we were 22 again on the baseball grandstand at West Point the night I graduated."

He often sent poems to her that he had written or jokes that he had heard. One such joke that he sent to her in a postscript went like this: "Here is a nasty story. You will like it. A wife once woke up in the night and said to her husband, "John, if that is your elbow sticking in my back, turn over. If it is not, I will."

During his first tour of duty at Fort Sheridan, while Beatrice was visiting relatives, he wrote to her, "Darling One: You are one fierce woman. What in the Hell do you mean by, 'Doing what I like best to do—reading'? I would a damned sight rather look at something else than a book, and you know what it is, too. It looks like a skunk . . . ."

Their marriage was as a marriage ought to be. It was a full partnership, vital to endure all hardships. Each personality complemented, enhanced, and strengthened the heart, the very soul of the other.

On one occasion, when asked if it didn't add to her concern for her husband to know that the very lives of many thousands of American soldiers depended upon him and his personal judgment, Beatrice replied very simply and matter of factly, "I always think how lucky they are to be with General Patton." She was always giving to him what was not possible to supply through logistics. She was giving him faith and courage.

Beatrice was more than just "Mrs. Patton." She was in every sense of the word a rugged individualist, a great person in her own right. She came from the same tough stock that had sculpted a new land of freedom out of the harsh environment that the New World offered to the Pilgrims.

She had a great deal of her father in her. Once, when one of his mills burnt down, Frederick Ayer was asked, "Do you wish, sir, to be driven down to the mills?" He inquired, "Was anyone killed or seriously hurt?" The answer was no. He said, "Then what use is served by looking at ruins? No, order my carriage, I will go to the station. I'll take the train into Boston and just borrow the money to build a new and better plant."

Mr. Ayer was indeed an individualist. He was the first New England businessman to give female employees a monthly day off with pay at a time of their own choosing, although other manufacturers claimed that he was insane and that it would ruin his business. He also ignored their advice when he helped to finance Alexander Graham Bell and the New York subway system.

Beatrice had the same grit and determination, the same practicality, that her father had.

During WWII Beatrice was very popular with the War Department. She was asked, and she consented, to make a number of tours all over the country speaking at Army camps, women's clubs, and factories, and giving radio addresses. She would tell how proud she was of everyone, of the young Army wives, of the women of America, and of how everyone had to work together, as a team, to believe and sacrifice for victory.

Later on, after George had died in 1945, Beatrice became a very forceful and persuasive public speaker in defense of the draft. She advocated and debated the cause of universal military training in the United States. Her argument, in accordance with her late husband's beliefs, was that if strong measures were enacted it would prove convincingly to the Russians that the United States government meant what it said. She was completely outspoken in the conviction that her husband's judgments, especially those concerning the Russians, were ultimately sound.

Beatrice was popular, in and out of the Army, long before WWII. She had translated a number of French books of instruction and regulations for the United States Army. She was completely bi-lingual in English and French, as was her husband.

Beatrice was gifted in many ways and was very versatile. She was a fine writer. While stationed in Hawaii, she wrote two books. The first, a book published in French called, *Légendes Hawaiiennes,* was a complete collection of Hawaiian fairy tales, legends, and historical stories of great importance to Hawaiian culture. It grows in importance as the years pass, when considering the declining number of full-blooded Hawaiians who remain in the Islands and the commercialization that has overtaken the tropical paradise.

Her other book written at that time is entitled *Blood of the Shark.* It is a historical novel about an English seaman around the time of James Cook's expeditions. The Englishman makes a decision to remain in Hawaii and marry one of the daughters of the King of the Islands. The book tells the story of his subsequent life.

Beatrice later put together another volume which consisted of stories that her father, who died in 1917 at the age of 96, had told her about the Ayer family and their New England heritage. This book, named *Reminiscences of Frederick Ayer,* was privately published by Beatrice, primarily for family consumption. It is a very interesting book, revealing some of the hardships encountered by the early New Englanders.

In addition to her work as a translator for the Army and her own writing, Beatrice was an excellent musician who composed many pieces of music for her family. For her husband she had written a song called, "Song of the Armored Force" in 1941. It is a rousing piece which originally began with pistol shots and a siren, much the same as the cannon fire of the 1812 Overture. Today, that musical piece is called the "Second Armored Division March." It is still the official song of the Second Armored Division. This was the first division that Patton commanded. It is noteworthy that history was made in 1974 when Patton's son, George S. Patton III, assumed command of the same unit. It was the first time in American Army history that a son took command of a unit previously commanded by his father. There can be little doubt as to why the unit continues to be referred to as "Patton's Own."

Beatrice had many talents, too many to detail in a book of this scope. She was an expert equestrian, thought by friends to be as good as her husband. She was an able sailor who owned her own sloop and won many cups racing it.

For her small size, Beatrice was, indeed, a daring and courageous adventuress. One of the true stories about her activities involved a new prototype of a tank that Walter J. Christie had been trying to sell to the United States Army. George had been working with and following the development of Christie's armored vehicles for a few years and he had arranged a trial demonstration to be viewed by a congressional committee and some of the higher echelon Army brass.

The locale was Fort Myer, Virginia, in April of 1932. The dignitaries present were from the "Military Affairs Committee," and the light tank was called the "Christie Crawler," after its inventor.

Overall, it was a very impressive demonstration of the tank's toughness, speed, and maneuverability. It ran in and out of deep tank trap ditches, through water, and over steep bunkers at high speed. Nothing like it had ever been seen anywhere in the world. After the show, George asked if any of the committee would like to try a ride in it to test its safety. When all present declined, he then strapped goggles and a helmet on his wife and let *her* ride the machine on a second run through the same course. She emerged from the turret afterwards, grinning broadly, cloaked in dust, but completely unbruised and happy. A congressman later came to George and confided to him, "It's a beautiful tank, Georgie, certainly the best we have ever seen. But we're not going to buy it, you know. I doubt that we would even if it were driven up the steps of the Capitol, loaded with votes. We just aren't going to spend the money."

It may be noted here that the British and French also decided against the tank. However, the Germans and the Russians thought it very worthwhile. They bought prototypes from Christie, who after offering them to his own country, and being turned down, had to sell them to keep from going bankrupt. It was the Christie tank that was the forerunner of the Panzer Division tanks which overran Europe, the backbone of the whole of German armor.

Of course, in any marriage of thirty years, especially a marriage of two people as individual as the Pattons, there must be disagreements. There were a number of explosive episodes during the Pattons' years together. One of them occurred in 1912 after George had placed fifth in the Military Olympics in Stockholm. He had attended the games at his own expense, and afterward, with permission from the War Department, he stayed in Europe to attend special fencing classes offered by the French Army School at Saumur. When the course ended, Beatrice spent many hours packing their belongings, and finally had everything crated and ready to board the ship. George came running into their flat with a couple of new French swords that he had just bought. He handed them to Beatrice, demanding that she open one of the crates and re-pack it with the new acquisitions. This was the last straw for Beatrice. She unsheathed one of the swords and chased "Saber George" around the room, using expletives that should have made her warrior husband proud. After she had treed him on top of the crates, stabbing at his legs, and making him dance a jig, he pleaded, "Goddammit, Bea, I'm sorry! I'll pack them myself!" And he did.

As quick as she was to lose her temper with George, she was just as quick to lose her temper in defense of her husband.

On one occasion, she inflicted substantial damage on the person of an officer who unjustly criticized her husband. It happened just after the Great War. George had parked their car and had just come in the door to join Beatrice for a dinner party. He was in full dress uniform with complete medals. A drunken Reserve Colonel saw him and made the mistake of remarking, "That man's one of those all chicken, chicken on his shoulder and chicken in the heart."

Beatrice had knocked him down and was on top of him, pounding his head on the oak floor, before George could get her to a neutral corner.

The bottom line is that Beatrice Patton was, although a fearsome individualist, an asset to George and his career. She adopted a "whither thou goest" attitude and never allowed anything to stand in his way. She was just as determined to stand by him as he was to become a great commander.

She and George loved each other solidly, firmly, and completely. Neither was ever out of the heart and mind of the other, even when separated by thousands of miles of ocean and a war. It was truly a marriage that worked because they made it work.

★★★ NEWS ITEM ★★★

DINAH WARBLES TO GERMANS BUT IT'S PATTON SHE DISARMS

New York, Sept. 24 (ANS)

Dinah Shore is back from France with a pearl-handled pistol presented by Lt. Gen. George S. Patton when she sang for his men and then turned loose on the Germans via the American Broadcasting station in Europe with some psychological lyrics especially tailored to the tune of "I'll Be Around."

She serenaded the Nazis, Miss Shore said, with "I'll Be Around When We Get Into Berlin, I'll Be Around, That's No Lie."

Singing and speaking in German, French, Danish, and English, the little Tennessee star said she had little trouble rolling foreign phrases across in her first spoken message to the Germans. Here's what she told them:

"German soldiers, here talks Dinah Shore. I have just returned from Paris where I sang for American troops. Meanwhile, our boys entered Germany to re-establish order, freedom, and justice. I hope they will succeed real soon for then you'll be able to return to your Fatherland and your families and start a new life."

General Patton's Address

I

The Background Research

Anyone who has ever viewed the motion picture "Patton" will never forget the opening. George Campbell Scott, portraying Patton, standing in front of a huge American flag, delivers his version of Patton's "Speech to the Third Army" on June 5, 1944, the eve of the Allied invasion of France, code-named "Overlord."

Scott's rendition of the speech was highly sanitized so as not to offend too many faint-hearted Americans. Luckily, the soldiers of the American Army who fought in WWII were not so faint-hearted.

After one of my lectures on the subject of General Patton, I spoke with a retired Major-General who was a close friend of Patton and who had been stationed with him in the 1930's in the cavalry. He explained to me that the movie was a very good portrayal of Patton in that it was the way he wanted his men and the public to see him, as a rugged, colorful commander. There was one exception, however, according to the Major General. In reality, Patton was a much more profane speaker than the movie dared to exhibit.

Patton had a unique ability with regard to profanity. During a normal conversation, he could liberally sprinkle four letter words into what he was saying, and his listeners would hardly take notice of it. He spoke so easily and used those words in such a manner that it seemed natural for him to talk that way.

He could, when necessary, open up with both barrels and let forth such blue-flamed phrases that they seemed quite eloquent in their delivery. When asked by his nephew about his profanity, Patton remarked, "When I want my men to remember something important, to really make it stick, I give it to them double

26

dirty. It may not sound nice to some bunch of little old ladies at an afternoon tea party, but it helps my soldiers to remember. You can't run an army without profanity; and it has to be eloquent profanity. An army without profanity couldn't fight its way out of a piss-soaked paper bag."

"As for the types of comments I make," he continued with a wry smile, "Sometimes I just, by God, get carried away with my own eloquence."

When I appeared on a local San Diego television show to discuss my Patton collection, a viewer who lived in a suburb of San Diego was very interested for personal reasons. Her husband had been a lieutenant assigned to General Patton's Third Army Headquarters, code named "Lucky Forward," and he had known the general quite well. He had recently died and had left to his wife a box that he had brought home with him from the European Theater of Operations.

The lady invited me to her home to inspect the box to see if there was anything in it that might be useful to me in my search for "collectables."

On opening the box, I was thankful at once, and I told her so. Inside was one of only a couple of hundred copies that had been printed of the Official United States Third Army After-Action Reports. It is a huge two-volume history of the Third Army throughout their 281 days of combat in Europe. She said that she had no use for it and that I could have it. I left with my new treasure.

When I arrived at my office and removed the foot-thick books from the box, I had an even greater surprise. Under the Reports lay a small stack of original Third Army memos and orders— and a carbon copy of the original controversial speech that had been typed by some unknown clerk at Lucky Forward and had been widely distributed throughout Third Army.

A few years earlier, I had discovered an almost illegible xerox of a carbon copy of a similar speech. This one came from the Army War College and was donated to their Historical Library Section in 1957.

I decided to do some research in order to obtain the best available version of the speech, and try to identify the "unknown soldier" who had clandestinely typed and distributed the famous document. I began by looking in my collection of

old magazines, newspapers, and the books that have been written about Patton since his death, and dozens of other books
which had references to Patton and his speech.

I discovered some interesting facts, the most interesting probably being that George C. Scott was not the first actor to deliver
the speech.

In 1951, the *New American Mercury* magazine had printed a
version of the speech which was almost identical with the version printed by John O'Donnell in his "Capitol Stuff" column
for the *New York Daily News* on May 31, 1945. According to the
editors of the *New American Mercury,* their copy was obtained
from Congressman Joseph Clark Baldwin, who had returned
from a visit to Patton's Headquarters in Czechoslovakia.

After publishing the speech, the magazine received such a
large reader response asking for reprints of it that the editors
decided to go one step further. They hired an actor described
as famous to make an unexpurgated recording of the Patton
speech. This recording was to be made available to veterans of
the Third Army and anyone else who would like to have one.
The term "famous" was the only reference made by the editors
to the actor who recorded the speech. In a later column they
explained, "We hired an excellent actor whose voice, on records, is almost indistinguishable from Patton's, and with RCA's
best equipment we made two recordings; one just as Patton
delivered it, with all the pungent language of a cavalryman,
and in the other we toned down a few of the more offensive
words. Our plan was to offer our readers, at cost, either recording."

Unfortunately, some years later there was a fire in the magazine's editorial offices that destroyed almost all of their old
records. The name of the actor was lost in that accident.

Only one set of master recordings of the speech was made.
The magazine Editors, not wanting to offend either Mrs. Patton
or her family, asked her sanction for the project. The editors
explained the situation in this way: "While we had only the
master recordings, we submitted them to our friend, Mrs. Patton, and asked her to approve our plan. It was not a commercial
venture and no profits were involved. We just wanted to preserve
what to us seems a worthwhile bit of memorabilia of the Second

World War. Our attorneys advised us that legally we did not need Mrs. Patton's approval, but we wanted it.

"Mrs. Patton considered the matter graciously and thoroughly, and gave us a disappointing decision. She took the position that this speech was made by the General only to the men who were going to fight and die with him; it was, therefore, not a speech for the public or for posterity.

"We think Mrs. Patton is wrong; we think that what is great and worth preserving about General Patton was expressed in that invasion speech. The fact that he employed four-letter words was proper; four-letter words are the language of war; without them wars would be quite impossible."

When Mrs. Patton's approval was not forthcoming, the entire project was scrapped, and the master recordings were destroyed.

Patton always knew exactly what he wanted to say to his soldiers. He never needed notes—he always spoke to his troops extemporaneously. As a general rule, Patton usually told his men some of his basic thoughts about the nature of war, strategy, and tactics. Instead of the generalized rhetoric of no substance often used by Eisenhower, Patton spoke to his men in simple, down-to-earth language that they understood. He taught them lessons he had learned that would keep them alive.

As he traveled through the battle areas, he always took the time to speak to individual soldiers, squads, platoons, companies, regiments, divisions, or whatever size group could be collected. About the only difference in the content of these talks was that the smaller the unit, the more the talk would focus on tactics. Often he would just give his men some sound, common sense advice that they could follow in order to keep from being killed or maimed.

The account of the speech that follows is a composite narrative. From innumerable sources—magazine articles, newspaper clippings, books, motion picture biographies and newsreels, I have put together the most complete version possible, encompassing all of the material that is available to date.

II

The Speech

Somewhere in England—June 5, 1944

The big camp buzzed with tension. For hundreds of eager rookies,· newly arrived from the States, it was a great day in their lives. This day marked their first taste of the "real thing." Now they were not merely puppets in khaki uniforms. They were not going through the motions of soldiering with three thousand miles of ocean between them and English soil. They were actually in the heart of England itself. They were waiting for the arrival of that legendary figure, Lieutenant General George S. Patton, Jr.—old "Blood and Guts" himself, about whom many a colorful chapter would be written for the school-boys of tomorrow. Patton of the brisk, purposeful stride. Patton of the harsh, compelling voice, the lurid vocabulary, the grim and indomitable spirit that had carried him and his army to glory in Africa and Sicily. They called him "America's fight-ingest general." He was no desk commando. He was the man who was sent for when the going got rough and a fighter was needed. He was the most hated and feared American on the part of the German Army.

Patton was coming and the stage was being set. He would speak in the context of an action that might have a far-reaching effect on the global war, and that, at the moment, was top-secret in the files in Washington, D.C.

The men saw the camp turn out "en masse" for the first time. Today their marching was not lackadaisical. It was serious, and the soldiers felt the difference. From the lieutenants in charge of the companies on down, they felt the difference.

In long columns they marched downhill from the barracks. They counted cadence while marching. They turned off to the left, up a rise and so into the roped-off field where the General was to speak. Gold braid and stripes were everywhere. Soon, company by company, the hillside was a solid mass of brown. It was a fresh, beautiful English morning. Tall trees lined the road and swayed gently in the breeze. Across the field, a farmer was calmly tilling the soil. High upon a nearby hill a group of British soldiers huddled together, waiting for the coming of the General. Military Police were everywhere, wearing their white leggings, belts, and helmets. They were brisk and grim. The twittering of the birds in the trees could be heard above the dull murmur of the crowd, and soft white clouds floated lazily overhead as the men settled themselves and lit cigarettes.

On the special platform near the speakers' stand, Colonels and Majors were a dime a dozen. Behind the platform stood General Patton's "Guard of Honor," all specially chosen men. At their right was a band playing rousing marches while the crowd waited, and on the platform a nervous sergeant repeatedly tested the loudspeaker. The moment grew near, and necks began to crane to view the tiny winding road that led to Stourport-on-Severn. A captain stepped to the microphone. "When the General arrives," he said sonorously, "the band will play the Generals March and you will all stand at attention."

By now the rumor had gotten around that Lieutenant General Simpson, Commanding General of the Fourth Army, was to be with General Patton. The men stirred expectantly. Two of the big boys in one day!

At last, the long black car, shining resplendently in the bright sun, roared up the road, preceded by a jeep full of Military Police. A dead hush fell over the hillside. There he was! Impeccably dressed. With knee high, brown, gleaming boots, shiny helmet, and his Colt .45 Peacemaker swinging in its holster at his right side.

Patton strode down the incline and then straight to the stiff-backed "Guard of Honor." He looked them up and down. He peered intently into their faces and surveyed their backs. He moved through the ranks of the statuesque band like an avenging wraith and, apparently satisfied, mounted the platform with Lieutenant General Simpson and Major General Cook, the Corps Commander, at his side.

Major General Cook then introduced Lieutenant General Simpson, whose army was still in America, preparing for its part in the war.

"We are here," said General Simpson, "to listen to the words of a great man. A man who will lead you all into whatever you may face with heroism, ability, and foresight. A man who has proven himself amid shot and shell. My greatest hope is that some day soon, I will have my own army fighting with his, side by side."

General Patton arose and strode swiftly to the microphone. The men snapped to their feet and stood silently. Patton surveyed the sea of brown with a grim look. "Be seated," he said. The words were not a request, but a command. The General's voice rose high and clear.

"Men, this stuff that some sources sling around about America wanting out of this war, not wanting to fight, is a crock of bullshit. Americans love to fight, traditionally. All real Americans love the sting and clash of battle. You are here today for three reasons. First, because you are here to defend your homes and your loved ones. Second, you are here for your own self respect, because you would not want to be anywhere else. Third, you are here because you are real men and all real men like to fight. When you, here, everyone of you, were kids, you all admired the champion marble player, the fastest runner, the toughest boxer, the big league ball players, and the All-American football players. Americans love a winner. Americans will not tolerate a loser. Americans despise cowards. Americans play to win all of the time. I wouldn't give a hoot in hell for a man who lost and laughed. That's why Americans have never lost nor will ever lose a war; for the very idea of losing is hateful to an American."

The General paused and looked over the crowd. "You are not all going to die," he said slowly. "Only two percent of you right here today would die in a major battle. Death must not be feared. Death, in time, comes to all men. Yes, every man is scared in his first battle. If he says he's not, he's a liar. Some men are cowards but they fight the same as the brave men or they get the hell slammed out of them watching men fight who are just as scared as they are. The real hero is the man who fights even though he is scared. Some men get over their fright in a minute under fire. For some, it takes an hour. For some, it takes days. But a real man will never let his fear of death overpower his honor, his sense of duty to his country, and his innate manhood. Battle is the most magnificent competition in which a human being can indulge. It brings out all that is best and it removes all that is base. Americans pride themselves on being he-men and they *are* he-men. Remember that the enemy is just as frightened as you are, and probably more so. They are not supermen.

"All through your Army careers, you men have bitched about what you call 'chicken shit drilling.' That, like everything else in this Army, has a definite purpose. That purpose is alertness. Alertness must be bred into every soldier. I don't give a fuck for a man who's not always on his toes. You men are veterans or you wouldn't be here. You are ready for what's to come. A man must be alert at all times if he expects to stay alive. If you're not alert, sometime, a German son-of-an-asshole-bitch is going to sneak up behind you and beat you to death with a sockful of shit!" The men roared in agreement.

Patton's grim expression did not change. "There are four hundred neatly marked graves somewhere in Sicily," he roared into the microphone, "all because one man went to sleep on the job." He paused and the men grew silent. "But they are German graves, because we caught the bastard asleep before they did." The General clutched the microphone tightly, his jaw out-thrust, and he continued, "An Army is a team. It lives, sleeps, eats, and fights as a team. This individual heroic stuff is pure horseshit. The bilious bastards who write that kind of stuff for the *Saturday Evening Post* don't know any more about real fighting under fire than they know about fucking!"

The men slapped their legs and rolled in glee. This was Patton as the men had imagined him to be, and in rare form, too. He hadn't let them down. He was all that he was cracked up to be, and more.

"We have the finest food, the finest equipment, the best spirit, and the best men in the world," Patton bellowed. He lowered his head and shook it pensively. Suddenly he snapped erect, faced the men belligerently, and thundered, "Why, by God, I actually pity those poor sons-of-bitches we're going up against. By God, I do." The men clapped and howled delightedly. There would be many a barracks tale about the "Old Man's" choice phrases. They would become part and parcel of Third Army's history and they would become the Bible of their slang.

"My men don't surrender," Patton went on. "I don't want to hear of any soldier under my command being captured unless he has been hit. Even if you are hit, you can still fight back. That's not just bullshit either. The kind of man that I want in my command is just like the lieutenant in Libya, who, with a

Luger against his chest, jerked off his helmet, swept the gun aside with one hand, and busted the hell out of the Kraut with his helmet. Then he jumped on the gun and went out and killed another German before they knew what the hell was coming off. And, all of that time, this man had a bullet through a lung. There was a real man!''

Patton stopped and the crowd waited. He continued more quietly, "All of the real heroes are not storybook combat fighters, either. Every single man in this Army plays a vital role. Don't ever let up. Don't ever think that your job is unimportant. Every man has a job to do and he must do it. Every man is a vital link in the great chain. What if every truck driver suddenly decided that he didn't like the whine of those shells overhead, turned yellow, and jumped headlong into a ditch? The cowardly bastard could say, "Hell, they won't miss me, just one man in thousands." But, what if every man thought that way? Where in the hell would we be now? What would our country, our loved ones, our homes, even the world, be like? No, Goddamnit, Americans don't think like that. Every man does his job. Every man serves the whole. Every department, every unit, is important in the vast scheme of this war. The ordnance men are needed to supply the guns and machinery of war to keep us rolling. The Quartermaster is needed to bring up food and clothes because where we are going there isn't a hell of a lot to steal. Every last man on K.P. has a job to do, even the one who heats our water to keep us from getting the 'G.I. Shits.' ''

Patton paused, took a deep breath, and continued: "Each man must not think only of himself, but also of his buddy fighting beside him. We don't want yellow cowards in this Army. They should be killed off like rats. If not, they will go home after this war and breed more cowards. The brave men will breed more brave men. Kill off the goddamned cowards and we will have a nation of brave men. One of the bravest men that I ever saw was a fellow on top of a telegraph pole in the midst of a furious fire fight in Tunisia. I stopped and asked what the hell he was doing up there at a time like that. He answered, 'Fixing the wire, Sir.' I asked, 'Isn't that a little unhealthy right about now?' He answered, 'Yes, Sir, but the goddamned wire has to be fixed.' I asked, 'Don't those planes strafing the road bother you?' And he answered, 'No, Sir, but you sure as hell do!' Now, there was a real man. A real soldier. There was a man who devoted all he had to his duty, now matter how seemingly insignificant his duty might appear at the time, no matter how great the odds. And you should have seen those trucks on the road to Tunisia. Those drivers were magnificent. All day and all night they rolled over those son-of-a-bitching roads, never stopping, never faltering from their course, with shells bursting all around them all of the time. We got through on good old American guts. Many of those men drove for over forty consecutive hours. Those men weren't combat men, but they were soldiers with a job to do. They did it, and in one hell of a way they did it. They were part of a team. Without team effort, without them, the fight would have been lost. All of the links in the chain pulled together and the chain became unbreakable."

The General paused and stared challengingly over the silent ocean of men. One could have heard a pin drop anywhere on that vast hillside. The only sound was the stirring of the breeze in the leaves of the bordering trees and the busy chirping of the birds in the branches of the trees at the General's left.

"Don't forget," Patton barked, "you men don't know that I'm here. No mention of that fact is to be made in any letters. The world is not supposed to know what the hell happened to me. I'm not supposed to be commanding this Army. I'm not even supposed to be here in England. Let the first bastards to find out be the goddamned Germans. Some day I want to see them raise up on their pissed-soaked hind legs and howl, 'Jesus Christ, it's the Goddamned Third Army again and that son-of-a-fucking-bitch Patton.'

"We want to get the hell over there," Patton said. "The quicker we clean up this goddamned mess, the quicker we can take a little jaunt against the purple pissing Japs and clean out their nest, too. Before the goddamned Marines get all of the credit."

The men roared their approval and cheered delightedly. This statement had real significance behind it. Much more than met the eye, and the men instinctively sensed the fact. They knew that they themselves were going to play a very great part in the making of world history. They were being told as much right now. Deep sincerity and seriousness lay behind the General's colorful words. The men knew and understood it. They loved the way he put it, too, as only he could.

Patton continued quickly, "Sure, we want to go home. We want this war over with. The quickest way to get it over with is to go get the bastards who started it. The quicker they are whipped, the quicker we can go home. The shortest way home is through Berlin and Tokyo. And when we get to Berlin," he yelled, "I am personally going to shoot that paper hanging son-of-a-bitch Hitler. Just like I'd shoot a snake!

"When a man is lying in a shell hole, if he just stays there all day, a German will get to him eventually. The hell with that idea. The hell with taking it. My men don't dig foxholes. I don't want them to. Foxholes only slow up an offensive. Keep moving. And don't give the enemy time to dig one either. We'll win this war, but we'll win it only by fighting and by showing the Germans that we've got more guts than they have; or ever will have. We're not going to just shoot the sons-of-bitches, we're going to rip out their living goddamned guts and use them to grease the treads of our tanks. We're going to murder those lousy Hun cocksuckers by the bushel-fucking-basket. War is a bloody, killing business. You've got to spill their blood, or they will spill yours. Rip them up the belly. Shoot them in the guts. When shells are hitting all around you and you wipe the dirt off your face and realize that instead of dirt it's the blood and guts of what once was your best friend beside you, you'll know what to do!

"I don't want to get any messages saying, 'I am holding my position.' We are not holding a goddamned thing. Let the Germans do that. We are advancing constantly and we are not interested in holding onto anything, except the enemy's balls. We are going to twist his balls and kick the living shit out of him all of the time. Our basic plan of operation is to advance and to keep on advancing regardless of whether we have to go over, under, or through the enemy. We are going to go through him like crap through a goose; like shit through a tin horn!

"From time to time there will be some complaints that we are pushing our people too hard. I don't give a good goddamn about such complaints. I believe in the old and sound rule that an ounce of sweat will save a gallon of blood. The harder *we* push, the more Germans we will kill. The more Germans we kill, the fewer of our men will be killed. Pushing means fewer casualties. I want you all to remember that."

The General paused. His eagle-like eyes swept over the hillside. He said with pride, "There is one great thing that you men will all be able to say after this war is over and you are home once again. You may be thankful that twenty years from now when you are sitting by the fireplace with your grandson on your knee and he asks you what you did in the great World War II, you *won't* have to cough, shift him to the other knee and say, 'Well, your granddaddy shoveled shit in Louisiana.' No, sir, you can look him straight in the eye and say, 'Son, your granddaddy rode with the great Third Army and a son-of-a-goddamned-bitch named Georgie Patton!'"

★★★ NEWS ITEM ★★★

GENERAL PATTON'S RIDE

June 8, Boston, - (AP)-
Listen, my children, and you'll be told
Of the midnight ride of Patton bold;
On the seventh of June in forty-five
It was partly ride and partly jive.
Said his countrymen, "Here comes Blood and Guts"
Who made Hitler look like plain Ambrose Glutz;
Forget the lanterns and all such stuff—
He throws off lights that are quite enough!
One, if by land, and two, if by sea;
And three if done by 'lectricity!
Meanwhile his friends in alley and street
Gathered pell-mell, hot-dogs to eat,
As they waited along the crowded course
Of a man who could do it without a horse.
No Charleston to Concord shall mark this verse;
For Patton, he rode in complete reverse.
A flash and a roar through a village street,
A man and a gun and perpetual heat.
It was three by the village clock
When he crossed the bridge at Concord town;
His very manner packed a sock
That made the northwest wind pipe down.
The farmer's dog barked not at all—

It scrammed straight through a fieldstone wall.
It was two o'clock by the village clock
When he motored into Lexington;
You could see the villages reel and rock
As they caught a glimpse of his ivory gun.
It was one by the village clock
When old Medford saw him slam straight through;
"Wottaman!" declared the cheering flock,
"A Paul Revere with a sockeroo!"
It was noon at Charleston or thereabouts
When they saw the stars on his iron hat
And cheered this man who had knocked the Krauts
So often down on their rear-ends flat.
So to his home rode Patton, George,
A grin on his face and a smile of joy
As people rushed from mill and forge
To join in a welcome of "Attaboy!"
A scrapper hot who had made the grades
A colorful Paul Revere, in spades!

The General's Personal Sidearms

General Patton, in December of 1944, explained to Major-General Robert M. Littlejohn, "I want the men of Third Army to know where I am, and that I risk the same dangers that they do. A little fancy dress is added to help maintain the leadership and fighting spirit that I desire in the Third Army."

Over the years, that "fancy dress" included a number of personal weapons definitely not government issue.

The best remembered "trademark" of General Patton is the ivory-handled Colt .45 Peacemaker that he wore.

During the early days of WWII, when the news media were discovering that Patton was good copy, Patton was often referred to as "two-gun" Patton, alluding to the supposition that Patton wore a pair of ivory-handled Colt .45's all the time. These reports are not wholly correct on two counts.

First, Patton neither owned nor wore two "matching" Colt .45's. The pistol commonly thought to be a Colt was actually a Smith & Wesson .357 Magnum. And it was never worn as often as the Colt.

Secondly, the "two-gun" image of Patton is largely a creation of some inventive reporter. According to extensive research, there exists only one photograph of Patton wearing two ivory-handled revolvers at one time. Of course, Patton never said anything to hamper the image created by the media, since it served his purpose. The photograph spoken of was taken of Patton standing on the beach on the day of his landing at Fedala, North Africa, with his Western Task Force in November of 1942. It was the first major American naval invasion in the history of the United States.

It has been reported that another photograph of Patton wearing two pistols does exist, taken during maneuvers at the Desert Training Center in California in 1942, but that photograph has yet to be located.

39

Periodically, Patton would wear the Smith & Wesson .357 Magnum in place of the Colt .45, but that was an exception rather than the rule. As proved by "wear marks," the Colt .45 was the usual weapon worn in the right holster of the set. The Smith & Wesson .357 fits the left holster exactly.

Although the Colt .45 and Smith & Wesson .357 are the so-called "favorites" worn by the General, over the years Patton collected and used many different pistols. In Europe during WWII Patton had a small .32 caliber Colt automatic pistol which he called his "social pistol." He usually wore this .32 in a small clip-holster in his right hand trouser pocket when he was in the rear areas. He wore it inside his jacket as an additional "safety precaution" when he was in the front lines. On rare occasions, such as the formal ceremony when Patton turned over the command of the Third Army to Lt. General Lucian K. Truscott, Patton wore a more "subdued" weapon, a Colt .38 snub-nosed Detective Special with black, hard-rubber grips.

Since he was a general when he entered the action of WWII, Patton had the prerogative of designing his own uniform. This privilege allowed him to wear such pistols and accoutrements as he desired.

As a captain at the outbreak of WWI, the "Great War," Patton was required to wear the regulation uniform. Accordingly he sailed to France aboard the liner Baltic with the Army issue Model 1911 Colt .45 automatic pistol. The pistol was "regulation" with one exception. Patton had managed to replace the issue grips with ivory grips in which his initials were deeply engraved.

This same Colt .45 automatic was often worn by Patton during the Army's preparatory maneuvers and war games that took place in 1941 and 1942 in both Tennessee and Louisiana.

On the cover of *Life* magazine's "Defense Issue," dated July 7, 1941, Patton is seen in the turret of his command tank. He is wearing the M1911 Colt .45 automatic in a government issue shoulder holster. The tank is adorned with red, white, blue, and yellow stripes, along with two flags attached to the sides at the tank's front; one flag bears the two stars of a Major-General; the other is the flag of the Second Armored Division.

In accordance with his plan, it was impossible for Patton's troops not to know who or where he was.

A photograph of Patton in front of his Desert Training Center command tank appears on the cover of *Newsweek* magazine, dated July 26, 1943. In this photograph Patton is wearing yet another of his pistols. Another Colt, this one is a semi-automatic .22 "Woodsman" target pistol, with a long barrel which required a special holster.

While at the Desert Training Center in California in 1942, Patton seems to have favored this .22 pistol, probably because he was not in actual combat and in the desert he could use it for "plinking." There is an abundance of jack rabbits, varmints, and rattlesnakes in the desert to keep a shooter's eye and hand in practice.

The Smith & Wesson .357 Magnum that Patton owned was shipped to him from the Smith & Wesson factory on October 18, 1935. It was a newly developed gun manufactured especially for the new cartridge that Smith & Wesson had created. It was the most powerful handgun in the world at the time. Although Patton's Colt .45 was chambered for a special large revolver cartridge weighing 255 grams and developing enormous shocking power, he purchased the Smith & Wesson as what he called a "killing gun."

The newly introduced Smith & Wesson firearm was a double-action revolver with a special chrome-nickle-steel alloy hammer and cylinder, which were necessary to withstand the great pressure developed by the cartridge in firing. Because of the two types of metal in the gun, the originals were unique in that they were "two-tone," with the frame a blued gun metal and the hammer and cylinder an almost white alloy. They originally retailed at $60.00. It was offered as the most powerful handgun ever made. Today it is still advertised as one of the most powerful in the world, but the price has risen astronomically.

Upon leaving the factory, the revolver had standard walnut stocks, but they were soon replaced with the initialed ivory grips so loved by the General.

Throughout WWII, Patton predominantly wore the Colt .45 Peacemaker, but at the start of 1945 it seemed to be headed for retirement.

General Kenyon Joyce, a longtime friend of Patton, acquired and sent to the General a pocket-type pistol. It was a Remington

Model 51 .380 automatic. It had been a difficult gun to locate as it had not been manufactured since 1935, but one was found by the Remington firm. It was re-conditioned and engraved on it was, "To George Patton/From his shooting partner of many years/Kenyon Joyce." Patton wore it from time to time.

Patton's "special" weapons deserved something better than ordinary in the way of accoutrements, so "special" belts and holsters were selected that would enhance their appearance, much as a beautiful setting displays a gem.

The belt and holsters for Patton's Colt .45 and Smith & Wesson .357 were made by S.D. Myers of El Paso, Texas. S.D. "Tio" Myers had started his leather business as a saddle maker in Sweetwater, Texas in 1897. In 1920 he moved his business to El Paso where it remained until his death. Then his son took over the business, and he ran it until he retired in 1978.

The belt and holsters are made of light brown hide. The holsters have flat, closed tips with a safety strap to fit around the hammer of the pistol to prevent accidental discharging.

The belt is 1¹⁵⁄₁₆ inches wide, and its buckle has a convex brass disc marked with the letters "US." The buckle was taken from a Model 1910 officer's web belt.

Other items made to fit the belt are a "#4 Hand Cuff Case" in which Patton carried a lensatic compass; a "#19 Belt Slide Loop" which holds 12 cartridges; and a small leather box used as a first aid kit.

These pieces of equipment, along with the Colt .45 and Smith & Wesson .357 Magnum, fell into disuse when Patton began to favor a smaller, lighter Colt .380 automatic.

In the book, *Patton and His Pistols,* it is reported that Patton began to favor the small Remington that General Joyce had sent to him. According to that book, it is the Remington that replaced the Colt .45 revolver as Patton's favorite. That, however, is incorrect. Upon very close examination of the photos available of Patton wearing an automatic pistol, some discrepancies are noted in the claims made by the authors.

Plainly visible are features of the Colt .380 displayed on the automatic—the inlaid ivory stars which are discernibly different from the Remington .380. The butt is straight; the grip rivets are of a light color and are located at the rear, middle portion of the handle. The "wear marks" of the filled holster indicate, in a very pronounced way, a fully extended barrel of the same size as the portion near the trigger housing. These features are indicative of the Colt .380 automatic pistol.

Conversely, the Remington automatic has a curved butt; its grip rivets are of a dark color and are located at the top and bottom of the handle. It has a longer, tapered barrel which would not completely fill the bottom of the holster used by Patton, and is therefore not of sufficient size to create the wear marks which are shown on the holster.

For carrying the Colt .380, Patton used the new "General Officers" belt, sometimes called the "Marshall Belt," because General George C. Marshall personally had them created for general officers. This belt, like the stars of rank, were and are today considered as part of the insignia of a General Officer in the U.S. Army. It is made of soft rolled leather 1¾ inches wide, and the buckle is convex, bearing the U.S. Army eagle with laurel wreaths curving up either side.

Along with the belt were issued two holsters. One was made to fit the M1911 Colt .45 automatic and one to fit the newly issued Colt .380 automatic. The Colt .380 automatic greatly resembled a small version of the M1911 Colt .45, which it was since it was designed from similar specifications.

One of the most probable reasons that Patton liked the small Colt was its size and weight. It was a mere 13 ounces, as compared to the Colt .45's 38 ounces and the 41 ounces of the Smith & Wesson .357 Magnum. Though small, it was a hard hitting pistol.

Patton liked the Colt .45, but it was a very heavy sidearm. To his nephew, Fred Ayer, Jr., he explained, "People ask me why I swagger, swear, wear flashy uniforms, and sometimes two pistols. Don't you think these guns get awfully heavy, wearing them all the time? Well, I'm not sure whether or not some of it isn't my own fault. However that may be, the press and others have built a picture of me. So, now, no matter how tired or discouraged, or really ill I may be, if I don't live up to that picture, my men are going to say, 'The old man's had it. The old son-of-a-bitch has had it.' Then their own confidence, their own morale will take a big dip."

With the "Marshall" belt and the Colt .380 adorned with three stars, Patton had a classy, effective, and attractive combination. It could easily supersede the Colt .45 revolver and at the same time it was a complementary addition to Patton's colorful, cavalier uniform.

Most people, and especially Patton fans, are aware that Patton hated having his pistols referred to as "pearl-handled."

Of the 1,500 Colt .380's obtained by the Army for issue to General Officers, only one of them was different. Someone along the supply line had removed the standard grips from the pistol to be issued to General Patton, and had replaced them with pearl grips, undoubtably in an attempt to please the general.

In its original condition, the pistol had black, hard rubber grips. Patton replaced them with grips different from the usual ivory grips with his initials. This pistol had black grips with three large inlaid ivory stars. Upon his promotion to full General in 1945, Patton again replaced the grips. These new ones had four large inlaid stars.

In photographs of Patton after his acquiring this pistol, he is rarely seen without it.

Patton took violent offense at any reference to his pistols being pearl handled. He said, "Only a pimp in a New Orleans whorehouse or a tin-horn gambler would carry a pearl-handled pistol." In no uncertain terms he would have the offender know that his revolver was indeed *"ivory-god-fucking-damn-handled"* and with that he would turn on his heel and leave.

There were two very plausible reasons for Patton's disapprobation of pearl grips. One was that Patton, being a firm believer in luck, considered pearl to be unlucky. The other was that, as a young lieutenant, he spent years on border patrol in Texas and New Mexico. That territory in those days was still the "Old west" and many a time personal opinions were supported with a few ounces of hot lead. Patton personally knew and associated with many of the types about whom movies are made today. One of them was a town marshall named Dave Allison who had, while Patton was stationed at the town of Sierra Blanca, killed a gang called the "Orozco outfit." With no help and at a distance of 60 yards he had shot all six of them squarely through the head. Patton often went hunting with the marshall and they were good friends.

Truthfully, in those "old days" only pimps and tin-horn

gamblers did carry pearl-handled sidearms.

The Colt Revolver

Name:	Colt Single Action Army Revolver Model 1873
Caliber:	.45
Barrel Length:	4-3/4 inches
Overall Length:	10-1/4 inches
Weight:	38 ounces
Finish:	Silver
Stocks:	Ivory Carved Eagle on left hand stock. GSP in black enamel on right hand stock.
Purchase Date:	March 5, 1916
Cost:	$50
Serial Number:	332088

The Smith & Wesson Magnum

Name:	Smith & Wesson Double Action Revolver Model 27
Caliber:	.357
Barrel Length:	3-1/2 inches
Overall Length:	8-7/8 inches
Weight:	41 ounces
Finish:	Blue/Nickle Alloy
Stocks:	Ivory, GSP on right hand stock
Purchase Date:	October 18, 1935
Cost:	$60
Serial Number:	47022

The Colt Automatic

Name:	Colt Automatic Pistol Model 1908
Caliber:	.380
Barrel Length:	2-1/4 inches
Overall Length:	4-1/2 inches
Weight:	13 ounces
Finish:	Deep Blue
Stocks:	Black/Inlaid Ivory Stars (4) on right grip
Serial Number:	135170

General Specifications

Pistol	Type	Caliber	Length mm	Weight gm	Barrel mm	Maga-zine Capacity
Colt Match Target	Auto	.22	305	1105	152	10
Colt 1903 Pocket	Auto	.32	113	368	54	7
Colt 1908 Hammerless	Auto	.380	190	879	115	6
Colt Detective Special	Rev	.38	171	595	54	6
Colt Single Action	Rev	.45	260	1020	120	6
Colt Army M1911	Auto	.45AC	216	1105	114	7
Remington 1908 Model 51	Auto	.380	168	598	89	8
Smith & Wesson Magnum	Rev	.357	285	1245	152	6

★★★ NEWS ITEM ★★★

"COME AND GET US, GEORGIE PATTON," PRISONERS' REFRAIN

Siegenhain, Germany, April 3 - (AP) -

Americans freed from the German prison camp near here had a theme song: "Come and get us, Georgie Patton."

Sung to the tune, "Glory, Glory, Hallelujah," the words were:
We're a bunch of Yankee soldiers living deep in Germany,
We're eating soup and black bread and a beverage they call tea,
And we'll keep on singing till Patton sets us free,
So we can come rambling home.
Come and get us, Georgie Patton,
Come and get us, Georgie Patton,
Come and get us, Georgie Patton,
So we can come rambling home.

The rescue was made by Gen. Patton's Sixth Armored Division.

SHAEF's
Three Major Errors

I
The Falaise Pocket

On June 6th, 1944, the Allied Forces launched "Operation Overlord," the invasion of Normandy. This force, consisting of the First Army (American) and the Second Army (British) was commanded by General Montgomery.

On August 1, 1944, D-Day + 55, Patton's Third Army became officially operational.

Between July 5, when Third Army actually landed on French soil, and July 31, Third Army had advanced inland to the town of Avranches. The advance was a total of about 50 miles in 26 days.

In a comparison, Montgomery and his Second British Army had, since D-Day, advanced to the town of Caen, about 10 miles inland. A total of ten miles in 55 days. Montgomery's explanation for his slowness was that he was "re-grouping" in order to pivot at Caen and attack the Germans in force. This "pivoting on Caen" became a joke to the Americans.

By August 11, D-Day + 66, Patton and his Third Army had broken completely out of the Cherbourg peninsula. He had advanced south, west, east, and north. Third Army had ripped a hole through the German Seventh Army and had roared "hell for leather" through the towns of Avranches, Mortain, Fougères, Vitre, Mayenne, and Laval. They had made a sharp 90 degree turn at Le Mans and attacked north to the town of Aleçon. They had gone a total of 200 miles in 10 days.

Montgomery had finally "pivoted on Caen" and had advanced another 10 miles. A total of 20 miles in 66 days.

By August 15, D-Day + 70, Third Army units (the Second French Armored Division and the 90th American Infantry Division) had reached Argentan, a town about 12 miles from

Falaise. Canadian troops under Montgomery had reached the outskirts of Falaise. August 17, D-Day + 72, saw Patton's 90th Division and Second French Division joined by the 80th Infantry Division at Argentan. Montgomery's Second Army was still about 10 miles from Falaise.

At this point, there was a gap of 12 miles between Falaise and Argentan through which the German Seventh Army was escaping. Patton and his Third Army had moved 250 miles in 17 days. They had completely encircled the German Seventh Army, and were now ready to advance directly to Falaise. Blocking their escape and destroying them would be like shooting fish in a barrel.

Montgomery had moved about 20 miles in 72 days.

Third Army was poised and ready for one of the swiftest, greatest victories in all of history. To close the gap between the two towns would be a matter of hours. The 15th Corps had the tanks and troops necessary to put up a solid wall of men and armor. The Germans were completely confused and running for their lives. Then, the order arrived from **SHAEF**: *Halt!*

Patton and his Third Army were ordered *not* to seize Falaise.

What the Germans were powerless to do, SHAEF did for them.

There were two explanations given later for the order to stop Patton. First, SHAEF claimed that the British had "heavily sewn the Falaise area with time bombs." Secondly, Bradley claimed that he not only feared a head-on collision of the British and Americans, but he also was worried that the fleeing Germans might "trample" the Third Army in its rush to escape.

The first claim was an outright lie to cover political chicanery.

The second claim, advanced by Bradley, made no sense at all. They were noises made by a subordinate to obfuscate and justify an error on the part of his superiors. Had the proper order been issued, the British could have held their position and there would have been no possibility of a "collision" of British and American forces.

In regard to Bradley's anxiety about Third Army being "trampled," it is difficult to imagine two Infantry Divisions and an Armored Division being trampled by a thoroughly routed enemy. Evidently, the thought never occurred to Bradley that the enemy might consider surrendering.

The real reason behind the halting of Third Army was Montgomery. He insisted, or rather, demanded, that he be allowed to close the gap. He did not want Patton to spring the trap that Third Army had set. Monty wanted the glory and the credit for the "ripe plum" situation which had been created by Patton's brilliant leadership and Third Army's speed and daring execution. Monty achieved neither. He did not close the gap in time, and he allowed a great number of Germans to live to fight another day.

Montgomery failed to reach Falaise until the 19th of August, D-Day + 74. During that time, with Patton halted at Argentan, the great bulk of the German Army managed to escape through the 12-mile gap. What would have been one of the great and memorable victories of all time was lost because of one of SHAEF's oleaginous political schemes.

After this major blunder had occurred and had became part of history, Patton wrote in his diary: "The 15th Corps could have easily entered the town of Falaise and completely closed the gap to Argentan. This halt was a great mistake, as I was certain that we could have entered Falaise and I was not certain that the British would. As a matter of fact, we had reconnaissance parties near the town when we were ordered to pull back."

Patton was correct, yet his advice went unheeded.

II

Market-Garden and Out of Gas

What was probably the greatest error made in WWII by Eisenhower and the SHAEF planners was actually two directly related occurrences, one of which greatly affected the other.

To quote General Patton: "The 29th of August, 1944 was, in my opinion, one of the critical days of the war. Hereafter pages will be written on it, or rather on the events which produced it. It was evident that then there was no real threat against us as long as we *did not stop ourselves* or allow ourselves to be stopped by imaginary enemies. Everything seemed rosy when suddenly it was reported to me that the 140,000 gallons of gasoline which we were supposed to get for that day did not arrive. I presented my case for a rapid advance to the east for the purpose of cutting the Siegfried Line *before it could be manned*. It was my opinion that this was the *momentous* error of the war."

Patton thought that German resistance had collapsed and that nothing could stop the Third Army and the Allies if they proceeded with speed. What did stop them was once again the high command. Now, thirty-five years later, there is massive evidence to prove conclusively that Patton was correct. Eisenhower and SHAEF were wrong, again. One of Eisenhower's problems was that his SHAEF headquarters was located at Granville, near Cherbourg, a distance of 400 miles from the battle front.

The reason for Patton's halt was explained away as "lack of supplies." Another great lie. There was no lack of supplies. There was, however, a diversion of supplies.

One thorn in Patton's side was the person of General John C. H. Lee, the commander of COMZ, the supply command. With Patton in dire need of gasoline and other vital supplies, Lee decided that the end of August was the perfect time to move his non-combatant headquarters to greener pastures. What proved to be "just the ticket" was a move to newly liberated Paris. This, of course, meant newly liberated wine, newly liberated women, and newly liberated song. During the move, Lee used *hundreds* of trucks, *tons* of supplies, and *thousands* of gallons of gasoline that were desperately needed by the Third Army's thirsty tanks. Eisenhower, of course and as usual, remained silent. Bradley quietly remarked, "No one can compute the cost of that move in lost truck tonnage on the front."

It is interesting to consult a map of the European Theater of Operations as of the end of August, 1944. In northern France, from Dieppe to Nantes (north to south) were Crerar and the Canadian Army; Dempsey and the British Second Army; and Hodges and the First American Army. These three Armies constituting Montgomery's 21st Army Group occupied a front of about 150 linear miles. Contiguous to them on the south was Patton and Third Army. First Army received ample supplies. The boundary between First and Third Armies apparently was an insurmountable obstacle making utterly impossible any transport of supplies, especially gasoline.

It was evident to all commanders that what was actually needed was to discontinue Eisenhower's "Broad front" strategy (which he continually and pontifically quoted from Clausewitz). Reassessment of the situation demanded a "single thrust" strategy. There were decisive reasons why this thrust should have been headed by Patton. He, above all others, was capable of the direct, simple, and ruthless drive which would be required to accomplish the task. He was also the most adept at exploiting success.

Actually, Patton could have been supplied more easily than might be imagined. Had 21st Army group been halted instead of Third Army, supplies could have been sent directly behind and through 21st Army Group territory. When Third Army had advanced to the forefront, 21st Army Group could have then followed up Third Army's advancing rear to the south. They could then pivot to the north when Third Army had taken the northern position previously held by 21st Army Group. In other words, they could have switched places by means of a "pinwheel" maneuver.

The great need, therefore, was for Patton to orchestrate a single concentrated thrust so deep into Germany's heart that the enemy would have no chance of recovery. The timing was perfect, the day of August 29 was the day. It should have been ordered by SHAEF. Instead, Bradley, reluctantly following orders from above, cut Patton's gasoline supply from 400,000 gallons a day to almost nothing.

Fate had given Eisenhower the greatest cavalry leader and as great an Army as his nation had every produced. He failed at the decisive moment to use them. Why? The reason was *not* the supply situation. The reason was Field-Marshal Montgomery.

Eisenhower once again sided with Montgomery and the British so that Montgomery could attempt the "single thrust" attack, but not into Germany. The attack was to be in Holland. Montgomery used the term "dagger-like" thrust. Bradley remarked that it probably would be more like a "butter-knife" thrust.

Patton had often claimed that Eisenhower was more British than American and that he (Eisenhower) allowed the British to influence him too extensively. This is certainly true. One cannot fault the British nor even Montgomery for this. Men and nations have since the dawn of time pursued what they regarded as their own best interests, and that is understandable. The British were not at fault. Montgomery was not at fault. The entire blame lies squarely and solely with Eisenhower. He was a straw man who had never experienced the necessary command of troops. He utterly lacked "command presence" and personal confidence in his own decisions. According to General Patton, Eisenhower was always attempting to be popular, always wanting to be "one of the boys." He was, for his entire Army career, a staff officer. As General MacArthur had once said of him, "He was the best clerk I ever had." Had he been a better, more capable commander, had he some combat experience and more backbone, he might have been able to stand his ground and make the correct and necessary decision. Instead, he replaced pragmatism with politics. One of the influences that affected him greatly was his romantic involvement with an English-woman, his driver, Kay Summersby.

Eisenhower had decided to go along with Montgomery and his plan, code-named, "Operation Market-Garden." Montgomery demanded, and got, absolute priority for ETO supplies. He was assured by Bedell Smith, Eisenhower's Chief of Staff, that not only would he receive a thousand tons of supplies per day plus transport, but that Patton's drive to the Saar would be completely halted. Montgomery was elated.

Shortly after 10 A.M. on Sunday, September 17, 1944, from airfields all over southern England, the greatest armada of troop-carrying aircraft ever assembled for a single operation took to the air. "Market," which was the airborne phase of the operation, was monumental. It involved almost 5000 fighters, bombers, and transports and more than 2500 gliders. That Sunday afternoon, at 1:30 P.M., an entire Allied airborne army, complete with vehicles and equipment, began dropping behind the German lines. The target for this historic and tragic invasion from the sky was Nazi-occupied Holland.

On the ground, ready along the Dutch-Belgian border, were the "Garden" forces, massed tank columns of the British Second Army. At 2:35 P.M., preceded by artillery and led by swarms of rocket-firing fighters, the tanks began their dash into Holland along a strategic route that the paratroopers were already fighting to capture and hold open.

It staggers the imagination when considering what Patton could have accomplished with this massive force and number one priority.

On September 24, 1944, Operation Market-Garden was officially over. Here is what had happened:

Allied forces suffered more casualties in Market-Garden than in the mammoth invasion of Normandy. Most historians agree that in the twenty-four hour period of D-Day, total Allied losses reached an estimated 10,000 to 12,000 men. In the nine days of Market-Garden, combined losses amounted to MORE THAN 17,000 men.

British casualties were the highest—a total of 13,226. General Urquhart's entire division was destroyed almost to a man. In the 10,000 Arnhem force, which included a Polish division and glider pilots, casualties totaled 7,578. In addition to this figure, RAF pilot and crew losses came to another 294, making a total of 7,872. General Horrocks' 30th Corps lost 1,480 and the British 8th and 12th Corps another 3,874.

American losses, including glider pilots and the 9th Troop Carrier Command, are put at 3,974. General Gavin's 82nd Airborne Division had suffered a loss of 1,432. General Taylor's 101st Airborne lost 2,118. Air crew losses were 424.

Complete German figures are unknown. In Arnhem and Oosterbeek, admitted casualties came to 3,300 including 1,300 dead. After interviewing German commanders a conservative estimate was that Army Group B lost at least 7,500 to 10,000 men of which perhaps a quarter were killed. A total of 12,000 to 15,000 men. Less than the Allies.

What about Dutch civilian casualties? No one can say. Deaths in Arnhem and Oosterbeek are said to have been low, less than 500, but no one knows with any certainty. There have been casualty figures given as high as 10,000 in the entire Operation Market-Garden campaign, and as a result of the forcible evacuation of the Arnhem sector, together with deprivation and starvation in the terrible winter that followed the attack.

Had it been worth it? No. Operation Market-Garden was a prime example of a Pyrrhic victory.

After Market-Garden was over, Montgomery said, "In my

prejudiced view, if the operation had been properly backed from its inception, and given the aircraft, ground forces, and administrative resources necessary for the job—it would have succeeded in spite of my mistakes, or the adverse weather, or the presence of the 2nd and SS Panzer Corps in the Arnhem area. I remain Market-Garden's unrepentant advocate."

It seems incredible that with Patton stopped, with Montgomery enjoying absolute priority in supplies and weapons, and having at his disposal over 30,000 troops, the British commander still claims that his plan was "improperly backed." What more could he have asked for and gotten? The only other possible "resource" would have been for the Germans either to throw away their weapons or to shoot themselves.

Had Patton been given this kind of support, supplies, and equipment, he could have destroyed the entire German Reich within three months.

Perhaps Prince Bernhard of the Netherlands summed it up most succinctly when he stated, "My country can never again afford the luxury of another Montgomery success."

III

The Ardennes Offensive— The Battle of the Bulge

The "Battle of the Bulge" at Bastogne, Belgium was not initiated completely by the Germans. They had a healthy assist from their enemy, the Allies. It is another case of one thing affecting another. There were two occurrences which helped the Germans to launch their offensive on December 16, 1944.

The first was recorded by General Patton in his diary: "The 1st Army is making a terrible mistake in leaving the 8th Corps area static, as it is probable that the Germans are building up to the east of them."

What prompted Patton to this judgment were reports from his G-2 (Intelligence) officer, Colonel Oscar Koch. Ignoring daily intelligence reports from SHAEF, which was hundreds of miles behind the front lines, and who claimed that everything was fine and dandy, Koch had his own intelligence teams at work. One of these was nicknamed "Patton's Household Cavalry."

As early as December 12, 1944, Koch had begun preparing and transmitting reports to SHAEF regarding what he considered to be a dangerous buildup of Germans east of the 1st Army's 8th Corps. Eisenhower was very busy, occupied with major decisions such as who should be head nurse of SHAEF. Therefore, he ignored the warnings from those two upstarts, Koch and Patton. He mistakenly allowed Bradley to turn the 8th Corps area into a "rest station," thereby reducing both their discipline and fighting spirit.

The second occurrence was Bradley's breaking a promise that he had made to Patton. Patton explains: "Bradley called up at 1710 hours and, in my opinion, crawfished quite blatantly, in his forbidding me to use the 83rd Division. I believe that he had been 'overtalked' by either Middleton or Hodges, or by both. I was very sore at the time and I still regard it as a great mistake. If I had been able to use the two combat teams of the 83rd to attack Saarburg, that town would have fallen on the 12th or 13th and we probably would have captured the city of Trier. With Trier in our hands, Von Rundstedt's breakthrough could not have occurred. This is probably a case of, 'because of a nail, a shoe was lost, etc. . . .' "

In other words, had Patton been allowed to use the 83rd Division, as he had been promised, the Germans would not have had the ability to stage their offensive, let alone break through to Bastogne. Knowing Patton's perceptiveness, his intuitiveness, and above all, his track record, it is next to impossible not to believe him. Yet, he was once again ignored and put in his place by his "superiors," to use the word in a military sense only.

Patton, being the commander he was, envisioned what could and might happen if the Germans did decide to attack. He called his staff together for a meeting. By the time that Patton was called to attend the Allied meeting at Verdun, to discuss the "Bulge" situation, he was already prepared with two completely separate and distinct plans of action. All that was needed was for him to phone his Chief of Staff, utter one of two code words, and within a matter of minutes Third Army would be headed north toward Bastogne to ". . . rip out their living guts and grease the treads of our tanks with them."

This was the kind of planning that Patton and his staff did so well—the same staff that Bradley had termed "mediocre." In truth, it was the best and most loyal staff in the entire European Theater of Operations.

At one point, Patton proposed that the Germans be allowed to advance even further. Then he could attack their rear, cut off the salient at the base, and annihilate them. He was turned down.

Within less than 48 hours after that meeting, Third Army had 2 divisions attacking toward Bastogne, hitting them in the flank and abruptly stopping their offensive. Within a week Patton had moved the bulk of his Army, a quarter of a million strong, and including 133,000 tanks and trucks, between 50 and 70 miles to the north in the worst possible weather conditions over icy roads. It is little wonder that the Germans had such a healthy respect for Patton and a powerful fear of him. It is a wonder, though, how SHAEF could continually ignore him and his ideas.

By January 23, the Ardennes Offensive was *kaput*. The Germans had lost not only the battle, but also the war. The Germans knew it and Patton knew it. The only ones who did not know it were the masterminds of SHAEF.

After Patton had been called in to save the day, he was put back in his place. Though he had saved the Bastogne operations, he was informed that the major push would now be north of the Ruhr, meaning Montgomery.

In the aftermath of Bastogne, Patton continued to follow orders and to fight Germans. Montgomery made some noisy statements about how he had come to the rescue and saved the day for the unfortunate Americans. From his speech, one would almost get the impression that he might have used the term "colonists" in lieu of "Americans." This was too much even for some of the British. Winston Churchill, speaking before the House of Commons, publicly repudiated Montgomery and his statements. It might be mentioned that had Patton acted and spoken the way Montgomery did, he would have been immediately relieved of duty by Eisenhower, castigated (or castrated) by the press, and sent home in shame. Churchill not only repudiated Montgomery, but he reminded him and the British people that during the Bulge, for every British soldier in the line, there were 35 to 40 Americans; for every British casualty, there were 55 to 60 American casualties.

Worth mentioning here is an interesting insight into the kind of man that Eisenhower was. Only three months prior to the Battle of the Bulge, before Churchill found it necessary to defend the American soldier, and before Patton and his staff had performed a miracle with his great Third Army, Eisenhower had the gall to make the statement that ". . . Montgomery is the greatest living soldier in the world!" Patton—and even Bradley—was disgusted by Eisenhower's remark.

These, then, are the three major errors made by Eisenhower and SHAEF during WWII in the European Theater of Operations. There were others, but none which had such a widespread effect on the possible end of the war itself. Had Patton's advice been heeded, it is very probable that the war would have been concluded by the end of 1945.

★★★ NEWS ITEM ★★★

PATTON NAMED MAYOR
FOR TOWN IN KANSAS

Junction City, Kansas, June 23—(AP)—

General George S. Patton, Jr., asked for the job; so he can be Mayor of Junction City anytime he chooses. Patton, whose Third Army raced across France and Germany, was quoted in a magazine recently as saying he had no political ambitions except to be Mayor of Junction City. Today, Mayor Roy Moore submitted his resignation to take effect whenever his successor qualifies, and the City Council promptly named "Old Blood 'n Guts" to the office.

Some Misconceptions
(And Some Plain Old Lies)

In the past, it has very often been the usual and accepted attitude of people that Patton was effective only as a field commander; that he was not suited for higher command, or for tactical and strategic planning.

The consensus on Patton's lack of ability was perhaps summed up best by Eisenhower when he once remarked to him, "George, you are a great leader, but a poor planner." Patton's reply was that "... except for [Operation] Torch, which I planned and which was a great success, I have never been given the chance to plan."

In the months to come, after North Africa, Patton was never *officially* asked about plans for any Allied operation. In private, though, it was a very different story. Very often, others would come to him to ask his views concerning future plans. Bradley, especially, would come to Patton to ask his opinion about impending operations. Often he would not only ask Patton's opinion, but he would also "borrow" his thoughts. They would later turn up miraculously as Bradley's ideas. This situation became so bad that, eventually, Patton became fed up with Bradley receiving all of the credit for his ideas. As Patton put it, "I do not want any more of my ideas used without credit to me, as happens when I give them orally."

On the surface, this might seem to some people a selfish attitude, but some consideration of the situation will offer a better understanding. At Patton's expense, other General Officers were building their careers and gaining undue praise. Patton himself was being kept under wraps and he was being virtually ignored. Others of lesser ability were being promoted over him. In reality, he was pushing them up the ladder and they were taking the credit that was honestly due Patton.

Initially Patton did not mind Bradley's taking his ideas because as a soldier he realized that it would help the war effort. But as time passed it became evident that the Allies would, indeed, win the war. Patton felt that he had been pushed far enough and that he had been taken advantage of too much. When Patton personally proffered his plans he was ignored. When Bradley put forth Patton's plans as his own, they were readily accepted for consideration.

Operation Cobra, the breakout in Normandy by Patton's armored divisions, was actually a slightly altered version of one of Patton's plans, but it was fully credited to Bradley. Actually, it was the first in a series of bold and brilliant plans devised by Patton during 1944.

The third Army staff never doubted that Bradley was making good in France by expropriating their boss's ideas. Patton's aide, Colonel Charles Codman, wrote to his wife, "As of August 1st, General Bradley has adopted practically all of General Patton's plans."

On August 14, 1944, Patton wrote in his diary regarding the St. Lo breakthrough: "It is really a great plan, wholly my own, and I made Bradley think that he thought of it."

Patton eventually became disgusted with the hypocrisy of the higher command. He stopped telling any of his plans to Bradley.

In reality, Patton was probably the best planner in the European Theater of Operations. Indeed, his knowledge of strategy and tactics was, to say the least, equal if not superior to that of any of the high command such as Eisenhower, Bradley, Devers, Clark, and the British. Without exception, his intuitiveness and perceptiveness was never equaled by any of the "masterminds" at SHAEF.

Patton had worked long and hard over the years to become the competent soldier that he was. His years of dedicated study and application were not in vain. He had attended all of the Army's "command level" service schools. He not only graduated from them, but did so with honors.

In 1923, he completed the Field Officers Course at Fort Riley, Kansas.

In 1924, he was an honor graduate of the Command and General Staff College located at Fort Leavenworth, Kansas. While at the Command and General Staff College, Patton compiled an extensive notebook which he lent to Eisenhower when the latter attended the same school in 1926. Eisenhower graduated first in his class. He wrote to Patton thanking him for the loan of the notebook, saying that it had made all the difference in his class standing.

In June of 1932, Patton was a distinguished graduate of the Army War College at Washington, D.C. If measured by no other standard than by education alone, Patton was prepared for general officer rank.

December 12, 1917, was the date on a report entitled "Light Tanks." It was a 58-page report written by Patton, assimilating his most salient views concerning the new military arm then known as the "Tank Corps." His report was the foundation, the entire basis, for the whole U.S. Armored concept.

At the very beginning of the involvement of the United States in armor, Patton was not only the first soldier in the Tank Corps, but he was the Tank Corps. He personally created the basic tank training procedures, the training instructions, the training manuals, the regulations, and the actual methods of instruction. He also created in their entirety the Tables of Organization and Equipment for the Tank Corps. He was personally responsible for the original Tank Corps patch worn by members of the corps, which was the forerunner of today's Armored Division patches.

In 1936, while stationed in Hawaii, Patton forecast a doctrine of amphibious warfare that proved to be highly, and terribly, prophetic.

After studying and observing the Japanese in the Pacific, Patton's conclusion was that they could and would attempt an air attack in the near future against Pearl Harbor. He wrote a paper on the subject in which his prophesy proved to be almost exactly the same as the actual Japanese attack on December 7, 1941.

By the time of the invasion of Sicily in 1943, Patton was regarded as one of the leading amphibious experts in the entire U.S. Army. Unfortunately, he was to be excluded from any planning of European amphibious operations.

He wrote in 1936, of the Japanese: ". . . It is reliably reported that during the last four years three or more Japanese divisions were embarked, moved to the coast of Asia and disembarked without any military attaché, consular agent, foreign press correspondent or any other foreigner living in Japan being aware of the fact until the troops were in action in Asia. Some of the Mandated Islands, about which absolutely nothing is known, are only 2,500 miles distant [from Hawaii], seven days' steaming over the loneliest sea lanes in the world. Who can say that an expeditionary force is not in these islands now?"

He warned against a surprise attack by the Japanese after participating in an annual exercise in Hawaii in 1937. He had specifically investigated the possibility of Hawaii's vulnerability to attack. He wrote, "The vital necessity to Japan of a short war and of the possession at its termination of land areas for bargaining purposes may impel her to take drastic measures. It is the duty of the military to foresee and prepare against the worst possible eventuality."

Within four and a half years, Patton's warnings would prove themselves correct. He had made a very shrewd, perceptive estimate of Japanese planning. He was ignored.

In 1928, Patton did a study of tables of organization and equipment for an infantry rifle company, an infantry battalion, an infantry brigade, and an infantry division. He followed this with a comparison of the current division and his "proposed" division, illustrating that his recommended division would have a total strength of 9,715 men. The current division had 19,417 men. With Patton's proposed division, the firepower of the recommended organization would be far greater, yet have 10,000 fewer men.

This was precisely what the "triangular" division of World War II sought to attain—more bang with fewer personnel.

Patton was also among the first to experiment with many new types of equipment. He used a personal command plane for reconaissance. He experimented with radio equipment for "tank to tank" and "tank to command post" communication. He worked closely with J. Walter Christie in an attempt to create a new and better tank. He continually strove for better ways to accomplish his goal—destroying enemy forces. The research he did for papers, his magazine articles, and his official reports, all that he studied simply reinforced his firm beliefs in the importance of mobility, speed, and surprise. He believed in the importance of the soldier rather than the machine; the importance of command, communications, and the supply line; the importance of air warfare and ground mechanization; and the continuing importance of the offensive, the attack.

He never ceased to believe that it was immensely cheaper for a nation to create and keep active a strong military organization than it was to fight, let alone lose, a war.

Had Patton's acumen been put to good use, instead of being wasted by men of lesser ability—men who had political aspirations and who suffered from mediocrity—the war would have ended much sooner than it did, with the advantage of great savings in both lives and materials.

In WWII, alone, there were many examples of Patton's shrewdness, his "sixth sense" in combat. Both before the war and during the war he showed much farsightedness. Major errors occurred which could have been avoided in the ETO had Patton's advice been heeded.

In North Africa, the Allies were planning to attack the Germans in Tunisia on the 25th of December, 1943. Patton felt that this was, ". . . unwise, as, unless things have changed at the front, there is not enough force on our side to make a go of it. *Nous verrons.*"*

Patton was right.

A lack of Allied strength in personnel and supplies, due to congested railroads, insufficient trucks, and mud-inducing rains, forced Eisenhower to admit that it was a mistake. He called off the attack.

General Mark Clark, in August of 1943, was preparing an invasion of Salerno, Italy. The code name of his attack was "Avalanche."

In the event that something might happen to Clark, Patton was told to familiarize himself with the plans for Avalanche. In his diary of September 1, he writes, ". . . I was very tactful [to General Gruenther], but could not help calling his attention to the fact that the plan uses the Sele River as a boundary between the British X Corps and the U.S. VI Corps, with no one actually on, or near the river. I told him that the Germans *will* attack down that river. He said that their plans provided for ample artillery to be ashore by 0630 on D Day to stop any German counter-attack. Of course, plans never work out (as expected), especially in a landing. I suggested this, but it did not register. I can't see why people are so foolish. I have yet to

* We shall see.

be questioned by any planner concerning my experience at Torch, yet Torch was the biggest and most difficult landing operation attempted so far.''

True to Patton's prediction, the Germans did exactly as he said they would. Neither the Americans nor the British held the Sele River and the Germans counter-attacked down the river with such a strong drive that they came very close to completely dividing the Allied forces. The Allies' position was so precarious that it almost caused an evacuation of the beachhead.

It was at this same time in the war that Bradley was chosen for the command spot of the 12th Army Group in the ETO, even though Patton was the only *experienced* American Army Commander in the ETO, and had more combat experience as a top field commander than anyone else, especially those above him. Bradley was chosen because, in Eisenhower's estimation, he was "balanced," "sound in judgment," and "experienced." Also because Bradley was a favorite of General Marshall. Bradley, thought Eisenhower, would be less apt to make mistakes than would Patton. Yet, Patton had not made a single mistake in judgment in the field. Another reason for not choosing Patton was that Eisenhower felt he made "rash" or "spur-of-the-moment" decisions. That was wholly inaccurate and a bad assumption on Eisenhower's part. As Patton put it: "For years, I have been accused of making snap judgments. Honestly, this is not the case because I am a profound military student and the thoughts I express, perhaps too flippantly, are the result of years of thought and study."

The most probable reason for Bradley's being placed above Patton was simply that General Marshall wanted it, and what Marshall wanted, Eisenhower was in no position to refuse. Eisenhower was fearful of losing his own lofty position.

In a letter dated September 16, from Eisenhower to Marshall, Eisenhower states: "... his intense loyalty to you and to me makes it possible for me to treat him [Patton] much more roughly than I could any other senior commander. ...."

This passage offers very enlightening insight into the personality and ego of both Eisenhower and Marshall. Patton's firm belief in loyalty from the top to the bottom, as well as from the bottom to the top, was virtually wasted on men of their sort. It is apparent that, to them, loyalty was something to be used to attain personal goals. Instead of appreciating Patton, they chose to take advantage of him and his great ability—not only to use, but to abuse him, and his loyalty and friendship.

In an entry to his diary dated February 12, Patton writes, "Ike said to me, 'You are fundamentally honest on the larger issues, but are too fanatical in your friendships.' That seems a strange thing to say to a friend of almost twenty years, but then, Eisenhower was concerned more with his position and his personal ambition than he was with loyalty to an old friend.

Patton's diary entry of September 8 indicates another prediction of error. He states: "[The Italian] armistice was just declared. . . . I fear that as a soldier I have too little faith in political war. Suppose the Italians can't or don't capitulate? . . . It is a great mistake to inform the troops, as has been done, of the signing of an armistice. Should they get resistance . . . [during the landings at Salerno] it would have a very bad effect."

Again, Patton was right.

The surrender of the Italians was announced on September 8, in the evening, as Clark's 5th Army was approaching Salerno Bay. The news was broadcast over all of the ships' speakers. Immediately the troops assumed that there would be no active resistance against them during the landings and there was a letdown of fighting spirit. The officers were ignored when they warned that Germans and not Italians would be on the beaches. A great many lives were needlessly wasted by this foolish act.

Patton wrote in his diary of September 15, ". . . Just saw a dispatch from Navy in which it seems that Clark has re-embarked. I consider this a fatal thing to do. Think of the effect on the troops—a commander, once ashore, *must conquer or die*." Clark was apparently concerned about other matters that took precedence over the morale and well-being of his soldiers. Nor did his actions indicate too great a concern about gaining a victory.

A diary entry of January 20 mentions the Anzio landings, code named "Operation Shingle." Patton says, "Shingle is pretty dubious as the beaches are bad and largely unknown. . . . It seems inconceivable that the Germans will not guess that we are coming ashore at Anzio, but they have made so many foolish mistakes that we may get ashore unopposed after all."

Patton was right. That is exactly what happened.

Sometime later, in April of 1944, Patton at least had occasion to have a chuckle to himself. One of his soldiers had overheard a heated discussion between General Albert C. Wedemeyer and Eisenhower. The discussion was about Patton. The little talk ended with General Wedemeyer saying, "Hell, get onto yourself, Ike. You didn't make Patton, he made you!" That knowledge must have been quite a blow to Eisenhower's mushrooming megalomania.

Patton entered a comment about the Falaise Gap dated August 13. He says, "This [XV] Corps could easily advance to Falaise and completely close the gap, but we have been ordered to halt because the British sowed the area between with a large number of time bombs [dropped from the air]. I am sure that this halt is a great mistake, as I am certain that the British will not close on Falaise."

On September 17th, Patton wrote in his diary, concerning Montgomery and his "Operation Market-Garden": "To hell with Monty. I must get so involved that they can't stop me. I told Bradley not to call me until after dark on the 19th. He agreed."

From all appearances, Bradley was finally coming around to Patton's viewpoint. He, too, had experienced enough of Eisenhower's two-faced attitude to see the handwriting on the wall. In any case of differing viewpoints between the Americans and the British, the British invariably won. Eisenhower's strategy for getting along with the "Allies" was to give in to them on each and every point, even if it meant demoralization and humiliation for the American forces.

Eisenhower had, on numerous occasions, shown his timidity, his inadequacy, his inability to command, and his unwillingness to differ with the British. On February 3, 1943, Patton recalled that "Ike talked in glittering generalities and then said, as nearly as I can remember, 'George, you are my oldest friend, but if you or anyone else criticizes the British, by God, I will reduce him to his permanent grade and send him home.' " So much for fair and equal treatment of the Americans and the British.

In April of 1943, concerning a matter of American honor, Patton writes, "It is noteworthy that had I done what Coningham did, I would have been relieved. Ike told me later that he could not punish Coningham [for calling the Americans cowards] because he was a New Zealander and political reasons forbade it. Unfortunately, I am neither a Democrat nor a Republican—just a soldier."

Again, another Allied general, did the same thing. Patton writes on April 16, "Lt. General Cocran, the s.o.b., publicly called our troops cowards. Ike says that since they were serving in his corps, *that was O.K.* I told him that had I so spoken of the British under me, my head would have come off. He agreed, but does nothing to Cocran. Bradley, Hughes, General Rooks, and I and probably many more, feel that America is being sold out. I have been more than loyal to Ike. I have talked to no one and I have taken things from the British that I would never take from an American. If this trickery to America comes from above, it is utterly damnable. If it emanates from Ike, it is utterly terrible. I seriously talked to Hughes of asking to be relieved as a protest. I feel like Judas. Hughes says that he and I and some others must stick it out to save the pieces."

Patton says on April 27, 1944, "None of those at Ike's headquarters ever go to bat for juniors. In any argument between the British and the Americans, they invariably favor the British. Benedict Arnold is a piker compared with them, and that includes General Lee as well as Ike and Beedle Smith."

One good reason for Eisenhower to be so lacking in backbone was his fear of Montgomery, or rather, fear of the power that he thought Montgomery had. Patton's diary of May 4, 1943 states: "Bedell Smith . . . says that the reason everyone yields to Monty is because Monty is the National Hero and writes directly to the Prime Minister; and that if Ike crossed him, Ike would get canned."

Still another monumental error made by SHAEF and Eisenhower is the "Battle of the Bulge." The Germans called it the "Ardennes Offensive." As mentioned previously, on December 12, 1943, Patton wrote about the possibility of a growing German salient in the area of Bastogne. ". . . The First Army is making a terrible mistake in leaving the VIII Corps static, as it is highly probable that the Germans are building up east of them."

An interesting and noteworthy fact concerning Bastogne is

that Hodges and Bradley both received a Distinguished Service Medal for their part in the defense of that small town, although their laxity in leadership and command greatly assisted the Germans in launching their offensive. Patton and his Third Army received not as much as a polite thank you for their monumental and heroic part in coming to their rescue.

On the day that Patton's Third Army had taken the German city of Trier, Bradley sent orders *not* to try to capture it, since Patton had only two divisions. Bradley and his planners said that it would require at least three divisions to capture the historic city.

Once again, Patton was right.

He sent a reply to Bradley: "Have taken city with two divisions, shall I give it back?" He also entered in his diary, "I have certainly again proven that my military ideas are correct and I have put them over in *spite* of opposition from the Americans."

The fact is that Patton was consistantly correct in his military ideas. He was not only the best combat commander in the ETO; he was one of the best, if not the best, strategic and tactical planners in the ETO. Yet, repeatedly, he was ignored, though his record and opinions were continually proved to be right.

According to Patton, the basic, underlying truth in war is that at any given moment tactics must take primacy over strategy. As he so succinctly puts it, "Good tactics can save even the worst strategy. Bad tactics can ruin even the best strategy." That concept, as simple as it is, is perhaps the best strategy.

Any adequate general can decide where he wants to fight a battle, but the important thing is to get the needed supplies, men, and proper leadership to the right place at the right time. Then, and only then, can the enemy be annihilated. That is how a battle is won.

It seems likely enough that a man such as Patton, who, in addition to his obvious natural talent, studied and lived the history of war and warriors from Xenophon, Alexander, Scipio, and Napoleon to Lee and Grant, could not help but be a great strategist as well as a great tactician.

It is folly to believe that because Patton was never given the chance to plan high-level strategy, he should be excluded from the ranks of the great captains of war.

Perhaps the most unfortunate problem plaguing the Americans during WWII was the fact that the top leadership was made up of men who had never exercised command at any adequate level and had little, if any, actual combat experience.

Lack of command experience was indeed the case with Eisenhower. Consciousness of his own lack of experience of front-line fighting led him to accept advice rather than make his own decisions. He ran SHAEF more along the lines of a board room than a military headquarters. A supreme commander must not act as chairman of the board, but must be fully in command, making all decisions firmly, decisively, and alone. The fact is that Eisenhower, never really developed a sense of what really went on at the front end of his armies. Never having personally been through the rigors of combat, he deferred too much to the advice of others less qualified than Patton. Patton noted in his diary, "Ike . . . is very querulous and keeps saying how hard it is to be so high and never to have heard a hostile shot. He could correct that situation very easily if he wanted to. I also think that he is timid."

Later, when Patton was thoroughly fed up with Eisenhower and his pomposity, he wrote, "Ike is bitten with the Presidential Bug and is *yellow*." Patton's belief that Eisenhower coveted the Presidency was recorded as early as 1943, in Africa. During the time that Patton was planning his resignation from the Army he wrote: ". . . I shall prove even more conclusively that he lacks moral fortitude. This lack has been evident to me since the first landing in Africa, but now that he has been bitten by the Presidential Bee, it is becoming even more pronounced."

The entire problem of a high command with no practical experience of command but only "theoretical knowledge," as Patton puts it, may be summed up in a further quotation from Patton's diary. He says: "In this war, we were also unfortunate in that our High Command in the main consisted of staff officers who, like Marshall, Eisenhower, and McNarny, had practically never exercised command. I think it was this lack of experience which induced them to think of and to treat units such as Divisions, Corps, and Armies as animated tables of organization rather than the living entities that they are."

★★★ NEWS ITEM ★★★

"BLOOD AND GUTS" CREDITED— BOOK MAY BURN ARMY BRASS

New York, April 30 - (AP) -

General George S. Patton, even though dead, was right back today where he always liked to be—in the middle of a hot argument.

Col. Brenton G. Wallace, a staff officer under "Blood And Guts," has written a book called "Patton and the Third Army," which is sure to burn the Army's brass.

Wallace claims that Patton was chiefly responsible both for the planning and execution of the famous St. Lo breakthrough, which swept on past Avranches and eventually hurled all the German armies out of France.

Battle plan credit, up until now, has gone uncontested to shrewd General Omar N. Bradley, who later commanded the 12th Army Group, and many experts have laid the brilliant execution of the plan at the door of Lt. Gen. Joseph L. (Lightning Joe) Collins, a corps commander in the First Army.

But Wallace, who served as assistant chief of staff in G-3 (liason) for the Third Army writes: "The First Army was given credit, whereas Gen. Patton planned it and executed it and used not only First Army troops but also a number of his own Third Army units."

Wallace, however, gives Bradley credit for his foresight in placing Patton "in charge of the breakthrough itself."

The Slapping Incidents
The Whole Story

I

Thousands of words have been written about the "slapping incidents" which took place during August 1943 on the island of Sicily and almost ended the career of General Patton. Yet little has been written that takes account of all the facts, the whole story.

I will give all the significant facts, and name the principle persons involved and how they acted or reacted. It will be left to the reader to decide for himself whether Patton was justified in his actions or not.

First, the recorded information, which has been publicized to date. Thereafter, we shall review the rest of the story, which has never been brought to light before.

From a letter dated August 16, 1943, by Lt. Col. Perrin H. Long, Medical Corps, on the subject of "Mistreatment of Patients in Receiving Tents":

"Exhibit 1—Pvt. Charles H. Kuhl, L Company, 26th Infantry, 1st Division, was seen in the aid station on August 2, 1943. A diagnosis of 'Exhaustion' was made. He was evacuated to C Company, 1st Medical Battalion. There was a note made on the patient's Emergency Medical Tag that he had been admitted to Company C three times for 'Exhaustion' during the Sicilian Campaign. From C Company he was evacuated to the clearing company and there was put in 'quarters' and was given sodium mytal. On 3 August 1943, the following note appears on the E.M.T.: 'Psychoneurosis anxiety state—moderate severe (soldier has been twice before in hospital within ten days. He can't take it at the front, evidently. He is repeatedly returned).' He was evacuated to the 15th Evacuation Hospital. While he was waiting in the receiving tent, Lt. Gen. George S. Patton, Jr.,

71

came into the tent with the commanding officer and other medical officers. The general spoke to the various patients in the receiving tent and especially commended the wounded men. Then he came to Pvt. Kuhl and asked him what was the matter. The soldier replied, 'I guess I can't take it.' The general immediately flared up, cursed the soldier, called him all types of a coward, then slapped him across the face with his gloves and finally grabbed the soldier by the scruff of his neck and kicked him out of the tent. The soldier was immediately picked up by corpsmen and taken to a ward tent. There he was found to have a temperature of 102.2 degrees F and he gave a history of chronic diarrhea for about one month, having at times as high as ten or twelve stools a day. The next day his fever continued and a blood smear was found to be positive for malarial parasites. The final disposition diagnosis was chronic dysentery and malaria. This man had been in the Army eight months and with the 1st Division since about June 2d.

"Exhibit 2—Pvt. Paul G. Bennet, C Battery, 17th Field Artillery, was admitted to the 93rd Evacuation Hospital on 10 August '43. This patient was a 21 year old boy who had served four years in the regular Army. His unit had been with II Corps since March and he had never had any difficulties until August 6th, when his buddy was wounded. He could not sleep that night and felt nervous. The shells going over him bothered him. The next day he was worried about his buddy and became more nervous. He was sent down to the rear echelon by a battery aid man and there the medical officer gave him some medicine which made him sleep, but still he was nervous and disturbed. On the next day the medical officer ordered him to be evacuated, although the boy begged not to be evacuated because he did not want to leave his unit. Lt. Gen. George S. Patton, Jr., entered the receiving tent and spoke to all the injured men. The next patient was sitting huddled up and shivering. When asked what his trouble was, the man replied, 'It's my nerves,' and he began to sob. The General then screamed at him, 'What did you say?' The man replied, 'It's my nerves, I can't stand the shelling anymore.' He was still sobbing. The General then yelled at him, 'Your nerves, hell; you are just a Goddamned coward, you yellow son of a bitch.' He then slapped the man and said, 'Shut up that Goddamned crying. I won't have these brave men here who have been shot at seeing a yellow bastard sitting here crying.' He then struck the man again, knocking his helmet liner off and into the next tent. He then turned to the admitting officer and yelled, 'Don't admit this yellow bastard: there's nothing the matter with him. I won't have the hospitals cluttered up with these sons of bitches who haven't got the guts to fight.' He then turned to the man again, who was managing to sit at attention though shaking all over and said, 'You're going back to the front lines and you may get shot and killed, but you're going to fight. If you don't, I'll stand you up against a wall and have a firing squad kill you on purpose. In fact,' he said, reaching for his pistol, 'I ought to shoot you myself, you Goddamned whimpering coward.' As he left the tent, the general was still yelling back to the receiving officer to send that yellow son of a bitch back to the front line. Nurses and patients attracted by the shouting and cursing came from adjoining tents and witnessed this disturbance. The deleterious effects of such incidents upon the wellbeing of patients, upon the professional morale of hospital staffs, and upon the relationship of patient to physician are incalculable. It is imperative that immediate steps be taken to prevent a recurrence of such incidents."

These reports had been made through the normal chain of command and eventually reached the desk of General Omar Bradley who was at the time Patton's subordinate. Rather than show the reports to his superior, Bradley chose to secure them in his safe and forget the whole affair. Had he shown them to Patton, he would at least have let him know that his actions were being challenged by his medical officers and he could possibly have reconsidered his actions. As it turned out, the medical officers by-passed the normal channels and sent a second set of reports through medical channels to the High Command at Eisenhower's headquarters.

The reports above are verbatim according to the "medical authorities." Later, after talking with another medical officer present at one of the incidents, General Brenton Wallace reported, "As for the so-called 'slapping incidents': General Patton made frequent visits to the hospitals to see that the wounded were being properly cared for. One day he visited a large hospital in Sicily when he commanded the Seventh Army.

"As he came to the last ward, having been much distressed

by the sights he had seen of the severely wounded and how bravely they were bearing up, he saw suddenly a young soldier sitting on the edge of his cot, apparently crying.

"Patton went over and said, 'What's wrong, soldier, are you hurt?'

"Without rising, but burying his face in his hands, the soldier whimpered, 'Oh, no, I'm not hurt, but, oh, it's terrible—terrible—boo-hoo-hoo.'

"With that the general, disturbed after seeing all the badly wounded and mutilated soldiers, commanded, 'Stand up.'

"The soldier got to his feet and the general slapped him across the neck with his gloves, which he was carrying, and said, 'Why don't you act like a man instead of a damn sniveling baby? Look at these severely wounded soldiers, not complaining a bit and as cheerful as can be, and here you are, a Goddamned crybaby.'

"I was told by the medical officer that it was the best thing that could have happened to the boy and that he was discharged from the hospital in less than a week, perfectly normal and well."

It would appear from this account that there are, indeed, two sides to every story.

On August 17, 1943, General F.A. Blesse, the Chief Surgeon at AFHQ brought to General Patton a letter from Eisenhower. It read, "I am attaching a report which is shocking in its allegations against your personal conduct. I hope you can assure me that none of them is true; but the detailed circumstances communicated to me lead to the belief that some ground for the charges must exist. I am well aware of the necessity for hardness and toughness on the battlefield. I clearly understand that firm and drastic measures are at times necessary in order to secure the desired objectives. But this does not excuse brutality, abuse of the sick,* nor exhbition of uncontrollable temper in front of subordinates.

"In the two cases cited in the attached report, it is not my present intention to institute any formal investigation. Moreover, it is acutely distressing to me to have such charges as these

* The implied definition of sick is Eisenhower's. It was Patton's firm conviction that "battle fatigue" is not a sickness. He believed that all men are afraid in combat, but that only the coward allows his fear to overcome his sense of duty.

made against you at the very moment when an American Army under your leadership has attained a success of which I am extremely proud. I feel that the personal services you have rendered the United States and the Allied cause during the past weeks are of incalculable value; but nevertheless, if there is a very considerable element of truth in the allegations accompanying this letter, I must so seriously question your good judgment and your self-discipline as to raise serious doubts in my mind as to your future usefulness. I am assuming, for the moment, that the facts in the case are far less serious than appears in this report, and that whatever truth is contained in these allegations reports an act of yours when, under the stress and strain of winning a victory, you were thoughtless rather than harsh. Your leadership of the past few weeks has, in my opinion, fully vindicated to the War Department and to all your associates in arms my own persistence in upholding your pre-eminent qualifications for the difficult task to which you were assigned. Nevertheless, you must give to this matter of personal deportment your instant and serious consideration to the end that no incident of this character can be reported to me in the future, and I may continue to count upon your assistance in military tasks.

"In Allied Headquarters there is no record of the attached report or of my letter to you, except in my own secret files. I will expect your answer to be sent to me personally and secretly. Moreover, I strongly advise that, provided that there is any semblance of truth in the allegations in the accompanying report, you make in the form of an apology or other such personal amends to the individuals concerned as may be within your power, and that you do this before submitting your letter to me.

"No letter that I have been called upon to write in my military career has caused me the mental anguish of this one, not only because of my long and deep personal friendship for you but because of my admiration for your military qualities, but I assure you that conduct such as described in the accompanying report will not be tolerated in this theater no matter who the offender may be."

Eisenhower had decided that Patton was far too valuable to the war effort to lose. His audaucious, driving leadership was surely needed at this stage of the game. Eisenhower's plan was to have Patton apologize to the soldiers he had slapped and also to all of the personnel in his Army in Division formation. Knowing Patton's pride, he felt that this would be severe punishment, indeed. In Beatrice Patton's words, "The deed is done and the mistake made, and I'm sure Georgie is sorrier and has punished himself more than anyone could possibly realize. . . . I just hope they won't kick him to death while he's down."

Some of the correspondents at AFHQ, including Demaree Bess of the *Saturday Evening Post* had learned of the slappings. They were uncertain about the propriety of reporting the situation because they did not know whether or not Patton might be subject to a Court Martial for his actions. They contacted Eisenhower prior to submitting their accounts of the matter for publication. Eisenhower then had a meeting with three of the Senior Correspondents at AFHQ during which he explained the situation to them and the exact course of action that he had followed, hoping that the issue could be regarded as settled.

The correspondents decided as a group to drop the matter. They, too, thought Patton too valuable a man to lose.

Although Eisenhower thought that this course of action was best, Patton disagreed. Of course, being in the doghouse at the time, he thought silence better than a protest. Later, he would write in his diary: "I had been expecting something like this [the Drew Pearson attack] to happen for some time because I am sure that it would have been much better to have admitted the whole thing to start with, particularly in view of the fact that I was *right* in what I did. (Patton never admitted having been in error. In his "apologies" he actually only explained why he had done what he had done).

At this point, our story would seem to be finished. Fate, however, disposed matters otherwise. Figures would become involved whose presence in the case was curious indeed. One of those persons was a homosexual employee of the State Department who had no other relationship to General Patton than that they both worked for the same government. It is ironic that two men so opposed in their character and predilections should be involved in the same historical tragedy.

In the month of November, 1943, Drew Pearson broadcast the story of Patton and his slapping of two American soldiers.

Disregarding the fact that many other correspondents and news media people knew of the incidents and that the story was three months old, Pearson claimed the story as his personal "scoop." Pearson's broadcast, of course, created a sensation throughout the United States. Some Senators and Congressmen, upon hearing the broadcast, clamored for the dismissal of General Patton purely on the basis of Pearson's allegations, not waiting for any evidence nor the complete facts of the story. One Congressman went so far as to compare Patton to Hitler, and one newspaper ran a political cartoon of Patton in which the General bore a remarkable resemblance to "Der Fuehrer."

One of the reasons that Pearson's "scoop" caused a furor was his allegation that the Army in general, and Eisenhower in particular, had made an attempt to cover up the whole story.

Actually, there was no attempt at a cover-up. During Eisenhower's absence a press conference was held by General Bedell Smith (never one of Patton's best friends). During this conference, when asked about the slappings, Smith said that Eisenhower's letter to Patton was "private" rather than a public reprimand. Later, Eisenhower termed Smith's remarks a "mistake." Smith probably did not care too much, though, as he had no great liking for Patton. This apparently impressed Pearson as an attempt to keep the story from the American public.

Here we arrive at what the public now generally considers the end of the story. We know that Patton did slap two soldiers. He was reprimanded and made to apologize. He was relieved of his command of the Seventh Army. He later went on to vindicate himself by further examples of the dynamic leadership he had always shown. His Third Army would go farther, faster, kill more enemy, take more prisoners, and conquer more territory than any other Army in history. All of this with Patton in the vanguard of the attack.

II

There are some questions which should be asked concerning the personalities with which we are dealing. First, there was that of Patton himself. He was known to be a hard taskmaster and stern disciplinarian. He demanded and received the utmost from his men. He was, in fact, even harder on himself than he was with his subordinates. Patton was the personification of the warrior spirit—aggressive, driving, and impervious to enemy opposition. He was absolutely dedicated to Allied victory—and one of its principal architects. He strove for the perfection of leadership indicated in his own words: "It lurks invisible in that vitalizing spark, intangible, yet as evident as the lightning; the warrior soul."

There is, then, a question which must be asked, even if only rhetorically. Why was everyone surprised when he acted as he did? Eisenhower, Bradley, Marshall, all of his colleagues who had either known him personally or known of him during his thirty years in the Army had also known of his volatile nature and his flaring temperament (which was largely a matter of deliberate policy). The public knew of his personality because of the mass press coverage about his style of leadership. The media not only knew of his brash actions and his powerful personality, but condoned and encouraged it because he was "good copy." They actually helped to create the image of the "fighting general" that fit Patton so well. Why, then, were all of these poeple so surprised and upset when Patton acted like Patton? The only possible answer is: human nature. A child thinks little of the danger of a fascinating, shiny, new fishhook, yet he cries when its sharp point becomes imbedded in his finger.

Patton knew war for what it was, and he knew that to fight a war successfully required a measure of ruthlessness. In his diary he wrote, "I believe that in war the good of the individual must be subordinated to the good of the Army. I love and admire good soldiers and brave men. I hate and despise slackers and cowards."

On the day that one of the slappings occurred, Patton had written, "At another evacuation hospital saw another alleged 'nervous patient'—really a coward. I told the doctor to return him to his company and he began to cry so I cursed him and he shut up. I may have saved his soul, if he had one."

When the criticism about his harshness with his men arose, he wrote in his diary, "For every man I have criticized in this Army, I have probably stopped, talked to, and complimented a thousand. But people are more prone to remember ill usage than to recall compliments."

Regarding Drew Pearson, he wrote, "My men are crazy about me, and this is what makes me most angry with Drew Pearson." And later he noted appositely, "If the fate of the only successful general in this war depends on the statement of a discredited writer like Drew Pearson, then we are in a bad fix."

In December of 1943 the Gallup Poll showed the general's ratings to be "77% good, 19% bad, and 4% uncertain."

Patton's wife, Beatrice, wrote at the time to a friend: "I wonder that he [Pearson] does not die of his own poison. The only excuse, and it is not an excuse, that I can see for his existence, is that the world is made up of forces of good and forces of evil, and that without the latter there would be no struggle, and people might get soft. I cannot explain him any other way.

"I have followed his predictions now for some time, and am convinced that he is a traitor to America."

Whereas in Pearson's broadcast he claimed Patton to be the "most hated man" in his Army, Eisenhower, in his report to General Marshall states, "In every recent public appearance of Patton before any crowd composed of his own soldiers, he is greeted by *thunderous* applause." On December 1, 1943, Patton received a letter from an old friend, General Kenyon Joyce, who wrote, "George, tell them the exact truth in these words— 'I had been dealing with heroes. I saw two men whom I thought to be cowards. Naturally, I was not too gentle with them.' "

By the end of 1943, approximately 1500 letters had been received at the White House concerning Patton. Most of them favored his actions and understood his motives; some even called for his immediate promotion.

One of the interesting pieces of information which was not published during the public controversy was told to General Patton by General John A. Crance (Pvt. Bennet's Brigade Commander). He informed Patton that, ". . . The man (Bennet) was absent without leave (AWOL) and had gone to the rear by falsely representing his condition to the Battery Surgeon." Patton remarked, "It is a commentary on justice when an Army Commander has to soft soap a skulker to placate the timidity of those above."

Further evidence regarding the motives behind Patton's actions comes from Maj. Gen. Clarence R. Huebner. After the war he had mentioned the possibility that he might have been partly responsible for the slapping incidents. Patton had once asked Heubner how things were going. Heubner replied, "The front lines seem to be thinning out. There seems to be a very large number of 'malingerers' at the hospitals, feigning illness in order to avoid combat duty."

Patton, of course, would not stand for this sort of thing. One of his maxims was, "Cowardice is a disease and must be checked immediately, before it becomes epidemic." In a special memo to Seventh Army dated August 5, 1943, Patton says, "It has come to my attention that a very small number of soldiers are going to the hospital on the pretext that they are nervously incapable of combat. Such men are cowards and bring discredit on the army and disgrace to their comrades, whom they heartlessly leave to endure the dangers of battle while they themselves use the hospital as a means of escape. You will take measures to see that such cases are not sent to the hospital but are dealt with in their units. Those who are not willing to fight will be tried by Court-Martial for cowardice in the face of the enemy."

Had these orders been followed, the slappings would never have occurred.

III

Now we have a more complete picture of what occurred and how Patton and his friends reacted to criticism. We shall now see how Drew Pearson fits into this story and why he chose to attack the only "successful general" that the United States had at that time.

According to reports of Drew Pearson's personality, some of which came from his friends, he was as mean and vengeful as a copperhead snake. It made no difference who he bit as long as he bit someone. That was his nature. Pearson would attack friend or foe alike. The only requirement was that it benefit Pearson.

We now become involved with four other principle characters in our story. They are Franklin D. Roosevelt, President of the

United States; Cordell Hull, Secretary of State; Sumner Welles, Undersecretary of State; and Ernest Cuneo, Pearson's lawyer.

Pearson was pro-communist, pro-Chinese, and pro-Russian. As a friend of Russia, he demanded in 1943 that the Allied Command create a second front in Europe to assist our Russian "friends." When Pearson's demands were not met immediately, he became angry.

President Roosevelt was by no means an admirer of Cordell Hull. He had appointed Hull Secretary of State as a political move to placate Southern Democrats. Whereas Hull was more inclined to a "close-to-home" foreign policy, Roosevelt favored a "good neighbor" policy. Hull resisted all attempts to bring about that "good neighbor" policy. Roosevelt then turned to Sumner Welles, Undersecretary of State, who, like the President, favored a more flexible and conciliatory foreign policy. What Roosevelt succeeded in doing was to create a confrontation between Hull and Welles. Hull wanted very much to be rid of Welles and was willing to do just about anything to attain that goal. Roosevelt had known for some time that Welles was homosexual. He cared little about that. His attitude was that as long as Welles was doing an adequate job, his sexual preferences should be his own concern. Welles, backed up by Roosevelt, refused to budge from his position, and he held his ground against Hull until the latter part of 1943. At that time some friends of Hull (who were of course enemies of Welles) began to attack the latter. In newspaper columns they began to allude to his sexual preferences, claiming that he was a security risk. The American public was far less tolerant of homosexuality in those days than it is today. Welles finally resigned his post as Undersecretary, citing among other reasons the possibility of his being a security risk as the newspapers had suggested.

Welles's forced resignation infuriated Pearson, who was a close friend of his. In retribution, Pearson vociferously attacked Secretary Hull, stating that Hull had only one idea in mind—not to open a second front, to "bleed Russia white." In response the Secretary said, "Pearson's allegations are pure falsehood; monstrous and diabolical lies." Roosevelt, always the politician, then chimed in with Hull. Using one of his favorite labels, he blasted Pearson as a "chronic liar." Knowing Pearson's affection for the Russians, Roosevelt then added insult to injury by claiming that the Russians might be offended by Pearson's untrue remarks.

Pearson, since he was indeed friendly toward the Russians, began to feel anxiety about Roosevelt's remarks. He worried over the impact of the President's criticism because it could hurt his position with the Russians and also because it was a blow to his credibility with the public. He called an emergency meeting with his lawyer, Ernest Cuneo.

Cuneo suggested that Pearson might use a "distraction" to focus the public eye away from his lost battle. His idea was to create a sensational new diversion. This, then was the moment that Fate had in store. Now was the time that seemingly unrelated occurrences would be tied together to make history. Cuneo suggested that Pearson use the story of the "slapping incidents." There were a number of Washington correspondents, along with the North African correspondents, who had already heard the story, but they had declined to make it public. Pearson had no scruples about any story at any time. He was a master of yellow journalism, and he never failed to use that mastery for his own benefit. On November 21, 1943, Pearson broke his three month old "scoop." He also predicted in his broadcast that Patton would never again hold a responsible war assignment. He was wrong, as he often was.

Another columnist jumped on the story immediately. Walter Winchell claimed that Patton was going to be murdered by one of his own men. So much for media credibility.

It is difficult to believe that a muckraker like Drew Pearson and the resignation of a homosexual government employee could almost cause the destruction of the career of one of the greatest military figures in the history of the United States, but it is true.

It would at least be understandable and perhaps gratifying if it could be reported that Pearson had broadcast the story because he truly believed in the rights of soldiers, or that he deeply cared about those men. It would be nice to be able to say that he did it because it was "the right thing to do" and because of his moral convictions. Unfortunately, that is not the case. Pearson created a sensation not out of virtue, but out of necessity, his only motive being to salve his hurt pride and defend his injured reputation.

Patton probably understood the whole matter better than anyone. He firmly believed in fate. He wrote in his diary, "Well, pretty soon I will hit bottom and then bounce." The following day he wrote a poem entitled "Seven up." The last verse was;

> Yet, like the fabled Phoenix,
> the Seventh shall arise.
> Again to soar in triumph,
> Through flaming smoke-veiled skies.

He probably was also thinking of "his" destiny as well as that of the Seventh Army. Patton always tried to be optimistic.

So there is the final story—facts that have never before been publicly exposed.

In summary:

Patton was known to be the kind of man who would react violently when confronted with soldiers whom he thought to be cowards, yet everyone was surprised when he was true to his image.

Patton had received reports of malingering and had issued orders that offenders be dealt with at unit level. His orders were not followed.

One of the soldiers who was slapped was AWOL at the time of the incident, yet that fact was never publicized.

The "scoop" publicized by Pearson was three months old and had been avoided by other, more discreet journalists.

Pearson used the story not for some virtuous, moral purpose, but to divert attention from President Roosevelt's characterization of him as a "chronic liar."

It would be well to close with a repetition of one of Patton's observations. "If the fate of the only successful General in this war depends on the statement of a discredited writer like Drew Pearson, we are in a bad fix."

A Footnote to the Slapping Incidents

Since the writing of this chapter on the slapping incidents, some additional information has come to light.

Porter B. Williamson holds two degrees: one a B.A. in business, and the other a Ph.D. in law. He has for a number of years been a legal columnist and has written several books on the subject of law. He achieved national recognition in 1955 when he won a "citizens rights" case against the Department of Defense and the case was reported in the *Saturday Evening Post* magazine. He was also a young lieutenant who served as Adjutant and Military Legal Advisor to General Patton during the Desert Training Maneuvers in the California desert in 1942. He knows what he is talking about when discussing either civil or military law.

The following is an excerpt from a letter received from Mr. Williamson concerning Charles Kuhl specifically, and having some general relevance to the case of Paul Bennet, the two soldiers whom General Patton slapped:

"About Kuhl and his statement. I am enclosing his newspaper interview. His words are not clear from the copy. His exact words were, 'Maybe if I had handled it right I'd have gotten home a lot sooner.'

"From a local doctor (Hank Limbacher) who was serving in this field hospital, this information is available. Kuhl reported to the hospital with his helmet and no 201 (personal file) and without a rifle. He walked in under his own power. It was two days before they could locate his file. By this time he had been slapped by General Patton. This Evacuation Hospital was not inclined to 'enjoy the war' as many of the doctors were aginst war. Their general policy was to encourage 'combat fatigue.' Combat fatigue was a term used by the front line medics [for men] who had served on the front too long. Exhaustion is the term we would use today. For 'combat fatigue,' the soldier would be sent by his unit commander to the hospital for any medical reason and then to 'rest and relaxation.' This Evacuation Hospital put both deserters and the combat fatigue patients and the injured in the same wards.

"According to the Tucson doctor, Kuhl had no symptoms of any illness when he reported. Two days later, he was running a fever. In WWII we had a GI soap that was often used as a suppository to fake sick call. This was a yellow soap which we often mentioned as matching the courage of the soldier.

"If General Patton had not slapped Kuhl, his unit commander could and probably would have charged him with desertion. [Ladislas] Farago gives an account of how this reached politics on the highest (or lowest) level . . . . We were briefed in WWII that the automatic carried by the officers was to use on soldiers turning away from the enemy. This is a common understanding among the soldiers of many armies. Or [in other words] the officer can be the judge and jury and administer the sentence for the crime."

Mr. Williamson refers in his letter to the Articles of War, Courts Martial, U.S. Army. Three paragraphs of particular interest are Articles 58, 59, and 66. They read as follows:

Art. 58. Desertion—Any person subject to military law who deserts or attempts to desert the service of the United States shall, if the offense be committed in time of war, suffer death or such other punishment as a court martial may direct, and, if the offense be committed at any other time, any punishment, excepting death, that a court martial may direct.

ART. 59 Advising or Aiding Another to Desert—Any person subject to military law who advises or persuades or knowingly assists another to desert the service of the United States shall, if the offense be committed in time of war, suffer death or such other punishment as a court martial may direct, and, if the offense be committed at any other time, any punishment, excepting death, that a court martial may direct.

ART. 66 Mutiny or Sedition—Any person subject to military law who attempts to create or who begins, excites, causes, or joins in any mutiny or sedition in any company, party, post, camp, detachment, guard, or other command shall suffer death or such other punishment as a court martial may direct.

According to the information received from Mr. Williamson, from the remarks of Mr. Limbacher, and from verified accounts from the company records of the soldiers involved, General Patton could have legally shot both of them and, on technical grounds at the very least, been perfectly within his rights as a Commanding General.

★★★ NEWS ITEM ★★★

SLAP, OR SLUG, OR KICK, PATTON HIS MAN, A G.I. SAYS

New Orleans, La., Jan. 15 - (AP) -

T/Sgt. Sam H. Tarleton, fresh from the European fighting where he was wounded, came home today high in praise of "pistol packing" Lt. Gen. Patton.

The 3d Army boys, he said, think this about Patton: "He could slap me, slug me in the teeth, kick me, and then if he said, 'Fall in' I'd be at the head of the column."

"As for the Heinies, he doesn't give a damn for them," said the sergeant. "If there's a bogey man for Hitler, it's George S. Patton."

Patton's Resignation

"I have given this a great deal of thought," said the General. "I am going to resign from the Army. Quit outright, not retire. That's the only way I can be free to live my own way of life. That's the only way I can and will live from now on. For the years that are left to me I am determined to be free to live as I want to live and to say what I want to say. This has occupied my mind almost completely the last two months and I am fully convinced that this the only *honorable* and proper course to take."

This was an extremely difficult and painful decision for Patton. The Army *was* his life. He had lived as a soldier and warrior for over thirty years. If Patton felt that he must give up the Army to be able to speak freely, there must surely have been some compelling reasons. Reasons so important that he would be willing to withdraw entirely from the only way of life he had ever known.

In December of 1945, Patton was scheduled to go home to Hamilton, Massachusetts, to spend the holidays with his family. His plans were to fly to London where he would meet Admiral Hewitt and sail on Hewitt's flagship to the United States.

"When I get home," said Patton, "I am going through with my plan to resign from the Army. I'm going to do it with a statement that will be remembered a long time. If it doesn't make headlines, I will be surprised. I am determined to be free to live my own way of life, and I'm going to make that *unforgettably* clear."

Unfortunately, General Patton did not live to fulfill his decision. He was injured in an automobile accident on the ninth of December, 1945; he died on the twenty-first of December in the same year. He had a broken neck as a result of the accident, and he never recovered. He was buried on December twenty-fourth, Christmas Eve, in the United States Military Cemetary located at Hamm, Luxembourg. To this day, there are thou-

sands of visitors who make a special trip to the cemetary to see
his grave among the graves of the men with whom he fought
during the Second World War. Luxembourg observes "Patton
Day" every year in commemoration of the great achievements of
General Patton.

Patton felt that there were many things that had been with-
held from the American public during the war, and he strongly
believed that they had a right to know the truth. He felt that
someone had to stand up and fight for America and it might as
well be he, since no one else seemed willing to do so. He was
firmly convinced that the United States had an obligation to
win not only the war they had just fought but also the *peace*.

More detailed examinations of "winning the peace" and
"telling the truth" will be dealt with later in this book. At this
point, we shall examine the reasons behind Patton's planned
resignation from the service, the underlying reasons why he felt
that he must do something now and why he was willing to give
up thirty years of his life.

To some people this may all seem to have been born of
"bitterness" which grew within Patton after his ouster from
command of the Third Army in September of 1945. That is not
so. It was a situation that had been festering for some years,
even before the Western Task Force's invasion of North Africa
in 1942. If Patton could, indeed, be labeled "bitter," his bitterness was not without cause, and damn good cause.

Patton's one great desire in life was to be a combat commander, to "lead thousands of men in a desperate fight." Unlike
Eisenhower, who attended West Point in order to "get a free
education," Patton attended West Point (which he called "That
Holy Place") as the first step in the ladder to his only ambition
in life; the role of a combat commander: a *soldier* of the highest
caliber.

As was admitted even by his most ardent military detractors,
Patton was the best the United States Army had in the European
Theater of war. Probably in all theaters of war. As time passes,
and more facts come to light, we see that Patton was more right
more often than his fellow commanders, not only in military
matters, but also in his international political assessments. He
was more successfully consistent in his winning abilities than
any other military commander of the Second World War. Yet

he was forced to humble himself before men of lesser ability.

Often, Patton was charged with being egotistical about his own ability. It was often said that he was too "cocky" (a term used very often also when speaking of Third Army soldiers). In war, as in no other human endeavor, there is no room for false modesty, especially when the lives of thousands of men are at stake.

Patton, during WWII, was the butt of a great many personal slights from people who were supposed to be his friends. The seeds of bitterness were planted before the United States became fully immersed in the brutal struggle in Europe. At the time that Patton was a Major General, Dwight Eisenhower, Omar Bradley, William Simpson, Courtney Hodges, Jacob Devers, and Mark Clark had yet to receive their first star.

In April of 1945, when Eisenhower had five stars, and all of the others had received their fourth stars, Patton had yet to receive his fourth star.

Patton had been a full Colonel in the Tank Corps in WWI and upon the signing of the Armistice in 1918, was reduced to Captain, then the following day promoted to Major. This demotion was not due to any error or failure on his part; it was just customary Army procedure. Most officers were treated in this manner. It is the usual course for American politicians, after a war, to reduce in grade all military personnel, and to do their best to destroy the fighting ability of the military organization. It had been done in every war in which the United States had ever been involved, and continues to be the course of action today. It took twenty years for Patton to again become a full Colonel, advancing through each and every rank.

Both Bradley and Clark had been given a special assist up the ladder of success. They had been promoted directly from Lieutenant Colonel to Brigadier General by General George C. Marshall, bypassing entirely the rank of Colonel. Patton, Bradley, and Clark wore stars before Eisenhower did, yet Eisenhower was eventually moved ahead of them all.

In all aspects—knowledge, education, ability, effectiveness, leadership, and experience—Patton was head and shoulders above them all. Yet, he was the last of them to receive recognition by the high command. And he was the last to receive the four stars of a full general.

Patton had seen himself and the American Army continually being forced to accept secondary roles in combat. In North Africa, the II Corps, under British command, suffered a humiliating defeat. Patton was called in to restore the unit to fighting pitch.

In Sicily, American forces (Patton's Seventh Army) were relegated to a second-place position as "flank defenders" for Montgomery during his advance toward Messina, the capital of that island. Patton and the Seventh Army still managed to get to Messina before Montgomery could.

In Normandy, Patton landed with the Third Army after a beachhead had been established. He then broke out of the hedgerows and began attacking in four directions. To quote an old cavalry saying, "He attacked in all directions at once, with a saber in each hand, and a pistol in the other." In short order, he surrounded the entire German Seventh Army. Yet he was halted in his tracks by SHAEF, being ordered not to close the gap between the American and British Armies. It was left to Montgomery to do so. He did so about two weeks later, after most of the Germans had managed to escape to fight again.

Patton and the Third Army later reached and had begun to clear Paris before the other Allied forces. He was ordered not to enter Paris, but to give that privilege to the American First Army and the British forces.

Patton's Third Army was the most successful and the fastest moving army in the ETO, yet he was halted during a successful campaign again in September of 1944 so that Montgomery could launch his "Operation Market-Garden"—an attack which was supposed to clear the Germans out of Arnhem and open the way to Germany itself. This operation designed to attack deep into the Reich's territory succeeded only in killing or wounding about half of the thirty thousand Allied troops involved and many civilians.

Ignoring SHAEF's intelligence reports and relying upon his own, Patton expected and was prepared for the German offensive at Bastogne in December of 1944. Patton suggested that the Germans be allowed to advance a short distance further and that he could then hit them in their rear, cutting them off at the neck. Of course, his idea was rejected. His army then shifted ninety degrees to the north as ordered, and it hit the German offensive in the flank, stopping its advance immediately. When Patton indicated that he should be allowed to advance directly to Berlin after the Bastogne operation, he was once more overruled and told to head south. Later, he was ordered to the "Redoubt" area which (as Patton had predicted) proved to be non-existent.

It is noteworthy to mention that at the time of the Ardennes Offensive (the Battle of the Bulge), Patton was leading his army in combat. Bradley was in SHAEF headquarters in London, playing bridge with Eisenhower, when they received word of the German attack.

There were two incidents which occurred in WWII which caused problems for Patton because of his "comments." One of these was the "Knutsford Incident" in England. It was alleged that, at a gathering at a women's club, Patton said that Britain and The United States were destined to rule the world. This was not the major problem; the problem was that he had supposedly omitted mention of our friends, the Russians. The fact is that the story is untrue; he *had* mentioned the Russians and it was duly noted in the English papers. That mention of the Russians was omitted in the United States papers by the United States publishers and correspondents. They then claimed that Patton was the one who had failed to mention the Russians. Furthermore, Patton had at first refused to speak at the gathering. He was talked into it by one of the ladies of the club. He was promised that there would be no journalists present, that his remarks were to be "off the record," and that he would not be quoted.

The second of the incidents was the "September Affair" in which Patton supposedly compared Nazis to Republicans and Democrats. What makes the story even more disgusting is the fact that the United States Supreme Court now allows the Nazi Party to exist within our own borders today.

After the cessation of hostilities in Germany, the country was, of course, in chaotic turmoil. The only people who knew how to run things were Nazis, or those who had at least joined the Nazi Party in order to hold on to their jobs. Patton kept a certain number of these people in key positions in an effort to start the rebuilding of a destroyed country. Patton's wish was to build Germany as a buffer state against the real enemy that he envisioned, the Russians. As he said, "They do a damned good impression of the 'goose-step.' They strike me as a very great danger and threat to future world peace and world political reorganization. They are something to be feared." Patton wanted to be friends with the Germans. Although Patton was condemned for this line of thought, the U.S. would later spend billions of dollars to rebuild Germany almost exactly along the lines that Patton had proposed—except that now the plan is known as the "Marshall Plan," and of course, General Marshall is lauded as a great hero and humanitarian. Patton was doing exactly what was being done by all other U.S., British, and French commanders and civilian authorities throughout occupied Germany. Later, after the furor had died down, the Military Government was to actually put into effect the same "Nazi personnel" quota that had been created by Patton.

At a press conference, Patton was asked by a reporter, "Isn't this Nazi thing really just like a Republican-Democratic election fight? The 'outs' calling the 'ins' Nazis?" To this question, Patton answered, "Yes, that is about it."

This was immediately paraphrased by the media into "front page stuff," with headlines claiming, "PATTON CALLS REPUBLICANS AND DEMOCRATS NAZIS."

At this point, with the war over, Eisenhower no longer needed Patton to push him up the ladder of success. After a strained two and a half-hour meeting, the friendship between the two was ended. Patton was removed from command of the Third Army and given command of the 15th Army, a paper army.

Patton could not understand why this had happened. He had done nothing that the other commanders had not done. If he was wrong, why not they, too? He was hurt by Eisenhower's patronizing, "Messiah" attitude (as Patton termed Eisenhower's growing egomania). As early as 1942, Patton had predicted, again correctly, that Eisenhower was cherishing the idea of being President of the United States. Patton had given his utmost in loyalty and labor, yet he was subjected to a humiliating verbal spanking in private by Eisenhower and to degrading condemnation in public. Radio commentators attacked him, newspaper editorials insulted him, and opportunistic politicians ranted and raved for his scalp.

Patton had no chance to defend himself, since he had been

ordered by Eisenhower to remain silent and have no further press conferences. There was, however, concern on the part of many newspaper people that he might have been goaded into the situation. One of them was George E. Sokolsky. In an editorial in a Cincinnati newspaper, he raised some very interesting questions which were never answered.

Sokolsky wrote: "Patton has a side. The argument against General Patton was that although he was a wonderful commander in the field, he was a pretty poor administrator and that he does not understand politics at all. This is a generalized statement of what has been said on all sides, and having had some experience with propaganda, particularly of the whispering kind, I have become suspicious of the unanimous character of the above judgment. Too many who could not know have said the same thing; therefore somebody laid it down as something to be believed. It is a dictum of propaganda that if a lie is repeated often enough, it comes to be believed.

"So I have been making inquiries, and the story I get is that some newspapermen and left-wing government agents have been laying for George Patton because they do not like him. These leftwingers know that the general has a strong temper, which the Germans found troublesome on the field of battle, and therefore they needled him into outbursts of wrath at them, which, when generalized and repeated out of context, got him into trouble. I have not been in Europe and cannot speak from first-hand information, but I feel that is is simple justice to give the side that seems to have had no representation.

"A tricky reporter can, like a shyster lawyer, cross up an amateur whose business is not asking or answering questions.

"Businessmen have in recent years found that they have to hire public relations counsel to protect them against the kind of inquisition which involves a yes-or-no answer to the query, "Have you stopped beating your wife again"? Of course, no decent person asks such a question just as no decent person picks a pocket.

"On the particular occasion when General Patton got himself into a jam on account of which he was removed from his own heroic Third Army, he was put through the kind of criss-cross questioning which Mr. Roosevelt used to handle both brilliantly and gallantly, making the questioners look like natural-born dopes. Patton apparently lacks that skill. At one time he did say, 'Don't you put words in my mouth,' but that only encouraged his cross-examiners. I am told that they asked him long, involved questions, ending in the query, 'Isn't that so'? To that sort of thing, the interrogated should ask, 'Isn't what so'? but it is difficult to be both a gentleman and cagey, particularly when a rude fellow is blowing smoke of his pipe into your face.

"So they got into an argument as to whether Patton had or had not said that 98% of the Germans were Nazis. And when Patton complained that he was being made to say something that he had not said, he was forced to ask whether he was being called a liar and it was said in his presence that he was being so called—and to me, it is astonishing that somebody was not carried out pummeled beyond recognition.

"Now, according to the account which was given to me, a number of persons were present at this interview and some of them discussed Patton before and after it and much of the conversation is recorded in a form which makes ugly reading. The entire row means little, but the veracity of American reporting is involved. Some of those present avoided the entire matter because they felt that George Patton was subject to a Max Steuer cross-examination in the hope that he would lose his temper and ultimately say something that would make headlines if properly played up. It is an old journalistic trick to trap the unwilling and unwary victim of the genteel art of interviewing, but decent newspapermen permit a man to say what he wants to say. My own habit, when I was a reporter, was to request the interviewed to sign the interview as evidence of good faith on either side.

"I should like to see the heads of the three American news agencies, the Associated Press, the International News Service, and the United Press, investigate this situation thoroughly and make a public report concerning it."

Of course, the investigation requested by Mr. Sokolsky was never undertaken. Apparently the issue was not "newsworthy."

Patton felt that he deserved better treatment than that from the people he had served for almost forty years.

To him it was a confirmation that there was, indeed, in and out of the army, certain malicious and envious forces that were determined to destroy and to discredit him. His greatness had inevitably brought about the jealously of his professional peers and rivals who, by virtue of their own mediocrity, were unable to perceive the intrinsic quality of his leadership.

Throughout Patton's long and distinguished career, his perceptions, his military ability, his strategical and tactical ideas were always excellent. There were none better. Had he not been continually slighted and ignored, it is certain, upon consideration of the information available to us today, that the war would have been over at least six months earlier. There would have been not only the saving of untold lives, but also of millions of dollars of property destroyed during those last six months.

These, then, are some of the reasons behind Patton's decision to resign his commission in the Army. When viewed in a spirit of candor, there is little wonder that Patton might feel bitter.

★★★ NEWS ITEM ★★★

CMH FOR PATTON ASKED

Washington, Jan. 15 - (AP) -

Legislation awarding the Congressional Medal of Honor posthumously to General George S. Patton will be introduced in the House. Representative John E. Rankin (D-Miss) announced that he would sponsor the bill.

The Patton Philosophy

I

In the final analysis, then, what manner of man was Patton? Was he superhuman with powers not possessed by mortal men? Certainly not. He was a man, merely another human being. Had a bullet shattered his brain, he would have died as would any other man. In fact, the irony of his accidental death underlines his human frailty.

What did make him different, what set him apart from the average person, was his ambition. He was willing to put his life on the line to defend his beliefs. He spent every waking moment concentrating every fiber of his being toward one end result, forcing himself to be the warrior he so desperately desired and needed to be.

His driving ambition shows clearly in an entry made in the diary which he started when he entered his plebe year at West Point as a young man of nineteen. He writes, "By perseverance and study and eternal desire, any man may be great."

Here we will let Patton speak for himself, presenting some of Patton's salient views for the reader without editor's notes or comments. Though they come from numerous and various writings, they will be given in a manner that attempts to spotlight the General's most perceptive assessments about war, leadership, politics, and preparedness.

In general notes made by Patton for short speeches to military units, from personal correspondence, in essays written to crystalize his own thoughts, and in magazine articles he wrote which were published in the Army's professional publications, are to be found very perceptive insights and much valuable advice. Some ideas advanced by Patton are simply age-old truisms that have yet to be learned by present-day nations and politicians. To quote an old phrase, "Those who refuse to learn from history are doomed to repeat it."

Patton was keenly aware that the government of the United States has the habit of dismantling the fine armies that it creates in times of emergency. He had personally seen it happen after the signing of the Armistice on November 11, 1918, and he knew that it was going to happen after the end of the war with the Axis powers in 1945. Knowing that it was far more expensive to be unprepared and have to build a new army from nothing than it was to maintain a finely honed armed force that would be ready for use when it was needed, he correctly reasoned that, " . . . it is better and cheaper to have a strong Army and not need it than it is to need a strong Army and not have it." A good analogy would be that an automobile kept in proper running condition by good maintenance practices is much cheaper in the long run than is purchasing a new automobile each year. He agreed wholeheartedly with the precepts of General Leonard Wood who wrote that " . . . 'panic patriotism' appears from time to time when the clouds of possible trouble loom up heavier than usual. There is much discussion, but little accomplishment. Adequate national preparedness on sound lines will be secured only when there is a general appreciation of its vital importance for defense and of the further fact that it *cannot* be improvised or done in a hurry. In short, improvisation is inadequate and extremely expensive in both material and manpower."

II

"Twice in my lifetime, America, the Arsenal of Democracy, has come from behind to insure victory. Is it not evident that should another war arise, those producing it will make every effort to see that the Arsenal of Democracy is knocked out in the first round? How this can be done I do not know, but I do know that the progress made in airplanes and self-propelled missiles is such that the possibility of an early knockout cannot be discounted."

"Perhaps a good illustration of what I am trying to put across to you is this: When I went to school, and I presume that it is the same now, all of the children were taught how to form in column and march out of the building in an orderly manner in case of fire. This instruction did not, so far as I know, produce fires, but when fire occurred, the lives of the majority of the children were saved. If we go to the extreme of saying that preparedness produces wars, then the instruction in fire drills would produce fires. Therefore, we should not teach children that a fire may come, that the building may burn, and as a result of such teaching have the sad duty of removing the charred little bodies from the ruined schoolhouse."

"You men are all American citizens, and in your generation you will have a very large voice in determining the election of our public servants and the enforcement of our laws. I am sure that you have found out that discipline, self-reliance, mutual respect, and faith are necessary in the Army. These traits are just as necessary in civilian life. Laws which are not enforced had better not be promulgated."

"Referring again to the fire department aspect of the prevention of war, a very large proportion of the duties of the fire departments in large cities is not the extinguishing of fires, but their prevention through advice and supervision. You men are all potential firemen. You have put out the fire by your heroic efforts. It is now your duty as citizens to see that other fires do not occur, and that you and your children are not again called upon to extinguish them."

"I have been speaking to you, not as your Commanding General, but rather as an old man to young men. I am in no way trying to propagandize you, but as I said before, it is my considered opinion that my duty demands that I should explain to you things as I see them."

"Let me say that it is my profound hope that we shall never again be engaged in war, but also let me remind you of the words attributed to George Washington: 'In time of peace, prepare for war.' That advice is still good."

"I am firmly convinced that we must have universal training because the one hope for a peaceful world is a powerful America with the adequate means of instantly checking aggressors. Unless we are so armed, and prepared, the next war will probably destroy us. No one who has lived in a destroyed country can view such a possibility with anything except horror."

"Man is War. War is conflict. Fighting is an elemental exposition of the age-old effort to survive. If we again believe that wars are over, we will surely have another and damned quick. We had better look out for ourselves and make the rest of the world look out for themselves. If we attempt to feed the world, we will starve and perhaps destroy America. Roman civilization fell due to the loss of the will to conquer; satisfaction with the 'status quo'; and high taxes, which destroyed trade and private enterprise. These conditions eventually forced people out of the cities. The cycle is returning."

"It is very easy for ignorant people to think that success in war may be gained by the use of some wonderful invention like the atomic bomb rather than by hard fighting and superior leadership."

"There are a host of people who have to squat to piss who will say that this will be the 'last' war and that from now on we will only need world 'clubs.' They are the ones who will be responsible for the deaths of millions of people. The pacifists are always at it. I met a 'visiting fireman' of supposedly great eminence who told me that this was to be the *last* war. I told him that such statements since 2600 B.C. had signed the death warrants of millions of young men. He replied with the stock lie, 'Oh, but things are different now.' My God! Will they *never* learn?"

"There are all kinds of low class slime who are trying and will continue to try to wreck this country from the inside. Most of them don't know it, but they are actually working for the Russians. Some of them do know it, though. It doesn't matter whether they call themselves Communists, Socialists, or just plain foolish Liberals. They are destroying this country."

"Politicians are the lowest form of life on earth. Liberal Democrats are the lowest form of politicians. I really shudder for the future of our country. Someone must not only win the war, but also the *peace*."

"I believe that Germany should not be destroyed, but rather should be re-built as a buffer against the real danger, which is Russia and its bolshevism."

"The difficulty in understanding the Russian is that we do not take cognizance of the fact that he is not a European, but an Asiatic, and therefore thinks deviously. We can no more understand a Russian than a Chinese or a Japanese, and from

what I have seen of them, I have no particular desire to understand them except to ascertain how much lead or iron it takes
to kill them. In addition to his other amiable characteristics,
the Russian has no regard for human life and they are all-out
sons-of-bitches, barbarians, and chronic drunks."

"Russia *knows* what she wants. *World Domination.* And she is
laying her plans accordingly. We, on the other hand, and England and France to a lesser extent, don't know what we want.
We get less than nothing as a result. If we have to fight them,
now is the time. From now on, we will get weaker and they
will get stronger. Let's keep our boots polished, bayonets sharpened, and present a picture of force and strength to the Russians. This is the only language that they understand and respect. If we fail to do this, then I would like to say that we
have had a victory over the Germans, and have disarmed them,
but we have lost the war."

"The one thing that I could not say, and cannot yet say
publicly, is that my chief interest in establishing order in Germany was to prevent Germany from going communist. I am
afraid that our foolish and utterly stupid policy in regard to
Germany will certainly cause them to join the Russians and
thereby insure a communistic state throughout Western Europe.
We have destroyed what could have been a good race of people
and we are about to replace them with Mongolian savages and
all of Europe with communism."

"Poland is under Russian domination, so is Hungary, so is
Czechoslovakia, and so is Yugoslavia; and we sit happily by
and think that everybody loves us. It seems likely to me that
Russia has a certain sphere of influence in Korea, Manchuria,
and Mongolia."

"We promised the Europeans freedom. It would be worse
than dishonorable not to see that they have it. This might mean
war with the Russians, but what of it? They have no air force,
and their gasoline and ammunition supplies are low. I've seen
their miserable supply trains; mostly wagons drawn by beaten
up old horses or oxen. I'll say this; the Third Army alone and
with damned few casualties, could lick what is left of the
Russians in six weeks. You mark my words. Don't ever forget
them. Someday we will have to fight them and it will take six
years and cost us six million lives."

"The Russians are Mongols. They are Slavs and a lot of them used to be ruled by Ancient Byzantium. From Genghis Kahn to Stalin, they have not changed. They never will, and we will never learn—at least, not until it is too late."

"I am very much afraid that Europe is going bolshevik. If it does, it' may eventually spread to our country."

"The too often repeated remark that 'the country owes me a living' is nothing short of treason. The nation owes all of its citizens an *equal* chance, but it is not responsible for the faults and follies of those who fail to avail themselves of these opportunities."

"Do not talk or think of your rights or your fatigues or of what the other fellow has failed to do. War is the struggle of nations; you are in it, but as an individual, and your feelings as such do not exist. In doing your utmost, even unto death, you are conferring 'no favor. You are privileged to be able to do so much for your country."

"War is simple, direct, and ruthless. It requires a simple, direct, and ruthless man to wage it."

"There are apparently two types of successful soldiers. Those who get on by being unobtrusive and those who get on by being obtrusive. I am of the latter type and seem to be rare and unpopular; but it is my method. One must be singleminded. One must choose a system and stick to it. People who are not themselves are nobody."

"To be a successful soldier you must know history. Read it objectively. Dates and even the minute details of tactics are useless. What you must know is how man reacts. Weapons change, but man who uses them changes not at all. Save for appearances, the ancient Greek warrior and the modern rifleman are one. The emotions and consequent reactions which affected one affect the other. To win battles you do not beat weapons—you beat the soul of man, of the enemy man. To do that you have to destroy his weapons, but that is only incidental. You must read biography and especially autobiography. If you will do that you will find that war is simple. Decide what will hurt the enemy most within the limits of your capabilities to harm him and then do it. *Take calculated risks.* That is quite different from being rash. My personal belief is that if you have a 50% chance, take it! I know that the superior fighting qualities of American soldiers led by me will surely give that extra 1% necessary."

"In Sicily, I decided as a result of my information, observations, and a sixth sense that I have, that the enemy did not have another large-scale attack in his system. I bet my shirt on that and I was right. You cannot wage war safely, but no dead general has ever been criticized, so you always have that way out. I get criticized evey day for taking needless risks by being too often right up front. What good is a dead general? I say, what good is a general who won't take the same risks as his troops? I still get scared under fire. I guess I never will get used to it, but I still poke along."

"I am sure that if every leader who goes into battle will promise himself that he will come out either a conqueror or a corpse, he is sure to win. There is no doubt of that. Defeat is not due to losses but to the destruction of the soul of the leaders—the 'live to fight another day' doctrine."

"The most vital quality a soldier can possess is *self-confidence*, utter, complete and bumptious. You can have doubts about your good looks, about your intelligence, about your self-control, but to win in war you must have *no* doubts about your ability as a soldier."

"What success I have had results from the fact that I have always been certain that my military reactions were correct. Many people do not agree with me. They are wrong. The unerring jury of history writing long after we are dead will prove me correct."

"Note that I speak of military reactions. No one is born with them any more than anyone is born with muscles. You are born with the soul capable of correct military reactions or the body capable of having big muscles, but both qualities must be developed by hard work."

"The intensity of your desire to acquire any special ability depends on character and ambition. They are wonderful possessions."

"Soldiers, all men in fact, are natural hero worshippers. Officers with a flair for command realize this and emphasize in their conduct, dress, and deportment the qualities they seek to produce in their men. When I was a second lieutenant I had a captain who was very sloppy and usually was late, yet he got after the men for just those faults; he was a failure."

"The troops I have commanded have always been well dressed, been smart saluters, been prompt and bold in action because I have personally set the example in these qualities. The influence one man can have on thousands is a never ending source of wonder to me. You are always on parade. Officers who, through laziness or a foolish desire to be popular, fail to enforce discipline and the proper wearing of uniforms and equipment not in the presence of the enemy will also fail in battle. If they fail in battle they are murderers. There is no such thing as a good field soldier. You are either a good soldier or a bad soldier."

"I have used one principle in my operations which has been remarkably successful, and that is to 'Fill the unforgiving minute with sixty seconds worth of distance run.' That is the whole art of war, and when you get to be a general, remember it!"

"Remember four basic principles;

First; surprise. Find out what the enemy intends to do and do it first.

Second; Rock the enemy back on his heels. Keep him rocking. Never give him a chance to get his balance or to build up.

Third; relentless pursuit. "A *l'outrance* the French say, beyond the limit.

Fourth; Mop him up."

"Three vital qualities in an officer are:

Imagination; to think what the enemy would do and beat him to the draw.

Unselfishness; always give credit where it is due. If you win, give the credit. If you lose, take the blame.

Courage; to shoulder responsibility."

"So far as the atomic bomb is concerned, while it is a scientific invention of the first water, it is not as earth-shaking as you might think. When man first began fighting man, he used his teeth, toenails, and fingernails. Then one day a very terrified or very inventive genius picked up a rock and bashed a man in the head while the latter was gnawing at his vitals. The news of this unheard-of weapon unquestionably shocked Neolithic society, but they became accustomed to it, Thousands of years later, another genius picked up the splintered rib of a mastodon and using it as a dagger struck the gentleman with the rock. Again pre-historic society was shocked and said, 'There can be no more wars. Did you hear about the mastodon bone?' When the shield, slingshot, throwing stick, and the sword and armor were successively invented, each in its turn was heralded by the proponents as a means of destroying the world or of stopping war. When Samson slew the Philistines with the jawbone of an ass, he probably created such a vogue for the weapon that throughout the world no prudent donkey dared to bray. Certainly the advent of the atomic bomb was not half as startling as the initial appearance of gunpowder. In my own lifetime, I remember two inventions, or possibly three, which were supposed to stop war; namely the dynamite cruiser Vesuvius, the submarine, and the tank. Yet, wars go blithely on and will when our great-grandchildren are vey old men."

"Do not regard what you do as only a 'preparation' for doing the same thing more fully or better at some later time. Nothing is ever done twice. There is no next time. This is of special application to war. There is but one time to win a battle or a campaign. It must be won the first time."

III

Patton was one of the rare "Great Captains" of war. He truly had the instinct for battle. A gifted few in history have had this battle judgment, this quality—a combination of imagination, daring, and skill, and an instantenous appreciation for the task to be performed. It cannot be learned in a military school, though the background may be acquired there. Experience in battle is necessary, but study and experience are not enough. The leaders who have it stand out above all others. Patton stands out above all others.

★★★ NEWS ITEM ★★★

LATEST PATTON STORY

With Ninth Army, March, 23—(NANA)—

The latest General George S. Patton story runs somewhat like this:

Patton to soldier: "Why didn't you salute me, soldier?"

Soldier: "I didn't see you, Sir."

Patton: "Oh, that's all right; I was afraid you were mad at me."

The Secret of Victory
by George S. Patton, Jr.

Despite the years of thought and oceans of ink which have been devoted to the elucidation of war, its secrets still remain shrouded in mystery.

Indeed, it is due largely to the very volume of available information that the veil is so thick.

War is an art and as such is not susceptible of explanation by fixed formulae. Yet, from the earliest times there has been an unending effort to subject its complex and emotional structure to dissection, to enunciate rules for its waging, to make tangible its intangibility. One might as well strive to isolate the soul by the dissection of the cadaver as to seek the essence of war by the analysis of its records.

Yet, despite the impossibility of physically detecting the soul, its existence is proven by its tangible reflection in acts and thoughts.

So with war, beyond its physical aspect of armed hosts there hovers an impalpable something which on occasion so dominates the material as to induce victory under circumstances quite inexplicable.

To understand this "something" we should seek it in a manner analagous to our search for the soul; and so seeking we shall perchance find it in the reflexes produced by the acts of the "Great Captains."

But whither shall we turn for knowledge of their very selves? Not in the musty tomes of voluminous reports or censored recollections wherein they strove to immortalize and conceal their achievements. Nor yet in the countless histories where lesser wormish men have sought to snare their parted ghosts.

The great warriors were too busy and often too inept to write contemporaneously of their exploits (save in the form of propaganda reports). While what they later put on paper as biographies were retrospects colored by their vain strivings for enhanced fame, or by political conditions then confronting them.

War was an ebullition of their perished past. The violent simplicity in execution which procured success for them and which enthralled the world looked pale and uninspired on paper; so they "seasoned" it.

The race yearns to adore. Can it adore the simple or venerate the obvious? All mythology and folk lore rise in indignant protest at the thought. The sun gave light, therefore he was not hot gas nor a flame, but a god or a chariot. The ignis fatuus deluded men of nights. It was a spirit; nothing so simple as decomposition could serve the need.

So with the soldier. To pander to self-love and racial urge he attributes to his acts profound thoughts which never existed.

The white-hot energy of youth, which saw in obstacles but inspirations, and in the enemy but the gage to battle, becomes too complacent and retrospective with age. The result of mathematical calculation and metaphysical erudition; of knowledge he never had and plans he never made.

With the efforts of the historians, the case is even worse. Those who write at the time are guilty of partisanship and the urge of hero-worship. Those who write later are forced to accept contemporaneous myths and to view their subject through the roseate light which distance, be it of time or space, sheds ever to deprive us of harsh truth.

Further, the historian, no matter when he writes, is by nature a man of thoughtful and studious habits utterly incapable of appreciating the roaring energy of a soldier. The motive of his life is admiration for reflection and ordered calculation. Can he attribute to his subject virtues other than those which in himself he esteems most highly? So all unwittingly he is bound to limn for us soldiers as utterly unlike themselves as those prissy and high-minded youths who stalk the pages of juvenile romances in the garb of the fourteenth century and with the manners of the twentieth.

Colored by self-deception, shaded by scholarly bookworms, our soldiers stand before us as devoid of life as the toothless portraits of Washington which adorn the walls of half our schoolrooms.

In peace, the scholar flourishes, in war the soldier dies; so it comes about that we view our soldiers through the eyes of scholars and attribute to them scholarly virtues.

Seeking obvious reasons for the obscure, we analyze their conduct as told by historians and assign as reasons for their success, apparent, trivial things.

Disregarding wholly the personality of Frederick, we attribute his victories to a tactical expedient, the oblique order of battle.

Impotent to comprehend the character of Rome's generals a great historian coins the striking phrase: "At this time the Roman Legionary shortened his sword and gained an empire," and we swallow it, thereby avoiding thought.

Our research is further muddled by the fabled heroism of all former fighters. Like wine, accounts of valor mellow with age, until Achilles dead for three thousand years stands peerless.

Yet, through the murk of fact and fable rises ever to our view this truth: "The history of war is the history of warriors; few in number, mighty in influence."

Alexander, not Macdeonia, conquered the world. Scipio, not Rome, destroyed Carthage. Marlborough, not the Allies, defeated France. Cromwell, not the Roundheads, dethroned Charles.

Were this true only of warriors we might well exclaim, "Behold the work of the historian," but it is equally the case in every phase of human endeavor. Music has its myriad musicians, but only its dozen masters. So with painting, sculpture, literature, medicine, or trade. "Many are called, but few are chosen."

Nor can we concur wholly with the alluring stories in the advertising sections of our magazines which point the golden path of success to all and sundry who will follow that particular phase of "home education" that they happen to advocate. "Knowledge is power," but to a degree only. Its possession per se will raise a man to mediocrity, but not to distinction. In our opinion, indeed, the instruction obtained from such courses is of less moment to future success than is the ambition which prompted the study.

In considering these matters, sight should not be lost of the fact that while there is much similarity, there is also a vast difference, between the successful soldier and the successful man in other professions. Success due to knowledge and personality is the measure of ability in each case; but to all, except the soldier, it has vital significance only to the individual and to a limited number of his family and associates, while with the soldier success or failure means infinitely more as it must of necessity be measured not in terms of personal honor or affluence, but in the life, happiness, and honor of his men—his country.

Hence, the search for that elusive secret of military success; soul, genius, personality—call it what you will—is of vital interest to us all.

As has been shown, history and biography are of but limited assistance, and the situation is still further complicated by other circumstances which we shall now discuss.

First, we must get a harmonious arrangement between two diametrically opposed views: namely, that there is "nothing new under the sun," and, to coin a phrase, that there is "nothing old."

Referring to the first assumption, that of immutability, we refer to the tendency, well attested in the records of these historians, to consider the most recent past war as the last word, the sealed pattern of all future contests to insure peace.

For this theory we of the military profession are largely to blame. First we realize, none better, that in the last war it was necessary to make many improvisations and to ply our trade with ill-assorted tools. We then read our books and note with a thrill of regret that in the war next preceding our own experience, "Things ran with the precision of a well oiled machine," for so the mellowing influences of time have made it appear to our authors.

In our efforts to provide for the avoidance, in future, of the mistakes which we personally have encountered and to insure to ourselves, or to our successors, the same mathematical ease of operation of which we have read, we proceed to enunciate rules.

In order to enunciate anything we must first have a premise. The most obvious is the last war. Further, the impressions we gained there were the most vivid we have ever experienced; burned on the tablets of our memories by the blistering flash of exploding shell, etched on our souls by the incisive patter of machine gun bullets, our own experiences become the foundation of our thoughts and, all unconscious of personal bias, we of necessity base our conceptions of the future on our experience of the past.

Beyond question, personal knowledge is a fine thing, but unfortunately it is too intimate. When, for example, we recall a railroad accident, the picture that most vividly presents itself to us is the severed blue-grey hand of some child victim; not the misread signals which precipitated the tragedy.

So with war experiences. The choking gas that strangled us sticks in our memory to the more or less complete exclusion of the important fact that it was the roads and consequent abundant mechanical transportation peculiar to Western Europe which permitted the accumulation of enough gas shells to do the strangling.

Even when no personal experience exists, we are certain to be influenced by the most recent experience of others. Because in the Boer War the bayonet found no employment, we all but abandoned it, only to seize it again when the Russo-Japanese conflict re-demonstrated its value.

Going back further we might point to countless other instances of similar nature. Witness the recurrent use and disuse of infantry and cavalry as the dominant arm according to the most recent "lesson" derived from the last war based invariably on *special conditions*, in no way bound to recur, yet always presumed as immutable.

So much for the conservatives; now for the optimists; the "Nothing Old" gentry.

These are of several species, but first in order of importance come the specialists.

Due either to super-abundant egotism and uncontrolled enthusiasm or else to limited powers of observation of the activities of other arms, these people advocate in the most fluent and uncompromising manner the vast *future* potentialities of their own weapon. In the next war, so they say, all of the enemy will be crushed, gassed, bombed, or otherwise speedily exterminated, depending for the method of his death upon whether the person declaiming belongs to the tank, gas, air, or other special service.

Due to the (unfortunate) fact that many of them possess considerable histrionic ability and much verbosity, they attract public attention. The appeal of their statements is further strengthened because, in the first place, they deal invariably in mechanical devices which intrigue the simple imagination. In the next place the novelty of their schemes and assertions has a strong news interest which insures their notice by the press. This last fact is of peculiar advantage to the present crop of specialists because in the last war the maximum press activity was on the Western Front. Here the preliminary cavalry activities had ended before the shock of the world cataclysm had been sufficiently dissipated to permit detailed accounts, while due to necessary restrictions, correspondents could not witness infantry fights in detail and therefore filled their articles with accounts of the noisy or noisome activities of the special arms whose preliminary activities they could see and whose novelty assured public interest.

Earlier examples of this newspaper tendency to exploit the bizarre is instanced in the opening accounts of the Civil War where "Masked Batteries" and "Black Horse Cavalry" seemed to infest the whole face of nature. Or again, the undue importance attached to the "Dynamite Ship," the *Vesuvius* at Santiago or the storied prowess of the submarine just after its invention.

Mention of the optimists would be incomplete without some reference to those super visionaries, the Pacifists.

Like the Specialists, the stupendous nature of their claims gains a hearing and affects a due consideration of war by the fact that it influences the minds of potential soldiers and hampers the activities of the armed forces by way of reduced financial support. To these people the history of the race, from the fierce struggles in primordial slime to the present day, is a blank. At their bidding all is changed. In a moment, the twinkling of an eye, the lion loses his appetite and the lamb his fear. Avarice and ambition, honor and patriotism are no more, all merge in a supine state of impossible toleration. To them the millions who have nobly perished for an ideal are fools, and a sexless creature too debased to care and too indolent to strive is held up for emulation.

Nor are they deterred in their schemes for complete disarmament by the fear of cost to themselves or their country because, for themselves, they know that by benefit of sex, weak eyes, flat feet, or a limber conscience they will avoid the conflicts that their unarmed policy will produce. For their country they care not at all—let *it* perish; so long as *they* may survive.

Both the standpatters and the progressives have reason of sorts and as we have pointed out we must seek to harmonize the divergent tendencies.

A British writer has said, "The characteristic of war is its constant change of characteristic," but as is ever the case with aphorisms his remark needs explanation.

There is an incessant and constant change of "means" to attain the inevitable "end," but we must take care not to let these inevitable sundry means, past or predicted, attain undue eminence in the perspective of our minds. Since the beginning, there has been an unending cycle of them, and for each, its advocates have claimed adoption as the sole means of successful war. Yet, the records of all time show that the unchanging ends have been, are, and probably ever shall be, the securing of predominating force, of the right sort, at the right place, at the right time.

In seeking a premise for the enunciation of rules for the employment of this predominating force, we must cull from past experience, or study, the more permanent characteristics, select our weapons, and assign to them that importance which reason and the analogy of experience indicate that they will attain.

Bearing these considerations, and the definition of predominant force, in mind, we shall resume our search for the secret of victory.

No matter what the situation as to clarity of his mental perspective, the conscientious soldier approaches the solution of his problem more or less bemuddled by phantoms of the past and deluded by unfounded or unproven hopes for the future. So handicapped, he assumes the unwonted and labored posture of a student, and plans for perfection so that when the next war comes that part of the machine, for which he may be responsible, shall instantly begin to function with a purr of perfect preparation.

In this scholarly avocation soldiers of all important nations use at the present time what purports to be the best mode of instruction—the applicatory method. The characteristics of some concrete problem at first studied in the abstract and then tested by applying them with assumed forces and situations in solving analogous problems either on the terrain or on a map representation of it.

This method not only familiarizes the student with all of the tools and technicalities of his trade, but also developes the aptitude for reaching decisions and the self-assurance derived from demonstrated achievements.

But as always, there is a fly in the ointment. High academic performance demands infinite intimate knowledge of details and the qualities requisite to such attainments often inhabit bodies lacking in personality. Also the striving for such knowledge often engenders the falacious notion that capacity depends on the power to acquire such details, not the ability to apply them.

Obsessed with this thought, students plunge in deeper and ever deeper, their exertions but enmeshing them the more until like mired mastodons they perish in a morass of knowledge where they first browsed for sustenance.

When the prying spade of the unbiased investigator has removed the muck of official reports and the mire of self-laudatory biographies from the swamp of the World War, then the skeletons of many such military mammoths will be discovered. Amidst their mighty remains will lurk elusive the secret of German failure.

Beyond question, no soldiers ever sought more diligently for pre-war perfection. They built and tested and adjusted their mighty machine and became so engrossed in its visible perfection, in the accuracy of its bearings, and the compression of its cylinders, that they neglected the battery. When the moment came, their masterpiece proved inefficient through lack of the divine afflatus, the soul of a leader.

Truly, in war, "Men are nothing, a man is everything."

Here we must most vigorously deny that anything in our remarks is intended to imply belief in the existence of spontaneous untutored inspiration. With the single exception of the divinely inspired Joan of Arc, no such phenomenon has ever existed and as we shall show, she was less of an exception than a coincidence.

We require and must demand all possible thoughtful preparation, and studious effort possible, so that in war our officers may be equal to their mighty trust—the safety of our country.

Our purpose is not to discourage such preparation, but simply to call attention to certain defects in its pursuit. To direct it not towards the glorification of the means—study, but the end—victory.

In acquiring erudition, we must live on, not in, our studies. We must guard against becoming so engrossed in the specific nature of the roots and bark of the trees of knowledge as to miss the meaning and grandeur of the forests that they compose.

Our means of studying war have increased as much as have our tools for waging it, but it is an open question as to whether this increase in means has not perhaps obscured or obliterated one essential detail, namely the necessity for personal leadership.

Because Alexander as a boy learned the art from the stories told by Philip's veterans or the rhymed chronicles of mythological contests is no reason for assuming that, considering the time, he was less versed in the warfare of his day than was at our period the great military scholar and practitioner Ferdinand Foch. Simple as was the schooling of Alexander, his requirements were simpler.

All down the immortal line of mighty warriors the same is true. Hannibal, Caesar, Heraclius, Charlemagne, Richard, Gustavus, Turenne, Frederick, Napoleon, Grant, Lee, Hindenburg, Allenby, Foch, and Pershing, were all deeply imbued with the whole knowledge of war as practised at their several epochs.

But also, *and mark this,* so were many of their defeated opponents. As has been pointed out, the secret of victory lies not wholly in knowledge. It lurks invisible in that vitalizing spark, intangible, yet as evident as the lightning—the warrior soul.

There is no better illustration of the potency of this vitalizing element than is portrayed in the story of the "Maid of Orleans." For more than 90 years prior to her advent, the armies of France had suffered almost continuous defeat at the hands of their British opponents. The reason for this state of things lay not in the inferiority of French valor, but in the reappearance of the foot soldier armed with the missile weapon—the longbow—as the *temporary* dominating influence on the battlefield. As a result of the recurrence of this tactical condition, France suffered almost continuous defeats with the result that her people lost confidence. They developed an inferiority complex.

Then came Joan, whose flaming faith in her heaven-sent mission re-kindled the national spirit. Yet, as great as were her powers, it is idle to suppose that, all unschooled in war as she was, she could have directed, unaided, the energy that she produced.

Like the fire beneath the boiler, she produced the steam. Ready to her hand she found competent machinery for its utilization in the shape of those veteran soldiers, Dunois, La Hire, and Saint Railles.

The happy coincidence of her ignorant enthusiasm and their uninspired intelligence produced the phenomenal series of victories which freed France.

It seems a far cry from the Virgin Maiden to the professional pugilist, yet there is much in the way of similarity in their dominant characteristics. In all closely contested ring battles between opponents of equal weight (force) the decision almost invariably goes to the fighter who is better endowed with faith, self-confidence, and a courageous spirit. But, we must again point out that no pugilist, no matter how confident or courageous, has ever succeeded over an equal enemy unless to his spiritual attributes he has added the combined knowledge of, and skill at, his profession.

We shall now seek to evaluate and place in their just ratio the three essentials to victory; Inspiration, Knowledge, and Force (Mass).

Considering Napoleon as the apogee of military ability, we note that whereas he won many battles with numbers inferior to the enemy, he never lost a battle when he was numerically superior. In other words, even his transcendent ability was not equal, on every occasion, to the task of counterbalancing numerical inferiority.

Again, when he was confronted with the admittedly incapable Austrian generals of 1796, he destroyed armies; while later, particularly after 1805, his victories were far less overwhelming.

So it was with Caesar. Against the Nervae he was a consuming flame, yet against Romans a successful contender. Grant in the Wilderness was as nothing when compared to Grant at Donaldson or before Vicksburg.

The three preceding cases represent soldiers of the highest type both mentally and spiritually, but with perhaps a shade more emphasis on their spiritual side.

By way of contrast we may note how the learned, but uninspired, Prussians of 1870 triumphed over the poorly led French while, in 1914, their equally learned and uninspired descendents were far less successful in the face of better opposition.

We may therefore postulate that no one element, be it Soul, Knowledge, or Mass is dominant; that a combination of any two of these factors gives a strong presumption of success over an adversary relying on one alone, and that the three combined are practically invincible against a combination of any other two.

Comparing our own resources as to mass with those of any possible opponent or group of opponents, we strike at least a balance.

The demonstrated ability of our trained leaders in past wars show that, so far as education is concerned, our officers have no superiors and few equals. This being so, victory will fly to or desert our standards in exact proportion to the presence, or absence, in our leaders of the third attribute. Of what does it consist?

As has been noted, the records of all trades and professions show that it is the rare individual, rising like a mountain peak through the clouds of billowy mediocrity, who attains success.

He starts from the same upper reaches, be it hill or hero; yet the cataclysm which causes the former is as imponderable as the conditions which produce the latter. So it seems, yet as surely as the earthquake was the result of pre-ordained and computable contractions, so surely is the leader the product of obscure, yet ascertainable, circumstances.

The future happiness and existence of races cannot be relegated to the realm of uncertainty contained in that plausible but indefinite assurance that, "Genius is born, not made." If this were so, the World War, among other crimes, might well have had charged against it the sin of practicing an undue use of birth control. Certainly, despite a superabundance of educated aspirants, none of the participants produced an inspired leader.

It would be impious to attribute this dearth to God alone. The system of military education, and be it noted, the universal system [of the draft] must be at fault.

That "Man cannot live by bread alone," and that "As a man thinketh so is he," have been for generations droned from countless pulpits as the texts for prolix and unconvincing sermons until the cogency of the phrases has been somewhat dulled; yet, they contain an infinity of truth.

Dry knowledge, like dry rot, destroys the soundest fiber. A constant search for soul-less fundamentals, the efforts to regularize the irregular, to make complex the simple, to assume perfect men, perfect material, and perfect terrain as the prerequisites to war, has the same effect on the soldier student. Indeed, the statement that "Education is a device by which men fool themselves into a sense of efficiency" is too often apposite.

War is conflict. Fighting is an elemental exposition of the age-old effort to survive. It is the cold glitter of the attacker's eye, not the point of the questing bayonet, that breakes the line. It is the fierce determination of the driver to close with the enemy, not the mechanical perfection of tank, that conquers the trench. It is the cataclysmic ecstasy of conflict in the flier, not the perfection of his machine gun, which drops the enemy in flaming ruin. Yet, *volumes* are devoted to armaments; and only *pages* to inspiration.

Since, by necessity, limitations of map problems inhibit the student from considering the effects of hunger, emotion, personality, fatigue, leadership, and many other imponderable, yet vital, factors, he first neglects and then forgets them.

Obsessed with admiration for the intelligence which history has ascribed to past leaders, he forgets the inseparable connection between plans, the flower of the intellect, and execution, the fruit of the soul. Hooker's plan at Chancelorsville was masterly; its execution cost him the battle. The converse was true at Marengo. Yet, since the historian, through lack of experience and consequent appreciation of the inspirational qualities of generals, fails to stress them, he does emphasize their mental gifts which, since he shares, he values. The student blindly follows. Hugging the notion of "intelligence," he pictures armies of insensate pawns moving with the precision of machines and the rapidity of light, guided in their intricate and resistless evolutions over the battlefield by the cold effulgence of his emotionless cerebrations as transmitted to them by wire and radio through the inspiring medium of coded messages.

Doubtless, he further assumes the same superhuman intelligence will translate those somber sentences into words of fire, which shall electrify his chessmen into frezied heroes who, heedless of danger, shall dauntlessly translate the stillborn infants of his brain into heroic deeds.

Was it so with Caesar as he rallied the 12th Legion? Could the trackless ether have conveyed to his soldiers via the medium of radio waves the inspiration that Napoleon imparted by his ubiquitous presence when before Rivoli he rode five horses to death, "To see everything for himself"?

Staff systems and mechanical communications are valuable, but above and beyond them must be the *commander*. Not as a disembodied brain linked to his men by lines of wire and radio waves, but as a living presence, an all pervading *visible* personality.

The unleavened bread of knowledge will sustain life, but it is dull fare unless leavened by the yeast of personality.

Could seamanship and shooting have made the *Bonhomme Richard* prevail over the *Serapis* or have destroyed the French fleet in Abukar Bay if John Paul Jones and Horatio Nelson had been other than they were? What intellectual ghost replete with strategem could have inspired men as did these two who, in themselves, have epitomized not only knowledge of war, but the spirit of battle.

In defining the changeless characteristics of war we mentioned force, place, and time. In our calendar of warriors Napoleon Bonaparte and Stonewall Jackson stand preeminent in their use of the last of these—time. Of the first his soldiers boasted, "He wins battles more with our legs than with our bayonets." Jackson's men proudly called themselves "Old Jack's Foot Cavalry."

Libraries have been written on the deeds of both men. Shrewd critics have assigned success to all manner of things; as tactics, shape of frontiers, happily placed rivers, mountains or woods, intellectual ability, or to the use of artillery. All in a measure true, but none vital. Nor is it even in the speed of the operations that the secret lay, but in the inspiring spirit with which they

General Patton discussing with his staff the capture of Palermo, Sicily, July 1943.

Patton after landing at Gela, Sicily, July 1943.

Sicily, July 1943. British General Bernard L. Montgomery with General Patton.

Sicily, August 1943. General Montgomery and General Patton salute the colors at Seventh Army Headquarters.

*Palermo, Sicily, August 1943. British General Harold Alexander
with General Patton.*

General Mark Clark of the Fifth Army and General Patton of the Seventh Army, waiting for President Roosevelt at the airport, Castelvetrano, Sicily, December 8, 1943.

General Patton with General Archibald Roosevelt, Sicily, August 1943.

General Patton in Sicily, July 1943.

September 1944. **Left to right:** *General Omar M. Bradley, General O. P. Weyland, and General Patton at Patton's headquarters in France. Willie, Patton's bull terrier, sleeps in the foreground.*

Patton inspects a forward position and watches the fighting, European Theater, October 1944.

France, November 1944. General Patton congratulates the officers and men of XX Corps.

November 1944. French General Henri Giraud visits XX Corps Headquarters in France. Left to right: General Giraud, General Patton, Colonel William A. Collier and Major General Walton H. Walker of XX Corps.

August 1944. General Patton and General Bradley in a C-47, returning from a tour of Brittany.

France, December 1944. General Patton with General Alexander M. Patch, commander of the U.S. Seventh Army.

Patton with men of the 1503rd Engineers, who built the bridge
across the Sauer River between Luxembourg and Germany,
February 1945.

August 1945. General Patton rides the horse Hitler
had picked from the Vienna Riding School
to present to Emperor Hirohito.

*General Patton greets Lieutenant General Lucian K. Truscott,
who is to succeed him as commander of the Third Army.*

Left to right: *General Patton, Major General E. M. Harmon of XXII Corps,
and Brigadier General John L. Pierce of the 16th Armored Division,
Czechoslovakia, September 1945.*

*Germany, July 1945. Left to right: Major General Louis A. Craig,
II Corps; General Patton; Major General M. L. McBride,
80th Infantry Division.*

*General Patton holding a giant shotgun in front of his headquarters
in Herschfeld, Germany, April 1945. The gun was acquired
during his travels through Germany.*

*General Patton inspecting troops of the Third Army at
the Seine River, France, August 1944. The general is seen
adjusting the belt to his Colt .45 frontier model revolver.*

*May 1945. General Patton reprimands a driver of a tank of the 14th
Armored Division for having protective sandbags
on the front of his tank.*

May 21, 1945. General Bradley and General Patton leave General Eisenhower's headquarters in Reims, France. The Germans signed the surrender in this school building.

so innoculated their soldiers as to lift weary footsore men out
of themselves and to make them march, forgetful of agony, as
did Massena's division after Rivoli or Jackson's at Winchester.

No words ever imagined could have produced such prodigies
of endurance as did the sight of the boy general ill perched on
his sweating horse or of the stern puritan plodding ever before
them on Little Sorrel. The ability to produce endurance is but
an instance of that same martial soul which arouses in its
followers that resistless emotion defined as *"élan,"* the "will to
victory," or "viscousness," depending upon whether the vocabulary used is French, German, or Pacifist, respectively. However
defined, it is akin to that almost cataleptic burst of physical
and mental exuberance shown by the athlete when he breaks
a record or plunges through the tacklers, and by the author or
artist in the creation of a masterpiece. The difference is that in
the athlete or artist, the ebullition is auto-stimulated. With an
army it is the result of external impetus—*leadership.*

In considering war, we must avoid that adoration of the
material as exemplified by scientists who deny the existence of
aught they cannot cut or weigh.

In war tomorrow, we shall be dealing with men subject to
the same emotions as were the soldiers of Alexander; with men
but little changed for better or for worse from the starving,
shoeless Frenchmen of 1796. With men similar, except in their
arms, to those whom the inspiring powers of a Greek or a
Corsican changed at a breath to bands of heroes; all-enduring
and all-capable.

No! History as written and read does not divulge the source
of leadership. Hence, its study often induces us to forget its
potency.

As a mirror shows us not ourselves, but our reflection, so it
is with the soul and with leadership. We know them but by the
acts they inspire or by the results they have achieved.

Like begets like. In the armies of the great we seek the
reflection of themselves and we find: Self-confidence; Enthusiasm; Abnegation of Self; Loyalty; and Courage.

Resolution, no matter how so adament, mated to knowledge,
no matter how so infinite, never begat such a progeny.

Such offspring arises only from blood lines as elemental as
themselves. The leader must be incarnate of them.

Nor is the suggestion of Nicodemus as to re-birth (John Ill, 3-6) the only means of producing such a leader. There are certainly born leaders, but the soldier may still overcome his natal defects by unremitting effort and practice.

Self-confidence of the right sort, as differentiated from bumptious presumption based in ignorance, is the result of proven ability, the sense of conscious achievement. Its existence presupposes enthusiasm, for without this quality, no one could endure the travail of acquiring self-confidence. The enthusiasm which permits the toil and promises the achievement is simply an all-absorbing preoccupation in the profession elected.

Endurance, too, is linked with self-confidence. Mentally, it is the ability to subvert the means to the end, to hitch the wagon to a star and to attain it. Physically, it presupposes sufficient enthusiasm to force on nature, no matter how reluctant, the obligation of constant bodily fitness through exercise. The expanding waist line means the contracting heart line, both in length and vigor. Witness Napoleon at and after Jena.

Abnegation of self seems perhaps incongruous when applied to such selfish persons as a Frederick or a Napoleon, but this is not the case. Self can be subordinated to self. The Corsican leading his grenadiers at Lodi subordinated the life of Bonaparte to the glory of Napoleon.

Loyalty is frequently only considered as faithfulness from the bottom up. It has another and equally important application; that is from the top down. One of the most frequently noted characteristics of the great (who remained great) is unforgetfulness of and loyalty to their subordinates. It is this characteristic which binds, with hoops of iron, their juniors to them.

A man who is truly and unselfishly loyal to his superiors is of necessity so to his juniors, and they to him.

Courage, moral and physical, is almost a synonym of all the foregoing traits. It fosters the resolution to combat and cherishes the ability to assume responsibility, be it for successes or for failures. No Bayard ever showed more of it than did Lee after Gettysburg.

But, as with the Biblical candle, these traits are of no military value if concealed. A man of diffident manner will *never* inspire confidence. A cold reserve cannot beget enthusiasm, and so with the others, there must be an outward and visible sign of the inward and spiritual grace.

It then appears that the leader must be an actor and such is the fact. But with him, as with his bewigged compeer, he is unconvincing unless he lives his part.

Can a man then acquire and demonstrate these characteristics? The answer is: they *have*—they *can*. For, "As a man thinketh, so is he."

The fixed determination to acquire the warrior soul, and have acquired it to either conquer or perish with honor, is the *Secret of Victory*.

G. S. Patton, Jr.,
Major
March 26, 1926

★★★ NEWS ITEM ★★★

PATTON TAKES HOLIDAY
Londoners Recognize Famous General
In Delayed Victory Celebration

London, May 16—(AP)—

Hardhitting General George S. Patton, Jr., of the U.S. Third Army, flew to London from southwestern Germany today for a little delayed victory celebration of his own.

"Back to my friends," he grinned as London crowds recognized him on West End streets and gave him a welcome similar to that shouted at General Dwight Eisenhower last night.

Patton went to see the Alfred Lunt-Lynn Fontanne play "Love in Idleness" at the Lyric Theater, commenting; "I wanted to see the Lunts in this play not only because they're friends of mine, but because the first time I was in London last year I attended their other play. I was sorry to hear that their theater had been damaged by a flying bomb."

Between acts the audience recognized Patton and he received an ovation. He visited the Lunts in their dressing room after the performance. Lunt congratulated the General on his healthy appearance and Patton replied, "Yes, war seems to agree with me."

The Lunts will take their play and company to the continent to entertain troops, and Patton invited them to appear before the Third Army.

Several hundred persons cheered Patton as he left the stage door. "Where are your guns, General?" asked someone, referring to Patton's famous pistols. "I don't carry them now that the war is over," Patton answered with a grin.

Cheering crowds blocked the roads as the General was driven back to his hotel following the show. The car had difficulty moving as people ran out to peer at him. Patton smiled and waved to them. Another crowd jammed the hotel entrance.

Patton told reporters that he was greatly touched by the warmth of London's reception.

Appendix

During the last twenty years, I have avidly researched the life and career of General Patton. During those years, I have collected a massive amount of material from various sources — books, magazines, personal letters, personal interviews, and especially portions of the Patton Papers Collection which resides in the Library of Congress.

In addition to the items that I have obtained from the Patton Papers Collection, I have drawn very heavily from some sources which are the best available "in depth" research materials. The books which were used most in choosing quotes from the late General were:

> *The Patton Papers* (Volume One)
> by Martin Blumenson
> Houghton-Mifflin Company, 1972.

> *The Patton Papers* (Volume Two)
> by Matin Blumenson
> Houghton-Mifflin Company, 1974.

> *Before the Colors Fade*
> by Frederick Ayer, Jr.
> Houghton-Mifflin Company, 1964.

> *War As I Knew It*
> by General George S. Patton, Jr.
> Houghton-Mifflin Company, 1947.

I would like to thank the Houghton-Mifflin Company for allowing me to reprint the material in this section. I used the four above mentioned volumes to a great extent in my search for true "Patton-isms."

There is a voluminous amount of information concerning General Patton available today. This section of *The Unknown Patton* is designed to be a quick easy reference to the most pertinent, salient thoughts of General Patton for those who wish to understand the Patton "mystique," yet do not wish to involve themselves with lengthy research. This compendium should prove most helpful toward that end.

Those quotations run the gamut of Patton's career from his days as a young Plebe at West Point to the World War II battle-fields of Europe. These quotations, extracted from a span of many years with no attempt to date them, display the fact that Patton never deviated from his initial formulation of combat and war. His concept of battle did not alter from the time that he put on his first Plebe uniform at West Point in 1904 until his death in his "24 Star Patton Uniform" in 1945. His basic attitude toward war and the waging of war was ingrained in him at a very early age. His years of study and experience merely crystallized his thoughts, his command presence, and his knowledge of contemporary techniques, which was used to bring into play the new and amazing arsenal of WWII weaponry.

An additional, and extremely relevant point brought out by these quotations is the "prophetic" accuracy of Patton's view-point. Patton was cognizant of the impending dangers of Com-munism and the belligerent attitude of the Russians. He attempt-ed to warn the people of these dangers, but he was ignored. The press both attacked and ridiculed him; his superiors gagged and restrained him.

As the years go by, more information comes to light concern-ing the truth about the waging of WWII. The emergence of one point becomes clear — General Patton was the most correct and successful army commander that the United States had. His military decisions have, with each succeeding year, been proven correct, much more so than is the case with any other top echelon commander in WWII. His political observations and prophecies have also turned out to be more accurate than those of the "political analysts" of the post war era.

The bottom line is that had we listened more closely and carefully to General Patton, and had we paid heed to his warn-ings, the world would very probably not be in the condition in which it finds itself today.

FAMOUS QUOTATIONS
BY PATTON

ARNOLD, GENERAL HENRY H.

Hap Arnold is the only one who understands the Mongols except for me. But the rest are waking up.

BASTOGNE (ARDENNES OFFENSIVE)

The First Army is making a terrible mistake in leaving the VIII Corps static, as it is highly probable that the Germans are building up to the east of them.

When I said that I could attack on the 22nd of December, it created quite a commotion.

Ike said in departing, "Everytime I get a new star I get attacked." I replied, "And everytime you get attacked, I pull you out."

The 101st Airborne call themselves the triple B's. Battered Bastards of Bastogne. They did well, but like the Marines of the last war, they get more credit than they deserve.

I was more amused than surprised when Eisenhower failed to make any remark about my Bastogne operation; in fact, he made no reference whatever to the great successes of the Third Army.

Courtney Hodges and Omar Bradley both received Distinguished Service Medals for their unsuccessful defense of the 'Bulge.' I did not receive one for successfully defending it.

BATTLE FATIGUE

It has come to my attention that a very small number of soldiers are going to the hospitals on the pretext that they are nervously incapable of combat. Such men are cowards, and they bring discredit to the Army and disgrace to their comrades, whom they heartlessly leave to endure the dangers of battle, while they themselves use the hospitals as a means of escape.

General John A. Crane, to whose Brigade Private Bennet belongs, stated to me afterwards that the man was Absent Without Leave and that he had gone to the rear by falsely representing his condition to the Battery Surgeon. It is rather a commentary on justice when an Army commander has to soft soap a skulker to placate the timidity of those in command above.

The number of cases of "war wearies" (the new name for cowardice) and self-inflicted wounds have dropped materially since we got moving. People like to play on a winning team.

BRADLEY, GENERAL OMAR N.

I can't make out whether Ike thinks Bradley is a better close-in fighter than I am or whether he wants to keep in with General Marshall, who likes Bradley. I know that Bradley is completely loyal to me.

Keyes is very dashing. Bradley and Middleton are more methodical. All of them are infinitely loyal and of superior effectiveness.

I have a feeling, probably unfounded, that neither Monty nor Bradley are too anxious for me to have a command. If they knew what little respect I had for the fighting ability of either of them, they would be even less anxious for me to show them up.

It is really a great plan. Wholly my own, and I made Bradley believe that he thought of it.

Omar is O.K., but not dashing.

Bradley was picked for his present job of Army Group Commander long before the "slap." Bradley says that he will put me in the fight as soon as he can. He could do it right now and with much benefit to himself, if he had any backbone.

Bradley and Hodges are such nothings. Their virtue is that they get along by doing nothing.

Collins and Bradley are too prone to cut off heads. This type of leadership will make division commanders lose their self-confidence.

Bradley is a man of great mediocrity. On the other hand, he has many attributes which are considered desirable in a general. He wears glasses; he has a strong jaw; he talks profoundly and says little; and he is a shooting companion of our present Chief of Staff, General Marshall. Also, he is a loyal man. I consider him to be among our better generals.

We had quite a long talk and I told Bradley a lot of my best ideas to tell to General Marshall. I suppose I should have kept them to myself, but I am not built that way. The sooner they are put into effect, the better it will be for our Army.

His success is due to his lack of backbone and his subservience to those above him. I will manage without him. In fact, I always have. Even in Sicily he had to be carried. Personally, I fight every order that I do not like, which makes me very unpopular, but successful.

I do not wish any more of my ideas to be used without credit to me, which is what happens when I give them orally to Bradley.

BRITISH, THE

Alexander said that it was foolish to consider the British and Americans as one people, as we were each foreigners to the other. I said that it was a correct concept and the sooner that everyone recognized it, the better. I told him that my boisterous method of command would not work with the British no matter how successful it might be with Americans, while his cold reserve method would never work with Americans. He agreed.

It is noteworthy that Alexander, the "Allied Commander" of a British and American Army, had no Americans with him. What fools we are.

This is a horse race. The prestige of the United States Army is at stake. We must take Messina before the British do.

Alexander has no idea of the power and speed of an American Army. We can go twice as fast and hit harder than the British.

I am fed up with being treated like a moron by the British. There is no national honor nor prestige left to us. Ike must go. He is a typical case of a beggar on horseback; he could not stand the prosperity.

One can only conclude that where the Eighth Army is in trouble we are to expend our lives gladly; but when the Eighth is going well, we are to halt so as not to take any glory. It is an inspiring method of making war and shows rare qualities of leadership, and Ike falls for it! Oh, for a Pershing!

It is noticeable that most of the American officers here are pro-British, even Ike. I am not, repeat not, pro-British.

CHURCHILL, WINSTON SPENCER

He strikes me as cunning rather than brilliant, but he has great tenacity. He is easily flattered, all of them are.

Finally, the Prime Minister made a really great fighting speech, worth all that preceded it.

Later, when we were going along well and could easily have taken Berlin, Churchill asked Ike to do it. Ike replied by stating that it was Churchill's fault that the line had been established where it was. I believe that this was a great mistake on Ike's part because, had we taken the country to the Moldau River and Berlin, we would have saved a great deal of agricultural Germany and prevented what I believe historians will consider a horrid crime and a great loss of prestige by letting the Russians take the two leading capitals of Europe.

CLARK, GENERAL MARK WAYNE

Clark was trying to be nice, but it makes my flesh creep to be with him.

Ike and Clark were in conference as to what to do. Neither of them had been to the front, so they showed great lack of decision. They have no knowledge of men or war. Too damned slick, especially Clark.

As far as I am concerned, General Clark has explained nothing. He seems to me more preoccupied with bettering his own future than in winning the war.

Wayne has his camp in the garden of a palace after which Versailles was copied. It is very beautiful, but too far to the rear.

Things are going worse with the 5th Army. Last night they flew in a regimental combat team of the 82nd Airborne to help out. It is noteworthy that when I asked for similar assistance last month, I was told that the 82nd was too valuable to be wasted as infantry.

I just saw a dispatch from the Navy in which it seems that

Clark has re-embarked. I consider this fatal for a commander. Think of the effect on the troops. A commander, once ashore, must either conquer or die.

DARBY, LIEUTENANT COLONEL

Bradley wanted to get Lieutenant Colonel Darby to command the 180th Regimental Combat Team of the 45th Division with the rank of Colonel. Darby preferred to stay with the Rangers. This is the first time I ever saw a man turn down a promotion. Darby is a great soldier. I gave him the Distinguished Service Cross.

DISCIPLINE

Lack of discipline at play means the loss of the game. Lack of discipline in war means death or defeat, which is worse than death. The prize of a game is nothing. The prize of war is the greatest of all prizes—Freedom.

There is only one kind of discipline; perfect discipline. If you do not enforce and maintain discipline, you are potential murderers.

It is the common experience of mankind that in moments of great excitement the conscious mental processes of the brain no longer operate. All actions are subconscious, the result of habits. Troops whose training and discipline depend on conscious thought become helpless crowds in battle. To send forth such men is murder. Hence, in creating an Army, we must strive at the production of soldiers, so trained that in the midst of battle they will still function.

When at the beginning of the football season the quarterback barks his numbers at the crouching players he excites an innate opposition—the feeling of "why in the hell should I do what he says?" Yet until that feeling is banished by habit, the team is dead on its feet. The soldier at attention and saluting, is putting himself in the same frame of mind as the player; alert, on his toes, receptive. In battle, the officers are the quarterbacks, the men are the disciplined team on their toes, with that lightning response to orders which means victory, and the lack of which means death and defeat.

The purposes of discipline and training are: 1. To insure obedience and orderly movement. 2. To produce synthetic courage. 3. To provide methods of combat. 4. To prevent or delay the breakdown of the first three due to the excitement of battle.

There has been, and is now, a great deal of talk about discipline; but few people, in or out of the Army, know what it is or why it is necessary.

All human beings have an innate resistance to obedience. Discipline removes this resistance and, by constant repetition, makes obedience habitual and subconscious.

Unless you do your best, the day will come when, tired and hungry, you will halt just short of the goal you were ordered to reach, and by halting you will make useless the efforts and deaths of thousands.

I'll bet that the Tank Corps will have discipline if nothing else.

Battle is an orgy of disorder. No level lawn nor marker flags exist to aid us in strutting ourselves in vain display, but rather groups of weary, wandering men seeking gropingly for means to kill their foes. The sudden change from accustomed order to utter disorder, to chaos, but emphasizes the folly of schooling to precision and obedience where only fierceness and habituated disorder are useful.

Discipline, which is but mutual trust and confidence, is the key to all success in peace or war.

A mechanical army only manned by mechanics who were not at the same time soldiers, would be a mess.

Discipline must be a habit so ingrained that it is stronger than the excitement of battle or the fear of death.

This "Blood and Guts" stuff is quite distasteful to me. I am a very severe disciplinarian because I know that without discipline it is impossible to win battles, and that without discipline to send men into battle is to commit murder.

Personally, I am of the opinion that older men of experience, who have smelled powder and have been wounded, are of more value than mere youthful exuberance, which has not yet been disciplined. However, I seem to be in the minority in this belief.

Brave, undisciplined men have no chance against the discipline and valor of other men.

There was one cadet standing at attention when I was inspecting him who had a fly crawling around his eye and he never winked. I believe that this is the epitome of discipline.

I saw hundreds of men of the First Army doing nothing. I issued orders that we keep a close check on our men to see that they are gainfully employed.

I have never seen in any Army, at any time, including the German Imperial Army of 1912, as severe discipline as exists in the Russian Army.

DUTY, HONOR, COUNTRY

The duties of an officer are the safety, honor and welfare of your country first; the honor, welfare, and comfort of the men in your command second; and the officer's own ease, comfort, and safety last.

In my opinion, we will only win this war through blood, sacrifice, and courage. In order to get willing fighters, we must develop the highest possible "Esprit de Corps." Therefore, the removal of distinctive badges and insignia from the uniform is highly detrimental. To die willingly, as many of us must, we must have tremendous pride not only in our nation and in ourselves, but also in the unit to which we belong.

We must keep moving. Do not sit down. Do not say, "I have done enough." Always see what else you can do to raise hell with the enemy. You must have a desperate determination to continually go forward.

I wish to assure all of my officers and soldiers that I have never and will never criticize them for having done too much. However, I shall certainly relieve them for doing nothing.

Sometimes I think I will simply resign and not be a further party to the degradation of my country.

We must have more decorations and we must not give them out with a niggard hand. A young soldier upon being asked by Napoleon what he desired in recompense for an heroic act said, "Sire, the Legion of Honor," to which Napoleon replied, "My boy, you are over young for such an honor." The soldier again said, "Sire, in your service, we do not grow old." This story is as true as it is tragic. Our men do not grow old. We must exploit their abilities and satisfy their longings to the utmost during the brief span of their existence. Surely, an inch of satin for a machine gun nest put out of action is a bargain not to be lightly passed up.

EDDY, GENERAL MANTON S.

General Eddy is very nervous, very much inclined to be grasping and always worrying that some other Corps Commander is getting a better deal than he is, but when the decision is made, he always does as he is told.

EISENHOWER, GENERAL DWIGHT DAVID

Eisenhower is either unwilling or unable to command Montgomery.

Ike asked me to dinner. Butcher, a British aide-de-camp, a WAAC Captain, and Kay Summersby were also present. Ike was very nasty and show-offish. He always is when Kay is present. He criticized General Lee for his flamboyance, but he would give a million to possess it himself.

Ike said to me, "You are fundamentally honest on the larger issues, but are too fanatical in your friendships." It is a good thing for him that someone is.

I wish to God that Ike would leave and take Smith with him. They cramp my style. It is better to rule in hell than to serve in heaven.

Ike was quite apologetic about the "four star" business, but has, however, good reasons. That is, you must maintain the hierarchy of command or else relieve them, and he had no reason for relieving them. At the moment I am having so much fun fighting that I don't care what my rank is.

This so called "re-deployment" is really a vote catching program. Ike's people were here to explain the unexplainable.

If Ike, etc. don't like what I do, they can relieve me. Then I will resign, not retire, and I can tell the world a few truths which will be worth saying.

Ike has an unfortunate habit of underrating all Americans who come under him and overrating all British and all Americans who have served elsewhere.

I wish to God that Ike were more of a soldier, and less of a politician.

We suffer very much from lack of command. No one is running the show.

Ike has no conception of physical command. He has never

exercised it.

Of course, I was originally selected for "Torch" through the direct action of Ike and therefore I owe him a good deal. On the other hand, I have paid my way ever since.

His is the style of an office seeker rather than that of a soldier.

Neither Ike nor Brad has the stuff. Ike is bound hand and foot by the British and does not know it. Poor fool. We actually have no supreme commander. No one can take hold and say that this shall be done and that shall be done. It is very unfortunate and I see no solution to the situation.

I told him that if I were reduced to Colonel, I demanded the right to command one of the assault regiments; that this was not a favor, but a right.

Ike replied, "Don't I know it, but what can I do?" That is a hell of a remark for a "supreme commander."

Ike was very pontifical and quoted Clausewitz to us, who have commanded larger forces than Clausewitz ever heard of.

Ike kept talking about the future "Great Battle of Germany" while we assured him that the Germans have nothing left to fight with and if we push on now, there will not be a "Great Battle of Germany."

Ike is all for caution since he has never been to the front and has no feel for actual fighting.

At 0800 hours, we heard on the radio that Ike had said that "Monty" was the greatest living soldier and that he is now a "Field Marshal."

I wish that Ike were more of a gambler, but he is certainly a lion compared to Montgomery. And Bradley is better than Ike as far as nerve is concerned.

Ike is not well and is very querulous and keeps saying how hard it is to be so high and never to have heard a hostile shot. He could correct that situation very easily if he wanted to. I also think that he is timid.

I am flying to see Ike. He and Clark certainly need to know the facts of life. They send some of the most foolish instructions that I have ever read.

Ike was fine, except that he spoke of lunch as "tiffin," of gasoline as "petrol," and of anti-aircraft as "flak." I truly fear that London has conquered Abilene.

Ike is not as rugged mentally as I had thought. He vacillates and is not realistic.

Ike is getting megalomania.

I spent the night at Ike's. Lieutenant Kay Summersby came to supper. Ike and I talked until 0129 hours. He is beginning to see the light but is too full of himself. I was quite frank with him about the British and he took it.

Ike walked the floor for some time, orating, and then he asked me to mention how hard he worked, what great risks he had taken, and how well he had handled the British, in my next letter to General Marshall.

Ike needs a few loyal and unselfish men around him, even if he is too weak a character to be worthy of us. But if I do my duty I will be paid in the end.

It is always depressing to me to see how completely Ike is under the influence of the British. He even prefers steel tracks to rubber tracks on tanks because 'Monty' does.

We are in the clutches of the "masterminds" here with the inevitable result that we are changing our plans more often than we are changing our underwear. I have been consulted no more than I was when we landed in Sicily.

Ike and I dined alone and we had a very pleasant time. He is drinking too much but is terribly lonely. I really feel sorry for him. I think that in his heart he knows that he is really not commanding anything.

Ike told me that he had not yet decided which of us three, Hodges, Bradley, or I, should command the Army Group. Bradley will!

Ike is getting foolish and bothering about things such as who is to be head nurse; far below his dignity.

Ike has never been subjected to air attack or any other form of possible death. However, he is such a straw man that his future is secure. The British will never let him go.

At no time did Ike wish us luck and say that he was back of us. He is a fool.

Ike said, "You are a great leader, but a poor planner." I replied that except for "Torch" which I had planned and which was a high success, I have never been given a chance to plan.

Ike arrived. We had a scout car and a Guard of Honor for him. The Guard of Honor was from his old battalion of the 15th Infantry, the only unit he ever commanded.

Ike is now wearing suede shoes, à la British.

When I took Ike to my room to show him the situation, he was not much interested, but he began to compare the sparsity of my reports with the almost hourly news bulletins of the 8th Army under Montgomery.

Ike called up late and said that, "My American boss will visit you in the morning." I asked, "When did Mamie arrive?" Man cannot serve two masters.

Lieutenant General Cocran, the son of a bitch, called our troops cowards. Ike says that since they were serving in his

Corps it was O.K. I told him that had I so spoken of the British under me, my head would come off. He agreed, but does nothing to Cocran.

It is noteworthy that had I done what Cunningham did, I would have been relieved of duty. Ike told me later that he could not punish Cunningham because he was a New Zealander and political reasons forbade it. Unfortunately, I am neither a Democrat nor a Republican. Just a soldier.

Ike talked in glittering generalities and then said as nearly as I can remember, "George, you are my oldest friend, but if you or anyone else criticizes the British, by God, I will reduce him to his permanent grade and send him home."

Ike made the sensational statement that while hostilities were in progress, the one important thing was order and discipline, but that now that hostilities were over the important thing was to stay in with "world opinion." Apparently whether it was right or wrong.

Eisenhower was also quite anxious for me to run for congress. I presume in the belief that I might help him.

Ike is bitten by the Presidential Bug and he is *yellow*.

Apparently Ike has to a high degree the "Messiah Complex" for which he can't be blamed since everybody bootlicks him except me.

Eisenhower was more excited than I have ever seen him, and I believe that this can be traced to the fact that he is very much worried about the delay in getting appointed as Chief of Staff at home. He fears that if he stays here, he will lose some of his prestige.

How can anyone expect any backbone in a man who is already running for President?

I feel that as an American it will ill become me to discredit

Ike yet. That is, until I shall prove even more conclusively that he lacks moral fortitude. This lack has been evident to me since the first landing in Africa, but now that he has been bitten by the Presidential Bee, it is becoming even more pronounced.

FLINT, HARRY (PADDY)

Paddy Flint is clearly nuts, but he fights well.

GAY, GENERAL HOBART (HAPPY)

Hap Gay is not a world beater, but he is much better than many other Lieutenant Generals and far more loyal.

GERMANS AND GERMANY

The mention of Bitburg reminds me of an incident which I saw there, which is very illustrative of the Germans. I entered the town from the south while fighting was still going on along the northern edge, which was not too far distant, since Bitburg is a small place. In spite of the fact that shells were falling with considerable regularity, I saw five Germans, three women and two men, re-roofing a house. They were not even waiting for Lend Lease, as would be the case in several other countries which I could mention.

All Nazis are bad, but not all Germans are Nazis.

Actually, the Germans are the only decent people left in Europe. It's a choice between them and the Russians. I prefer the Germans.

We are turning over to the French several hundred thousand Prisoners of War to be used as slave labor in France. It is amusing to recall that we fought the Revolution in defense of the rights of man, and the Civil War to abolish slavery, and have now gone back on both principles.

It is no more possible for a man to be a civil servant in Germany and not have paid lip service to the Nazis than it is for a man to be a postmaster in America and not have paid at least lip service to the Democratic Party or the Republican Party when they are in power.

If we let Germany and the German people be completely disintegrated and starved, they will certainly fall for Communism and the fall of Germany for Communism will write the epitaph of Democracy in the United States.

HARMON, GENERAL ERNEST N.

If it is desired to have an Armored Corps, I should recommend General Harmon to command it.

HISTORY

So far as the Atomic Bomb is concerned, while it is a scientific invention of the first water, it is not as earthshaking as you might think. When man first began fighting man, he unquestionably used his teeth, toenails, and fingernails. Then one day a very terrified or else very inventive genius picked up a rock and bashed a man in the head while he was gnawing at his vitals. The news of this unheard-of weapon unquestionably shocked Neolithic Society, but they became accustomed to it. Thousands of years later, another genius picked up the splintered rib of a Mastodon and using it as a dagger, thrust it into the gentleman with a rock in his hand. Again, pre-historic society was shocked and said, "There will surely be no more wars. Did you hear about the Mastodon bone?" When the shield, slingshot, javelin and the sword and armor were successively invented, each in its turn was heralded by the proponents as a means of destroying the world or of stopping war. Certainly the advent of the Atomic Bomb was not half as startling as the initial appearance of gunpowder. I remember two inventions which were supposed to stop war; namely the submarine and the tank. Yet, wars go blithely on and will continue to do so when your great-grandchildren are very old men.

The great warriors of history were too busy and often too inept to write contemporaneously of their exploits. What they later put on paper was colored by strivings for enhanced fame or by political conditions then confronting their perished past. The violent simplicity in execution which procured for them a success and enthralled the world looked pale and uninspired on paper, so they invariably seasoned it.

Without benefit of aerial bombardment, ground smoke, artillery preparation and airborne assistance, the Third Army at 2200 hours, Thursday, 22nd March, 1945, crossed the Rhine River.

The 21st Army Group was supposed to cross the Rhine River on 24th March, 1945, and in order to be ready for this "earth-shaking" event, Mr. Churchill wrote a speech congratulating Field Marshal Montgomery on the "first" assault crossing over the Rhine River in modern history. This speech was recorded and through some error on the part of the British Broadcasting Corporation, was broadcast. In spite of the fact that the Third Army had been across the Rhine River for some *thirty-six hours*.

History is replete with accounts of military inventions, each heralded by its disciples as the "Dernier Cri," the "Key" to victory.

It took me a long time to realize just how much a student of medieval history could gain from observing the Arab.

I have a notion that usually the great things a man does appear to be great only after we have passed them. When they are at hand they are normal decisions and are done without knowledge. In the case of a General, for example, the almost superhuman knowledge which he is supposed to possess exists only in the mind of his biographer.

I believe that for a man to become a great soldier it is

necessary for him to be so thoroughly conversant with all sorts of military possibilities that whenever an occasion arises, he has at hand, without effort on his part, a parallel. To attain this end, I believe that it is necessary for a man to begin to read military history in its earliest and crudest form and to follow it down in natural sequence, permitting his mind to grow with his subject until he can grasp, without any effort, the most abstract question of the Science of War because he is already permeated with its elements.

We disregard the lessons of history.

I am convinced that more emphasis should be placed on history. The purpose of history is to learn how human beings react when exposed to the dangers of wounds or death, and how high-ranking individuals react when submitted to the onerous responsibilities of conducting war or the preparation of war.

Save for the appearances, the Hoplite and the Rifleman are one. The emotions and consequent reactions which affected one affect the other.

Caesar, utilizing the rapid marching and high battle mobility of his professional armies, defeated many mass armies, all of which invariably outnumbered him.

Genghis Khan, by the use of higher mobility, led his Mongols to victory over many weak nations.

HODGES, GENERAL COURTNEY

Even the tent maker admits that Courtney is dumb. He is also very jealous of me.

He is apparently less dumb than I considered him. I am personally very fond of him.

HUMOR

The following pun always elicited great applause in the Great War: "If the staff of life is bread, what is the life of the staff? One long loaf!"

Yesterday, the Field Marshal ordered SHAEF to have the Third Army go on the defensive, stand in place, and prepare to guard his right flank. The Field Marshal then announced that he will, after regrouping, make what he describes as a lightning thrust at the heart of Germany. "They will be off their guard," he said, "and I shall pop out at them like an angry rabbit."

In view of the prevalent opinion in America that soldiers are, of all persons, the least capable of discussing military matters and that their years of special training is nil compared to the innate military knowledge of lawyers, doctors, and preachers, I am probably guilty of a great heresy in daring to discuss tanks from the viewpoint of a tank officer.

I just took Trier with only two divisions. Do you want me to give it back?

Take this five-gallon gasoline can to Montgomery with this message: "Although I am sadly short of gasoline myself, I know of your admiration for our equipment and supplies and I can spare you this five gallons. It will be more than enough to take you as far as you probably will advance in the next two days."

One very funny thing happened in connection with the Moroccan troops. A Sicilian came to me and said that he had a complaint to make about the conduct of the Moroccans, or Goums, as they are called. He said that he well knew that all Goums were thieves, and also that they were murderers, and that sometimes they indulged in rape. These things he could understand and make allowances for but when they came into his house, killed his rabbits, and then skinned them right in his parlor, it was going too far.

General Anders of the Polish II Corps told me laughingly that if he got between a German Army and a Russian Army, he would have difficulty deciding which they should fight.

A man I once met while a young lieutenant in Texas was a panther hunter and he told me very strange adventures which others said were all true. He was very dark and commented on it saying, "Damn it, lieutenant, a feller took me for a Mex and I hadda shoot him three times afore he believed I was white." This impressed me very much and I assured him that he was the whitest man I had ever seen.

The reason stated for the column leaving the road was that in this way they could avoid ricochets. A more complete immunity could be secured by not enlisting in the Army.

One of our American officers the other day began copying the British and started putting the initials of his decorations after his name; so today I wrote him a letter, adding the simple initials 'S.O.B.'

The Third Army starts attacking in the morning, but we will go slow so the others can catch up.

The Germans have damn little arms left, unless they have reproducing tanks.

Soldiers are always contrary. I could issue them coats without buttons and I will bet that within twenty-four hours they would find some, sew them on, and keep them buttoned.

JENSON, CAPTAIN RICHARD N.

He was a fine man and officer. He had no vices. I cannot see the reason why such fine young men get killed. I shall miss him a lot.

KEYES, GENERAL GEOFFREY

Keyes is very dashing, Bradley and Middleton are more methodical. All of them are infinitely loyal and of superior effectiveness.

I was delighted to see him. I think he is one of the pleasantest
companions and most loyal friends that I have ever known.

KOCH, COLONEL OSCAR

Oscar Koch is the best damned intelligence officer in any United
States Army Command.

LEADERSHIP

In picking a Command Post, you must always have a road net
from which you can move forward to any portion of your line.
A Command Post situated at a spot where it is necessary to
move to the rear is disadvantageous. In this connection, it is
always best, where practicable, to drive to the front, so that the
soldiers can see you going in that direction, and to save time,
fly back by Cub plane so that you are never seen going to the
rear.

There is nothing harsh in brief words of command any more
than there is impoliteness in the brief wording of a telegram.
Commands simply express your desire, your signal, in the brief-
est and most emphatic language possible. If you are to obtain
obedience from your men, your language must express your
meaning concisely and with emphasis. Further, each meaning
must always be expressed in precisely the same language. In
this way, when you give commands in battle, the unreasoning
mind of the soldier will automatically carry out the set of
instructions to which he has become accustomed. It is inexcus-
able for you to express yourself in an ambiguous or hesitating
manner.

A man of diffident manner will never inspire confidence. A cold reserve cannot beget enthusiasm.

The leader must be an actor. He is unconvincing unless he lives the part. The fixed determination to acquire the "Warrior Soul" and having acquired it, to conquer or perish with honor is the secret of victory.

The greatest gift a general can have is a bad temper. A bad temper gives you a sort of divine wrath and it is only by the use of a divine wrath that you can drive men beyond their physical ability in order to save their lives.

There are apparently two types of successful soldiers. Those who get on by being unobtrusive and those who get on by being obtrusive. I am of the latter type and seem to be rare and unpopular, but it is my method.

My little dictionary does not have "sycophant" in it, but every one of my divisions have.

It seems very queer that we invariably entrust the writing of our regulations for the next war to men totally devoid of anything but theoretical knowledge.

Leadership is the thing that wins battles. I have it, but I'll be damned if I can define it. It probably consists of knowing what you want to do, and then doing it and getting mad as hell if anyone tries to get in your way. Self-confidence and leadership are twin brothers.

Among leaders of whatever rank there are three types; 10% genius, 80% average, and 10% fools. The average group is the critical element in battle. It is better to give such men several simple alternative solutions which, by repeated practice, they can independently apply than it is to attempt to think for them via the ever fallible means of communication.

Wars may be fought with weapons, but they are won by men. It is the spirit of the men who follow and the man who leads that gains the victory.

Through the murk of fact and fable rises to our view this one truth; the history of war is the history of warriors; few in number but mighty in influence. Alexander, not Macedonia, conquered the world. Scipio, not Rome, destroyed Carthage. Marlborough, not the Allies, defeated France. Cromwell, not the Roundheads, dethroned Charles.

It lurks invisible in that vitalizing spark, intangible, yet as evident as the lightning; the "Warrior Soul."

War is conflict. Fighting is an elemental exposition of the age-old effort to survive. It is the cold glitter of the attacker's eye that breaks the line, not the point of the bayonet.

The most vital quality which a soldier can possess is self-confidence; utter, complete, and bumptious. You can have doubts about your good looks, about your intelligence, or about your self-control, but to win in war, you must have no doubt about your ability as a soldier.

Each, in his appropriate sphere, will lead in person. Any commander who fails to obtain his objective and who is not dead or severely wounded, has not done his full duty.

It always made me mad to have to beg for opportunities to win battles.

Julius Caesar would have a tough time being a Brigadier General in my Army.

Inspiration does not come via coded messages, but by visible personality.

This habit of commanding too far down, I believe, is inculcated at schools and maneuvers. Actually, a general should command one level down and know the positions of units two echelons down.

LOYALTY

I prefer a loyal staff officer to a brilliant one.

When a man gets married, he must be just as careful to keep his wife's love as he was to get it. It would be very sad for both of them if he said to himself, "Now that I have you I need not worry about losing you." Don't do that, ever!

There has been a great deal of talk about loyalty from the bottom to the top. Loyalty from the top to the bottom is much more important, and also much less prevalent. It is this loyalty from the top to the bottom which binds juniors to their seniors with the strength of steel.

MARSHALL, GENERAL GEORGE CATLETT

All he did was to make excuses for the lack of discipline in the Air Force. There is no excuse. My troops are disciplined.

Marshall lacks imagination, but he has an unusual mind.

MAXIMS

There is nothing more pathetic and futile than a general who lives long enough to explain a defeat.

Success in war depends on the "golden rules of war": speed, simplicity, and boldness.

The enemy is as ignorant of the situation as are we.

You are not beaten until you admit it.

You don't have to hurry, you have to run like hell.

War is the only place where a man lives.

The flag is to the patriot what the cross is to the Christian.

Do your duty as you see it, and damn the consequences.

It is the unconquerable soul of man and not the nature of the weapon he uses which insures victory.

Lack of orders is no excuse for inaction. Anything done vigorously is better than nothing done tardily.

Aviation cannot take prisoners nor hold ground.

A tank which stops to fire gets hit.

A good solution applied with vigor now is better than a perfect solution applied ten minutes later.

We can conquer only by attacking.

Speed and ruthless violence on the beaches is vital. There must be no hesitation in debarking. To linger on the beaches is fatal.

Officers must assert themselves by example and by voice.

There is no "approved" solution to any tactical situation.

There is only one tactical principle which is not subject to change. It is, "To use the means at hand to inflict the maximum amount of wounds, death, and destruction on the enemy in the minimum amount of time."

In case of doubt, ATTACK!

We must remember that victories are not gained solely by selfless devotion. To conquer, we must destroy our enemies. We must not only die gallantly, we must kill devastatingly. The faster and more effectively we kill, the longer we will live to enjoy the priceless fame of conquerers.

Battle is the most magnificent competition in which a human being can indulge. It brings out all that is best; it removes all that is base.

It is easy to die for nothing, one should die for something.

The more senior the officer, the more time he has to go to the front.

As long as you attack them, they cannot find the time to attack you.

A pint of sweat saves a gallon of blood.

One continues to learn about war by practicing war.

The soldier is the Army. No Army is better than its soldiers.

Never stop until you have gained the top or the grave.

The world has no use for a defeated soldier and nothing too good for a victor.

Never stop being ambitious. You have but one life, live it to the fullest of glory and be willing to pay any price.

Genius is an immense capacity for taking pains.

Always do more than is required of you.

It is better to live in the limelight for a year than in the wings forever.

Fame never yet found a man who waited to be found.

Everything is a "final heat."

By perseverance, and study, and eternal desire, any man can become great.

Do not regard what you do only as "preparation" for doing the same thing more fully or better at some later time. Nothing is ever done twice. There is no next time. This is of special application to war. There is but one time to win a battle or a campaign. It must be won the first time.

There is but one international law; the best Army!

We will have no real Army until we have universal service.

In war, death is incidental; loss of time is criminal.

War means fighting and fighting means killing.

If a man thinks war long enough, it is bound to have a good effect on him.

Punishment is not for the benefit of the sinner, it is for the salvation of his comrades.

There are more tired Corps and Division commanders than there are tired Corps and Divisions.

Fatigue makes cowards of us all. Men in condition do not tire.

Cowardice is a disease and it must be checked before it becomes epidemic.

Haste and speed are not synonymous.

The true objective of armor is enemy infantry and artillery; and above all else, his supply installations and command-centers.

You must never halt because some other unit is stuck. If you push on, you will relieve the pressure on the adjacent unit and it will accompany you.

The sole purpose of the cannon on the tank is to let the tank get into where it can use its machine gun to kill the enemy.

The unleavened bread of knowledge will sustain life, but it is dull fare unless it is leavened with the yeast of personality.

To be a successful soldier, you must know history.

Like wine, accounts of valor mellow with age; until Achilles dead 3000 years stands peerless.

Many soldiers are led to faulty ideas of war by knowing too much about too little.

War is an art and as such it is not susceptible of explanation by fixed formulae.

In peace, the scholar flourishes. In war, the soldier dies. So it comes about that we view our soldiers through the eyes of scholars and attribute to them scholarly virtues.

Throughout history wars have been lost because of armies not crossing rivers.

An army is like a piece of cooked spaghetti. You can't push it, you have to pull it after you.

War is simple, direct, and ruthless. It takes a simple, direct, and ruthless man to wage it.

War is a killing business. You must spill the enemy's blood or they will spill yours.

The greatest privilege of citizenship is to be able to freely bear arms under one's country's flag.

All men are afraid in battle. The coward is the one who lets his fear overcome his sense of duty.

Go until the last shot is fired and the last drop of gasoline is gone. Then go forward on foot.

The hardest thing a general has to do is to wait for the battle to start after all of the orders have been given.

Americans do not surrender.

Never make excuses whether or not it is your fault.

If brevity is the soul of wit, then repetition is the heart of instruction.

The important thing in any organization is the creation of a soul, which is based on pride, in the unit.

Re-grouping is the curse of war and it is a great boon to the enemy.

It may be of interest to future generals to realize that one makes plans to fit the circumstances, and does not try to create circumstances to fit plans.

The only thing to do when a son of a bitch looks cross-eyed at you is to beat the hell out of him right then and there.

There is nothing democratic about war. It is a straight dictatorship. The use of force to attain the end desired.

As long as man exists, there will be war. The only way to avoid trouble is to have the best Army, Navy, and Air Force.

MIDDLETON, GENERAL TROY H., MILLIKEN, GENERAL JOHN

I had to use the whip on both Middleton and Milliken today. They are too cautious.

General Middleton is the most methodical; probably the best tactician, very firm in his relations with other Corps-Commanders.

MISCELLANEOUS

When men see a marked helmet, they know that it is an officer. These markings are not visible at a range beyond 200 yards, therefore, the timid excuse that they produce sniping is of no value. Sniping occurs beyond that range.

One man received a direct hit and we could not find him for three days, when we began to smell pieces of him; but we never found any portion of his body.

I found a chaplain who was poking around the command post while there were wounded being put into ambulances close by. I gave him hell.

A bunch from Ike's staff tried to put me on the spot for not disarming the French in Africa. I assumed the offensive, showing them that to disarm the French or to discredit them meant an Arab War which would demobilize sixty thousand American soldiers as a starter. All of them agreed with me at last.

Battle is not a terrifying ordeal to be endured. It is a magnificent experience wherein all of the elements that have made man superior to the beasts are present. Courage, self sacrifice, loyalty, help to others, and devotion to duty.

As you go in, you will perhaps be a little short of breath, and your knees may tremble. This breathlessness, this tremor, they are not fear. It is simply the excitement which every athlete feels just before the whistle blows. No, you will not fear for you will be borne up and exalted by the proud instinct of our conquering race. You will be inspired by magnificent hate.

Sometimes I wish that people would take this war more seriously.

I think that we will go forward like shit through a tin horn.

Peace is going to be a hell of a letdown.

The woods are full of corpses and it is going to stink some in the spring.

I saw a lot of dead Germans yesterday frozen in funny attitudes. I got some good pictures, but did not have my color camera, which was a pity, as they were a pale claret color.

Speaking in general, I find that moral courage is the most valuable and usually the most absent characteristic in men. Much of our trouble is directly attributable to the fear of "they."

In this war, we were also unfortunate in that our high command in the main consisted of staff officers who, like Marshall, Eisenhower, and McNarny, had practically never exercised command. I think it was this lack of experience which induced them to think of and treat units such as divisions, corps, and armies as animated "tables of organization" rather than as living entities.

One feature of the Great War which has left its mark is the evolution of the "specialist." These men are trained to do a special job, and are not trained to be soldiers.

Dear SHAEF, I have just pissed into the Rhine River. For God's sake, send some gasoline.

One sentinel, reinforced, stopped 17 Germans in American uniforms. 15 were shot, 2 died suddenly.

To me, the Egyptian pyramids were quite disappointing. They are not as big nor as impressive as those around Mexico City.

In Egypt, on a fresh water canal, I saw a man defecating in the water, while below him at a distance of not more than ten yards, women were washing clothes, and a short distance further downstream a village populace was drawing drinking water.

All of the animals are head shy and many are blind as a result of the cheerful Arab custom of beating them on the head with a stick.

It seems to me a certainty that the fatalistic teachings of Mohammed and the utter degradation of the Arab women are the outstanding causes for the arrested development of the Arab. He is exactly as he was around the year 700, while we have been developing.

The bridge had been partly destroyed by a German who was hiding in a foxhole. He had pushed the detonator and blew the bridge killing some Americans after the leading elements had passed. He then put up his hands and surrendered. The Americans took him prisoner, which I considered to be the height of folly.

On this day, we processed through the cages and photographed the two hundred thousandth German prisoner. When we sent this to Public Relations, 12th Army Group, they would not publish the picture, because since the man had a sign on him stating that he was the two hundred thousandth prisoner of war, they said he was being degraded, which is contrary to the Geneva Convention.

Major Murphy told me that he could not add smoke in the plan since the stencil had already been cut. That was one of the most foolish remarks that I heard during World War II.

We are losing all hardihood. Today at the races I saw a jockey fall and get killed. A large, healthy man near me shuddered and said that steeplechasing was so dangerous that it should be abolished. Such squeamishness is fatal to any race of people.

The enemy has been booby-trapping his dead, which has made our men very mad. The result is that there are more enemy dead than usual.

Yesterday, I drove over one of our local battlefields and I

could smell men for ten miles. It is a very strong and disgusting odor.

It is very patent that what our Military Government in Germany is attempting to do is undemocratic and follows practically Gestapo methods.

After the meeting, I signed a number of Courts Martial and discovered that it is the policy of the Theater Commander not to give the death sentence to any American soldier convicted of raping a German woman. This seemed somewhat at variance with Anglo-Saxon custom.

MISTAKES

The 15th Corps could have easily entered the town of Falaise and completely closed the gap to Argenten, but we were ordered not to do this. This halt was a great mistake as I was certain that we could have entered Falaise and I was not certain that the British would. As a matter of fact, we had reconnaissance parties near the town when we were ordered to pull back.

The 29th of August, 1944 was, in my opinion, one of the critical days in this war. Hereafter pages will be written on it, or rather on the events which produced it. It was evident that at that time there was no real threat against us as long as we did not stop ourselves or allow ourselves to be stopped by imaginary enemies. Everything seemed rosy when suddenly it was reported to me that the 140,000 gallons of gasoline which we were supposed to get for that day did not arrive. I presented my case for a rapid advance to the east for the purpose of cutting the Siegfried Line before it could be manned. It is my opinion that this was the momentous error of the war.

Bradley called up at 1710 hours and in my opinion crawfished quite blatantly, in his forbidding me to use the 83rd Division. I believe that he had been "overtalked" either by Middleton or Hodges, or both. I was very sore at the time, and I still regard it as a great mistake. If I had been able to use two combat teams of the 83rd to attack Saarburg, that town would have fallen on the 12th or on the 13th and we probably would have captured the city of Trier. With Trier in our hands, Von Rundstedt's breakthrough to Bastogne could not have occurred. This is probably another case of "on account of a nail, a shoe was lost," etc.

I had never heard that we fought to "de-Nazify" Germany. Live and learn. What we are doing is to utterly destroy the only semi-modern state in Europe so that Russians can swallow the whole.

MONTGOMERY, FIELD MARSHAL BERNARD LAW

We roll across France in less time than it takes Monty to say "re-group," and here we sit stuck in the mud of Lorraine.

We never had to re-group, which seemed to be the chief form of amusement of the British Armies.

Montgomery had the nerve to get someone in the United States to suggest that General Eisenhower was "overworked" and needed a Deputy Ground Force Commander for all of the troops in Europe, and that he, Monty, was "God's gift to war" in this respect.

Monty is trying to steal the show with the help of Eisenhower. He may do so, but to date we have captured three times as many enemy as our cousins have.

Mr. McCloy asked me what I thought of Monty. I said at first that I preferred not to answer, and then, when pressed, I said that I thought Monty was too cautious and would not take calculated risks.

During Montgomery's lecture, it was interesting to note that I was the only American Commander of the four American Commanders involved in the plan to be mentioned by name. The other three he mentioned by number of the Army.

I fear that after we land in France, we will be boxed into a beachhead, due to timidity and lack of drive, which is latent in Montgomery.

Bradley says he will put me in as soon as he can. He could do it now with much benefit to himself, if he had any backbone. Of course, Monty does not want me as he fears that I will steal the show, which I will.

Montgomery went to great lengths to explain why the British had done nothing.

To hell with Monty. I must get so involved that they can't stop me. I told Bradley not to call me until after dark on the 19th.

At 0800 we heard on the radio that Ike said that Monty was the greatest living soldier and that he is now "Field Marshal."

The "Field Marshal" thing made us sick—that is, Bradley and me.

This is another case of giving up a going attack in order to start one which has no promise of success except for the exaltation of Monty, who has never won a battle since he left Africa, and only El Alamein there. I won Mareth for him.

I can outfight that little fart, Monty, anytime.

We never met any opposition because the bigger and better Germans fight Monty. He says so. Also, he advertises so damn much that they know where he is. I fool them.

PACIFISM AND PACIFISTS

The pacifists are at it again. I met a "visiting fireman" of great eminence who told me that this was to be the "last war." I told him that such statements since 2600 B.C. had signed the death warrants of millions of young men. He replied with the stock lie, "Oh yes, but things are different now." My God! Will they never learn?

The pacifist actually refuses to defend what defends him; his country. In the final analysis this is the most basic immoral position.

Man is war. War is conflict. Fighting is an elemental exposition of the age-old effort to survive.

PATRIOTISM

In our schools the youth should learn to show reverence for our flag and not treat it only as a handsome decoration. Each day he should study and hear recounted some of the splendid deeds of patriotism with which our country abounds. Surely this is vital, for if the alphabet and the multiplication table develop the mind, is not the soul worthy of instruction?

The often repeated statement that the country owes the soldier something for his services is based on a misconception of duty and patriotism. The soldier, being a citizen, owes the country service and whatever he gets in return is a gift, pure and simple.

The too often repeated remark that "the country owes me a living" is nothing short of treason. The nation owes all of its citizens an equal chance, but it is not responsible for the faults and follies of those who fail to avail themselves of these opportunities.

My poetry, my rhymes, were written by a man who having seen something of war is more impressed with the manly virtues it engenders than with the necessary and much exaggerated horrors attendant upon it. They are offered to the public in the hope that they may help to counteract the melancholy viewpoint of many of our poets who write of the great wars. We should not dwell on sorrow that those slain in battle have died, but rather be thankful that they have lived.

The man who finds twenty dollars on the street or wins it at the slot machine thinks lightly of it, and before long it is as lightly spent. The same man who works and sweats for half a week for that same amount respects it and grudgingly parts with it when he has won it. So with patriotism. The light feelings of love and reverence for our country engendered by shouting for the flag on the 4th of July are too haphazard, too cheap. The man who has served a year with sweat and some discomfort feels that truly he has a part in his country, and that of a truth he has, and he is a patriot.

Back of us stretches a line of men whose acts of valor, of self-sacrifice, and of service have been the theme of song and story since long before recorded history began. Our professional ancestors were sung of by the blind poet Homer a thousand years before the Christ. The exploits of which he chanted, and others of like nature, were handed down by word of mouth or in everlasting marble to the time when they might be recorded in writing for the eternal inspiration of the race.

Do not talk or think of your rights or your fatigues or of what the other fellow failed to do. War is the struggle of nations; you are in it, but as an individual, and hence your feelings as such do not exist.

In doing your utmost, even unto death, you are conferring no favor. You are privileged to be able to do so much for your country.

PATTON, GEORGE SMITH, JUNIOR

It is really amazing what determination on the part of one man can do to many thousands.

I have written more damn letters, I suppose a thousand, to the mothers of private soldiers whom I happen to know have been killed, but that never comes out. I kick some son of a bitch in the ass who doesn't do what he should and it comes out all over the whole damned country.

If I could only steal some gasoline, I could win this war.

They all get scared, and then I appear and they feel better.

At the close of this war, I will remove my insignia and wrist watch. I will continue to wear my short coat so that everyone can kiss my ass.

If I were a liar, I would say that I planned it, but actually I was as lucky as hell.

I guess that I am the only one who sees glory in war.

I am not the first general to catch hell. Wellington had plenty of it, as did General Grant, and countless others.

I love and admire good soldiers and brave men. I hate and despise slackers and cowards.

Like all commanders, I am constantly faced with the problem of malingering. If it is not checked, it spreads like a prairie fire.

I can't see how people can be so dull and lacking in imagination. Compared to them I am a genius. I think I am.

I can't see why people are so foolish. So far, "Torch" was the biggest and most difficult landing operation attempted. It was a great success and I planned it. I have yet to be questioned by any of the current planners concerning my experience.

Personally, I have never voted and do not intend to do so.

I drove to the Rhine River and went across on the pontoon bridge. I stopped in the middle to take a piss and then picked up some dirt on the far side in emulation of William the Conquerer.

The Marines always go to town by reporting the number of men they have had killed. I always try to fight without getting our people killed.

I wonder if ever before in the history of war a winning general has had to plead to be allowed to keep on winning.

We can never get anything across unless we talk the language of the people we are trying to instruct. Perhaps that is why I curse.

For years I have been accused of making snap judgments. Honestly, this is not the case because I am a profound military student and the thoughts I express, perhaps too flippantly, are the result of years of thought and study.

I wish someone would listen to me. I have something which makes people reluctant to question me; perhaps I always have an answer based on truth and not based on "bootlick."

Sometimes I wish that I was retired, but I guess that I would not like that either. I would probably be content only if I were God; and someone probably outranks him, too.

The more I see of the so called great, the less they impress me. I am better.

Little Bea's husband is in Europe as a lieutenant colonel and Ruth Ellen's husband is soon to go. George is a plebe at West Point and I have only two polo ponies left. Why should I linger too long?

I'm a hell of a guy. I'm giving the men hell one minute and crying over them the next.

When I think of the greatness of my job, and realize that I am what I am, I am amazed. But, on reflection, who is as good as I am? I know of no one.

I am probably the most unpopular man, not only in the 2nd Armored Division, but in the whole Army. I get very tired of being the only person in this outfit who makes any corrections.

There seems to be an unwitting conspiracy to make me lose my self-confidence, but so far it has failed.

Tomorrow I shall have my new battle jacket. If I'm to fight I like to be well dressed.

I wish I were supreme commander.

The only question in my mind is being able to survive the lapses between campaigns when I always seem to get myself into trouble. I am like a puppy, always sticking my nose into trouble.

There is nothing to do at the moment except to be a secret weapon.

If they will let me fight, I will. But if not, I will resign so as to be able to talk and then I will tell the truth and possibly do my country more good.

Even I can be pushed just so far.

It is a horrid thought that one may be deprived of doing the only thing one is good at due to the exercise of "free speech."

I only wear the shiny helmet in the back areas and have never ridden in a tank in battle.

I have this place so well organized now that there is nothing for me to do and I am getting nervous again.

Sometimes I think that I am not such a great commander after all; just a fighting animal.

Truly, for so fierce a warrior, I have a damned mild expression.

Does my conscience hurt me for killing that man in Mexico? It does not. I feel about it just as I did when I got my first swordfish, surprised at my luck.

Sometimes I wonder if I can do all that there is to do, but I suppose I can. I always have so far.

I have always talked blood and murder and am looked on as an advocate of close-up fighting. I could never look myself in the face if I were a staff officer and comparatively safe.

The bullet went into the front of my left leg and came out just at the crack of my ass about two inches to the left of the rectum. It made a hole about the size of a silver dollar where it came out.

Lots of officers look forward to fishing, farming, etc., after the war. I don't. I look forward to fighting here, in Japan, or at home, for the rest of my days.

I continued to walk up and down the beachhead and soon shamed them into getting up and fighting.

One man had the top of his head blown off and they were just waiting for him to die. He was a horrid bloody mess and was not good to look at or I might develop personal feelings about sending men into battle. That would be fatal for a general.

I have trained myself so that usually I can keep right on talking when an explosion occurs quite close. I take a sly pleasure in seeing others bat their eyes or look around.

I hear the big guns and they have the damndest effect on me. I am scared, but I still want to get to the front.

I am not a brilliant soldier. So far, I have been quite successful because I am always fully confident that I can do what must be done and have had my sense of duty developed to the point where I let no personal interests or danger interfere.

There must be one commander for ground, air, and sea. The trouble is that we lack leaders with sufficient strength of character. I could do it and possibly will. As I gain experience, I do not think more of myself, but less of others. Men, even so called great men, are wonderfully weak and timid. They are too damned polite. War is simple, direct, and ruthless. It takes a simple, direct, and ruthless man to wage it.

Now there is nothing to stop me. We have fresh divisions arriving. We've mastered the air. We have, after some tough lessons, the best weapons in the world. We can march into Berlin, Vienna, Prague, and Belgrade with people throwing flowers in our path. But, from Washington or London or somewhere they'll stop us. Otherwise, it might offend the God-damned Russians. Before that happens, I'm hoping to get out of here to fight the Japs. If not, I'm going to resign and tell the people in my country what is the truth.

On the opposite side of the road was an endless line of ambulances bringing men back; wounded men. Yet, when the soldiers of the 90th Division saw me, they stood up and cheered. It was the most moving experience of my life, and the knowledge of what the ambulances contained made it still more poignant.

On the 10th, Bradley called up to ask me how soon I could go on the defensive. I told him that I was the oldest leader in age and in combat experience in the United States Army in Europe and that if I had to go on the defensive, I would ask to be relieved. I further suggested that it would be a good thing if some of his staff visited the front to see how the other half lived.

It has always been my unfortunate role to be the "ray of sunshine" and the "back slapper" before any action, both for those under me and also those above me.

I told Papa of my fear of cowardice and he said that while ages of gentility might make a man of my breeding reluctant to engage in a fist fight, the same breeding made me perfectly willing to face death from weapons with a smile. I think that is true.

Papa always told me that the first thing was to be a good soldier. Next was to be a good scholar.

It is hard to answer intelligently the question, "Why I want to be a solider." For my own satisfaction I have tried to give myself reasons but have never found any logical ones. I only feel that it is inside me. It is as natural for me to be a soldier as it is to breathe, and it would be as hard to give up all thought of being a soldier as it would be to stop breathing.

Being a soldier and being a member of the Army in time of peace are two different things. I would accept the latter only as a means to the former.

No sacrifice is too great if by it you can attain your goals. Let people talk and be damned. You do what leads to your ambition and when you get the power, remember those who laughed.

I don't ever expect to be sixty years old. Not that it is old, but I simply prefer to wear out from hard work before then.

I do not fear failure. I only fear the slowing up of the engine inside of me which is pounding, saying, "Keep going, someone must be on the top, why not *you*?"

The only way for a soldier to die is by the last bullet of the last battle of his last war.

I have studied the German all of my life. I have read the memoirs of his generals and political leaders. I have even read his philosophers and listened to his music. I have studied in detail the accounts of every damned one of his battles. I know exactly how he will react under any given set of circumstances. He hasn't the slightest idea of what I'm going to do. Therefore, when the time comes, I'm going to whip the Hell out of him.

It's God awful. It's terrible, that's what it is. I can see it in a vision. It comes to haunt me at night. I am standing there knee deep in the water and all around me as far as the eye can see are dead men, floating like a school of dynamited fish. They are all floating face up with their eyes wide open and their skins a ghastly white. They are looking at me as they float by and they are saying, "Patton, you bastard, it's your fault. You did this to me. You killed me." I can't stand it, I tell you. By God, I won't go.

In any war, a commander, no matter what his rank, has to send to certain death, nearly every day, by his own orders, a certain number of men. Some are his personal friends. All are his personal responsibility; to them as his troops and to their families. Any man with a heart would like to sit down and bawl like a baby, but he can't. So, he sticks out his jaw, and swaggers and swears. I wish some of those pious sob sisters at home could understand something as basic as that.

As for the kind of remarks I make, why sometimes I just, by God, get carried away with my own eloquence.

People ask why I swagger and swear, wear flashy uniforms and sometimes two pistols. Well, I'm not sure whether or not some of it isn't my own fault. However that may be, the press and others have built a picture of me. So, now, no matter how tired, or discouraged, or really even ill I may be, if I don't live up to that picture, my men are going to say, "The old man's sick, the old son of a bitch has had it." Then their own confidence, their own morale will take a big drop.

I get criticized every day for taking needless risks by being too often right up front. What good is a dead general? I say, what damn good is a general who won't take the same risks as his troops?

You must be single minded. Drive for the one thing on which you have decided. You will find that you will make some people miserable; those you love and very often yourself. And, if it looks like you are getting there, all kinds of people, including some whom you thought were loyal friends, will suddenly show up doing their Goddamndest, hypocritical best to trip you up, blacken you, and break your spirit. Politicians are the worst; they'll wear their country's flag in public, but they'll use it to wipe their asses in the caucus room, if they think that it will win them a vote.

It is hell to be old, passé, and to know it.

Sometimes I think that I will simply resign and not be a further party to the degradation of my country.

During the course of the dinner which I had with Eisenhower on a purely social basis, I stated that I could not hereafter eat at the same table with General Bedell Smith.

If a man has done his best, what else is there? I consider that I have always done my best. My conscience is clear.

I will resign when I have finished this job, which will be not later than December 26th. I hate to do it, but I have been gagged all of my life and whether they appreciate it or not, Americans need some honest men who dare to say what they think, not what they think people want them to say.

In the summer of 1918, a group of soldiers of the 301st Tank Brigade, which I commanded, was having 37mm gun practice which I was observing. One defective round exploded in the muzzle, wounding two or three men. The next round exploded in the breech, blowing off the head of the gunner. The men were reluctant to fire the next round, so it was incumbent on me, as the senior officer present, to do so. In fact, I fired three rounds without incident. This restored the confidence of the men in the weapon. I must admit that I have never in my life been more reluctant to pull a trigger.

I still get scared under fire. I guess I never will get used to it, but I still poke along. I dislike the strafing most.

POLITICS AND POLITICIANS

Someday I'm going to bust loose across France and be heading hell bent for Berlin. Then either some coward or some dirty politician is going to become worried and order me to stop.

Any politician should be put in jail who votes for an appropriations bill and fails to vote the tax to pay for it.

There is something very phoney about all of our British and American efforts. Our strategy seems to be based on votes, not victories.

It is my belief that when the catchword "De-Nazification" has worn itself out and when people see that it is merely a form of stimulating Bolshevism, there will be a flop of the pendulum in the opposite direction.

The whole thing is a deliberate misquote with the intent of getting me into trouble because I am not "pink."

The point which I was and am still trying to bring out is that in Germany practically all or at least a very large percentage of the trades people, small businessmen, and even professional men such as doctors and lawyers, were beholden to the Nazi party. Without the patronage of the Nazi party, they could not carry on their business and work at their professions. Therefore, many of them were forced to give lip service to the party. I would extend this to mean that any dues paying by them was nothing but a form of blackmail and a means of holding onto their jobs. If we kick out these people, we will retard the reorganization of Bavaria to the extent that we will certainly be guilty of the deaths by starvation and freezing, of many women, children, and old men this winter.

The utterly un-American and almost Gestapo methods of De-Nazification were so abhorrent to my Anglo-Saxon mind as to be practically indigestible.

It is strange that in a battle situation I am perfectly willing to chop off heads, but in peacetime my Anglo-Saxon ancestry makes me reluctant to remove people without due process of law.

Everyone seems to be much more concerned and interested in the effects which his actions will have on his political future than in carrying out the motto of the United States Military Academy: "Duty, Honor, Country."

The noise created against me is only the means by which the Jews and Communists are attempting, and with good success, to implement a further dismemberment of Germany.

The whole damned world is going communist.

It is interesting to note that everything for which I have been criticized in the handling of the Germans has subsequently been adopted by our Military Government. I stated that if we took all of the small Nazis out of every job, chaos would result, and it did. The Military Government the other day announced that from two to five percent of Nazis would be permitted to stay in government offices.

Politicians are the lowest form of life on the earth. Liberal Democrats are the lowest form of politician.

The radio this morning said that the C.I.O. wants a bigger "New Deal." Where in hell do they think the money comes from? Or, do they simply want to destroy our form of government and go communist? If they knew as much about Russia as I do, they would not be so crazy to be communists.

PROPHECIES

It seems likely to me that Russia has a certain sphere of influence in Korea, Manchuria, and Mongolia.

There will be those who now and later will vilify and misrepresent me.

I have a hunch that my "Mexican Automobile Battle" was a forerunner of my involvement with tanks. Who can say?

Roman civilization fell due to the loss of the will to conquer, satisfaction with the "status quo," and high taxes, which destroyed trade and private enterprise. These conditions eventually forced people out of the cities. The cycle is returning.

If we again believe that wars are over, we will surely have another and damned quick. Man is War and we had better remember that! Also, we had better look out for ourselves and make the rest of the world look out for themselves. If we attempt to feed the world, we will starve and perhaps destroy America.

The Germans attacked down the Sele River just as I told Gruenther they would, and they have apparently cut the X Corps and the VI Corps in two. The only comfort I got out of it is the fact that my military judgment proved correct. I hope they can stop them. A withdrawal would hurt our prestige and surely prolong the war.

Someone must win the war and also the peace.

I am very much afraid that Europe is going Bolshevik, which, if it does, may eventually spread to our country.

I really shudder for the future of our country.

The Russians give me the impression of something that is to be feared in future world political reorganization.

ROOSEVELT, FRANKLIN DELANO

A great politician is not of necessity a great military leader.

ROOSEVELT, GENERAL THEODORE R.

He was one of the bravest men that I ever knew.

RUSSIAN AND RUSSIANS

We promised the Europeans freedom. It would be worse than dishonorable not to see they they have it. This might mean war with the Russians, but what of it? They have no Air Force anymore, their gasoline and ammunition supplies are low. I've seen their miserable supply trains; mostly wagons drawn by beaten up old horses or oxen. I'll say this; the Third Army alone with very little help and with damned few casualties, could lick what is left of the Russians in six weeks. You mark my words. Don't ever forget them. Someday we will have to fight them and it will take six years and cost us six million lives.

One form of securing testimony used by the Russians is to hang a man by his wrists with bandages so that they will not cut or leave marks. Then, two small incisions are made into the lower abdomen to allow a portion of the intestines to hang out. After the man has taken all that he can stand without dying, he is cut down, the incisions are sewn up, and he is restored to health with the promise that the operation will not be repeated IF he does as he is told.

I believe that by taking a strong attitude with the Russians, they will back down. We have already yielded too much to their Mongolian nature.

If it should be necessary for us to fight the Russians, the sooner we do it, the better.

We could have arrived sooner but for the fact that if one flies over Russian occupied territory they shoot at you. Nice friends.

If we have to fight them, now is the time. From now on, we will get weaker and they will get stronger.

It is said that for the first week after the Russians took Berlin, all women who ran were shot and those who did not were raped. I could have taken Berlin if I had been allowed.

The Russians have a lot of new heavy tanks of which they are very proud. The Marshal asked me how I liked them. I said that I did not and we had quite an argument. Apparently I am the first person ever to disagree with him.

At the dinner I stated that in my opinion Germany was so completely blacked out that so far as military resistance was concerned, they were not a menace and that what we had to look out for was Russia. This caused a considerable furor.

I believe that Germany should not be destroyed, but rather should be rebuilt as a buffer against the real danger, which is Russia and its Bolshevism.

Let's keep our boots polished, bayonets sharpened, and present a picture of force and strength to the Russians. This is the only language that they understand and respect. If you fail to do this, then I would like to say that we have had a victory over the Germans, and have disarmed them, but we have lost the war.

I have never seen in any army at any time, including the German Imperial Army of 1912, as severe discipline as exists in the Russian Army. The officers, with few exceptions, give the appearance of recently civilized Mongolian bandits. The men passed in review with a very good imitation of the goose step. They give me the impression of something that is to be feared in future world political reorganization.

SHAEF—HIGH COMMAND

We are in the clutches of the masterminds here with the inevitable result that we are changing our plans more often than our underwear. I have been consulted no more than I was when we went to Sicily.

All of them at SHAEF are scared to death to say anything which might be quoted.

None of those at Ike's headquarters ever go to bat for juniors in any argument with the British. They invariably favor the British. Benedict Arnold was a piker compared to them. That includes General Lee as well as Smith and Ike.

At the moment, I am being attacked on both flanks, but not by the Germans.

May God deliver us from our friends; we can handle the enemy.

If they would give me enough gasoline, I could go anywhere I wanted to.

I have to battle for every yard. It is not the enemy who is trying to stop me, it is "they."

It is too bad that the highest levels of command have no personal knowledge of war.

I told Bradley to tell them all to go to hell and we will resign. I would lead the procession.

SLAPPING INCIDENT

I am convinced that my actions in this case were entirely correct, and that had other officers had the courage to do likewise, the shameful excuse of battle fatigue instead of cowardice would have been infinitely reduced.

Over 80% of the letters that I have received are for me. Only one letter by a person of education is hostile. The rest are cranks and unsigned, mostly.

Ike and Beedle are not at all interested in me, but simply in saving their own faces. I might act the same if the case were reversed, but I doubt it.

General Joyce, to whom I talked about the Drew Pearson incident remarked, "George, just tell them the exact truth in these words; 'I had been dealing with heroes. I saw two men whom I thought were cowards. Naturally, I was not too gentle with them." This is exactly true, but there is no use in repeating it.

The thing which hurts me is that as far as I can see, my side of the case has never been heard. It is like taxation without representation.

I hear that the Gallup Poll says that I am 77% good, 19% bad, and 4% uncertain.

Apparently Drew Pearson has made certain allegations against me in Washington. I had been expecting something like this to happen for some time because I am sure that it would have been much better to have admitted the whole thing to start with, particularly in view of the fact that I was right.

If the fate of the only successful general in the war depends on the statement of a discredited writer like Drew Pearson, we are in a bad fix.

For every man that I have criticized in this Army, I have probably stopped, talked to, and complimented a thousand, but people are prone to remember ill usage more than to recall compliments.

SMITH, GENERAL WALTER BEDELL

On the way back, we met General Bedell Smith and General Lemnitzer. They were headed for Messina and I just heard the full story of Smith's actions. One of our batteries of 155mm guns let go, firing into Italy. Smith thought that it was enemy shells arriving and he jumped from the car into a ditch in one long leap, and he refused to leave it, even when Lemnitzer and

Murnane told him that it was quite safe. When I got back, he was still pale, grey, and very shaky.

Beedle also said that due to my "unfortunate" remarks, the permanent promotion of himself and me might never come off. How sad!

Smith is certainly an S.O.B. of the first type; selfish, dishonest, and very swell-headed.

During the course of the dinner which I had with Eisenhower on a purely social basis, I stated to him that I could not hereafter eat at the same table with General Bedell Smith.

SOLDIERS, AMERICAN

Of course, our men are willing to die, but that is not enough. We must be eager to kill, to inflict on the enemy, the hated enemy, all possible wounds, death and destruction. If we die killing, well and good. But, if we fight hard enough, viciously enough, we will kill and live to kill again. We will live to return to our families as conquering heroes.

When the great day of battle comes, remember your training. And remember, above all, that speed and vigor of attack are the sure roads to success and that you must succeed. To retreat is as cowardly as it is fatal.

We are ready. I shall be delighted to lead you men against any enemy. I am confident that your disciplined valor and high training will bring victory.

Put your heart and soul into being expert killers with your weapons.

To achieve harmony in battle, each weapon must support the other. Team play wins. You "musicians" of Mars must not wait for the band leader to signal to you. You must, each of your own volition, see to it that you come into this concert at the proper time and at the proper place.

There is a growing instance in this division of a disease common to this motorized age. It is called "waffle ass" and results from sitting down too much.

The fear of having their guts explored with cold steel in the hands of battle-maddened men has won many a fight.

To me, it is a never ending marvel what our soldiers can do.

Now that sounds like "what a great man George Patton is," but I did not have anything to do with it. The people who actually did it are the younger officers and the soldiers of the Third Army.

I believe that in war, the good of the individual must be subordinated to the good of the Army.

This ovation is not for me, George S. Patton. George S. Patton is merely a hook on which to hang the Third Army.

The soldier is the army. No army is better than the soldiers in it. To be a good soldier, a man must have discipline, self confidence, self respect, pride in his unit and in his country. He must have a high sense of duty and obligation to his comrades and to his superiors.

All of our soldiers do not drink like beasts. In fact, the lack of drinking in our Army is remarkable. They do, however, act like babies.

Who ever saw a dirty soldier with a medal?

The psychology of the fighting man is a strange thing. Early, well before dawn, I watched men of an almost green division, who were soaking wet and cold, cross a swollen river in the face of steep hills which were packed with concrete gun emplacements, machine guns, mines, and barbed wire. They crossed without hesitation and they walked right through that concentration of fire. They never hesitated once. Later in the day, I came across another outfit which was stalled along an open road. Do you know what was holding them back? It was a length of yellow string which was tied across their path between trees. No one in the outfit dared to touch it. I guess that it is the unknown which a man faces that he is scared of.

Anything that my men fight for and capture, they are entitled to and that includes fraternization.

The spirit of the men in the Evacuation Hospitals was improving and the incidence of "battle fatigue" and of "self-inflicted wounds" had dropped materially. Soldiers like to play on a winning team.

Men who are apt to die in battle are entitled to what pleasures they can get.

There were about three hundred 500 pound bombs and seven tons of 20mm high explosive shells piled on the sand and these soldiers had dug themselves foxholes in between the bombs and the boxes of ammunition.

It was funny to see our men sitting down among the German corpses and eating their lunches. Our men are pretty hard.

It was the superior fighting ability of the American soldier, the wonderful efficiency of our mechanical transport, the work of Bradley, Keyes, and the Army Staff that did the trick. I just came along for the ride. I certainly love war.

One poor fellow had lost his right arm and he cried. Another had lost a leg. All of them were brave and cheerful. A first sergeant who was in for his second wound laughed and said that after he received his third wound he was going to ask to go home. I had told General Marshall months ago that an enlisted man who had been hit three times should be sent home.

Our men are really grim fighters. I would hate to be the enemy.

This war makes higher demands on courage and discipline than any war of which I have known. But, when you see men who have demonstrated discipline and courage, killed and wounded, it naturally raises a lump in your throat and sometimes produces a tear in your eye.

SPAATZ, GENERAL CARL

General Spaatz came to see me. As usual, he was dirty and unshaven.

SUMMERSBY, LIEUTENANT KAY

Ike asked me to dinner; Kay, Butcher, a British aide-de-camp, and a WAAC captain were present. Ike was very nasty and show-offish. He always is when Kay is present.

Prince Bernhard of Holland decorated a number of SHAEF officers, including Lieutenant Summersby. The last one was in a high state of nerves as a result of hearing that General Eisenhower is not returning.

TRUSCOTT, GENERAL LUCIAN K.

His promotion has been well deserved and he has invariably done a good, though never brilliant, job. I am very proud of him.

UNIVERSAL MILITARY SERVICE

I am firmly convinced that we must have a universal system of training. The only hope for a peaceful world is a powerful America with the adequate means to instantly check aggressors. Unless we are so armed and prepared, the next war will probably destroy us. No one who has lived in a destroyed country can view such a possibility with anything except horror.

Fires are not put out by disbanding the fire department and wars are not prevented by destroying a country's armed forces.

We will have no real Army until we have universal service.

WALKER, GENERAL WALTON H.

Walker is a very fine soldier. He has never complained about any order that he has received.

Walker called up later and asked if he could continue a serious attack. I told him to go ahead.

Milly and Troy are starting again Sunday and Walker keeps pitching all the time.

General Walker is always the most willing and most cooperative. He will apparently fight anytime, anyplace, with anything that the Army Commander desires to give to him.

WAR, STRATEGY, AND TACTICS

Exploitation signifies that the situation is such as to at least justify the hope that there is something to exploit. In other words, that the crust has just been broken, and we are about to eat the pie.

Due to subconscious memories of prehistoric arboreal existence, man possesses an inherent instinct for secretive movements. Owing to this fact, instructors are prone to display exaggerated interest and ingenuity in "hide and seek" tactics.

Overstressing the value of concealment has a further disadvantage due to the psychological effect produced on the soldier. Just as children often create terrors from the fertility of their own imaginations, so do soldiers create in themselves visions of an omnipresent and deadly enemy.

In battle, the soldier enters a lottery with death as the stake. The only saving clauses in this gamble lie in time and the demoralizing effect produced on the enemy by the rapid and uninterrupted advance of the attacker.

My policy of continuous attack is correct. The farther we press, the more stuff we find abandoned that should not be abandoned. The Italians are fighting very well in the face of defeat. They must crack soon.

Sitting on a tank watching the show is fatuous; killing wins wars.

Each time we fight with only one weapon when we could use several weapons, we are not fighting and winning a battle; we are making fools of ourselves.

People must try to use their imagination. When orders fail to come they must act on their own best judgment. A very safe rule to follow is that in case of doubt, push on a little further and then keep on pushing.

I am obsessed with the idea that tanks should be used as quail shooting weapons, and not as buffaloes.

You can kill more soldiers by scaring them to death from behind with a lot of noise than you can by attacking them from the front.

I think that it is worthy to note that the primary function of an Armored Force is to disrupt command, communications, and supply.

Death in battle is a function of time. The longer troops remain under fire, the more men get killed. Therefore, everything must be done to speed up movement.

I am sometimes appalled at the density of human beings. I am also nauseated by the fact that Hodges and Bradley state that all human virtue depends on knowing infantry tactics. I know that no general officer and practically no colonel needs to know any tactics. The tactics belong to battalion commanders. If generals knew less tactics, they would interfere less.

We received a number of replacement captains. I initially assigned them to companies under lieutenants until they had learned the ropes. While this is not authorized in the regulations, I did it in both this and the First World War, and it works.

One of the chief defects of an airborne division is the fact that it never has anything it needs after it lands. No tanks, no adequate artillery, and no transportation.

General Eddy called me to state that his allowance of shells for the 16th was nine thousand, but I told him to go ahead and shoot twenty thousand, because I see no need in hoarding ammunition. You either use it or you don't. I would lose more men by shooting nine thousands rounds a day for three days than I would by shooting twenty thousand in one day, and probably would not get as far. I believe in fighting until lack of supplies forces you to stop, then digging in.

Throughout history, campaigns and wars have been lost due to an army stopping on the wrong side of a river.

The tank must be used boldly. It is new and always has the element of surprise. It is also terrifying to look at as the infantry soldier is helpless before it.

Civilization has affected us. We abhor personal encounter. Many a man will risk his life, with an easy mind, in a burning house, who would recoil from having his nose punched. We have been taught restraint from our emotions, to look upon anger as low, until many of us have never experienced the God sent ecstasy of unbridled wrath. We have never felt our eyes screw up, our temples throb, and have never had the red mist gather in our sight. But, we expect that a man shall, in an instant, in the twinkling of an eye, divest himself of all restraint, of all caution, and hurl himself upon the enemy, a frenzied beast, lusting to probe his enemy's guts with three feet of steel or to shatter his brain with a bullet. Gentlemen, it cannot be done without mental practice. Therefore, you must school yourselves to savagery. You must imagine how it will feel when your sword hilt crashes into the breastbone of your enemy. You must picture the wild exaltation of the mounted charge when the lips are drawn back into a snarl and the voice cracks with passion. At one time, you must be both a wise man and a fool.

Strategy and tactics do not change. The means only of applying them differ.

The fierce frenzy of hate and determination flashing from the bloodshot eyes squinting behind the glittering steel is what wins wars.

Volumes are devoted to armament; pages to inspiration.

Since the necessary limitations of map problems inhibit the student from considering the effects of hunger, emotion, personality, fatigue, leadership, and many other imponderable yet vital factors, he first neglects, and then forgets them.

The fixed determination to acquire the warrior soul, and having acquired it, to conquer or perish with honor, is the secret of success in war.

War is not a contest with gloves. It is resorted to only when laws, which are rules, have failed.

The atomic bomb is simply a new instrument in the orchestration of death, which is war.

Use steamroller strategy; that is, make up your mind on course and direction of action, and stick to it. But in tactics, do not steamroller. Attack weakness. Hold them by the nose and kick them in the ass.

Since our progress from now on had to be along the lines of what General Allen called the "rock soup" method, I will describe it. A tramp once went to a house and asked for some boiling water to make rock soup. The lady was interested and gave him some water, into which he placed two polished stones. He then asked if he might have some potatoes to flavor it a little, and then some carrots, and finally some meat. In other words, in order to attack, we had to first pretend to reconnoiter, then reinforce the reconnaissance, and finally put on an attack; all depending upon what amount of gasoline and ammunition we could secure.

I also re-read the *Norman Conquest* by Freeman, paying particular attention to the roads used by William the Conqueror during his operations in Normandy and Brittany. The roads used in those days had to be on ground which was always practicable.

War is just like boxing. When you get your opponent on the ropes you must keep punching the hell out of him and not let him recover.

Remember this; no set piece of tactics is of any merit in itself unless it is executed by heroic and disciplined troops who have self-confidence and who have leaders who take care of them.

We all feel that indiscriminate bombing has no military value and that it is cruel and wasteful and that all such efforts should always be on purely military targets and on selected commodities which are scarce of the enemy. In the case of Germany, the target would be oil.

War is the culmination of convergent commercial and political interests. Wars are fought by soldiers, but they are produced by businessmen and politicians.

Commanding an army is not such a very absorbing task except that one must be ready at all hours of the day and night to make some momentous decision, which frequently consists of telling somebody who thinks that he is beaten that he is not beaten.

WEAPONS

While in France in 1918, I was directed to report on the military value of a machine going by the euphonious name of the "moving fort and trench destroyer." An elaborate set of blueprints accompanied the description of the horrid instrument. Those prints depicted a caterpillar propelled box of generous proportions covered with two inch armor and bearing in its bosom six 75's, 20 machine guns, and a flame-thrower, while in the middle was a rectangular box 6 by 3 by 2 feet in size with the pathetic epitaph, "engine not yet devised." I do not know if atom bursting was known at that date, but if it was, I feel certain that an engine actuated by that sort of power must have been intended as no other form of power occupying so small a space could have propelled the 200 tons of estimated weight of the "fort."

Certainly, the advent of the atomic bomb was not half as startling as the initial appearance of gunpowder. In my own lifetime, I can remember two inventions, or possibly three, which were supposed to stop war; namely the dynamite cruiser *Vesuvius*, the submarine, and the tank. Yet, wars go blithely on and will still go on when your great-grandchildren are very old men.

Wars may be fought with weapons, but they are won by men. It is the spirit of the men who follow and the man who leads that gains victory.

Today, machines hold the place formerly occupied by the jawbone of an ass, elephant, armor, longbow, gunpowder, and submarine. They, too, shall pass.

The wrestling adage, "There is a block for every hold" is equally applicable to war. Each new weapon demands a new block and it is mightily potent until that block is devised.

The glory of the skyrocket elicits our applause; the splash of its charred stick is unnoticed.

The initial appearance of each new weapon or military device has always marked the zenith of its tactical effect, though usually the nadir of its technical efficiency.

Each form of specialist, like the aviators, the artillerymen, or the tanks, talk as if theirs was the only useful weapon and that if there were enough of them used, the war would soon end. As a matter of fact, it is the doughboy, in the final analysis, who does the trick.

It is very easy for ignorant people to think that success in war may be gained by the use of some wonderful invention rather than by hard fighting and superior leadership.

GENERAL ORDERS ISSUED BY PATTON

HEADQUARTERS
THIRD UNITED STATES ARMY
APO 9563
U. S. Army

6 March 1944

SUBJECT: Letter of Instruction No. 1.
TO: Corps, Division, and Separate Unit Commanders.

1. GENERAL

This letter will orient you, officers of the higher echelons, in the principles of command, combat procedure, and administration which obtain in this Army, and will guide you in the conduct of your several commands.

2. COMMAND

a. *Leadership*

(1) Full Duty.

Each, in his appropriate sphere, will lead in person. Any commander who fails to obtain his objective, and who is not dead or severely wounded, has not done his full duty.

(2) Visits to the front.

The Commanding General or his Chief of Staff (never both at once) and one member of each of the general staff sections, the signal, medical, ordnance, engineer, and quartermaster sections, should visit the front daily. To save duplication, the chief of staff will designate the sector each is to visit.

The function of these staff officers is to observe, not to meddle. In addition to their own specialty, they must observe and report anything of military importance. Remember, too, that your primary mission as a leader is to see with your own eyes and to be seen by the troops while engaged in personal reconnaissance.

b. *Execution*

In carrying out a mission, the promulgation of the order represents not over 10 percent of your responsibility. The remaining 90 percent consists of assuring, by means of personal supervision on the ground, by yourself and your staff, proper and vigorous execution.

c. *Staff Conferences*

Daily, at the earliest possible moment that the G-2 and G-3 can get their maps posted, a staff conference will be held, attended by the Commanding General, the Chief of Staff, and the heads of all general staff sections, the Surgeon, the Signal Officer, the Ordnance Officer, the Engineer Officer, and the other special staff heads when called on. Also present at this conference will be the staff officers described in paragraph 2a(2) above, who visited the front on the previous day. Any person present with a statement to make will do so briefly (n.b. if a staff inspector saw anything during his visit to the front requiring immediate action he would have reported the fact to the Chief of Staff immediately on his return). The Commanding General then gives his intentions and the Chief of Staff allocates the sectors for the day's staff inspectors.

d. *Rest Periods*

Staff personnel, commissioned and enlisted, who do not rest, do not last. All sections must run a duty roster and enforce compliance. The intensity of staff operations during battle is periodic. At the Army and Corps levels the busiest times are the periods from one to three hours after daylight, and from three to five hours after dark. In the lower echelons and in the administrative and supply staffs, the time of the periods is different but just as definite. When the need arises, everyone must work all the time, but these emergencies are not frequent; *"unfatigued men last longer and work better at high pressure."*

e. *Location of Command Posts*

The farther forward the Command Posts are located the less time is wasted in driving to and from the front. The ideal situation would be for the Army Command Post to be within one half hour's drive in a Command and Reconnaissance car of the Division Command Post. The driving time to the front from the Command Post of the lower units should be correspondingly shorter.

Much time and wire is saved if Command Posts of higher units are at or near one of the Command Posts of the next lower echelon.

All Command Posts of a division and higher units must have at least two echelons; the forward one—and that is the one referred to in this paragraph (e)—should be kept as small and mobile as possible with the minimum amount of radio traffic.

3. COMBAT PROCEDURE

a. *Maps*

We are too prone to believe that we acquire merit solely through the study of maps in the safe seclusion of a Command Post.

Maps are necessary in order to see the whole panorama of battle and to permit intelligent planning.

Further, and this is very important, a study of the map will indicate where critical situations exist or are apt to develop, and so indicate where the commander should be.

In the higher echelons, a layered map of the whole theater to reasonable scale, showing roads, railways, streams, and towns is more useful than a large-scale map, cluttered up with ground forms and a multiplicity of non-essential information.

b. *Plans*

Plans must be simple and flexible. Actually they only form a datum plane from which you build as necessity directs or opportunity offers. They should be made by the people who are going to execute them.

c. *Reconnaissance*

You can never have too much reconnaissance. Use every means available before, during, and after battle. Reports must be facts, not opinions; negative as well as positive. Do not believe intercepts blindly; crosscheck—sometimes messages are sent out to be intercepted.

d. *Orders*

(1) Formal Orders

Formal orders will be preceded by letters of instruction and by personal conferences. In this way the whole purpose of the operation will be made clear, together with the mission to be accomplished by each major unit. In this way, if communication breaks down during combat, each commander can and must so act as to attain the general objective. The order itself will be short, accompanied by a sketch—it tells *WHAT* to do, not *HOW*. It is really a memorandum and an assumption of responsibility by the issuing commander.

(2) Fragmentary orders

After the initial order, you will seldom get another formal order, but you will get many fragmentary orders in writing, or orally, by phone or personally.

Take down all oral orders and repeat them back. Have your juniors do the same to you.

Keep a diary with all orders and messages and the resulting action pasted in in sequence.

Keep your own orders short, get them out in time, issue them personally by voice when you can. In battle it is always easier for the senior officer to go up than it is for the junior to come back for the issuance of orders.

A division should have twelve hours, and better, eighteen hours, between the physical receipt of the order at Division Headquarters and the time it is to be executed.

(3) Warning Orders

Warning orders are vital and must be issued in time. This requirement applies not only to combat units, but also to the Surgeon, the Signal Officer, the Quartermaster, the Ordnance Officer, and the Engineer Officer who must get warning orders promptly. They, too, have plans to make and units to move. If they do not function, you do not fight.

Orders, formal or otherwise, concerning units further down than the next echelon of command are highly prejudicial.

(4) Keep Troops Informed

Use every means before and after combat to tell the troops what they are going to do and what they have done.

4. ADMINISTRATION

a. *Supply*

(1) General

The onus of supply rests equally on the giver and the taker.

Forward units must anticipate needs and ask for supplies in time. They must stand ready to use all their means to help move supplies.

The supply services must get the things asked for to the right place at the right time. They must do more; by reconnaissance they will anticipate demands and start the supplies up before they are called for.

The DESPERATE DETERMINATION to *succeed* is just as vital to supply as it is to the firing line.

(2) Replacements

Replacements are *spare parts*, supplies. They must be asked for in time by the front line, and the need for them must be anticipated in the rear. An educated guess is just as accurate and far faster than compiled errors. During lulls, you can balance the account. Keep your combat units full. A company without riflemen is just as useless as a tank without gasoline.

(3) Hospitals

Evacuation or Field Hospitals must be kept close to the front. Visit the wounded personally.

b. *Decorations*

Decorations are for the purpose of raising the fighting value of troops; therefore they must be awarded promptly. Have a definite officer on your staff educated in writing citations and see that they get through.

c. *Discipline*

There is only one kind of discipline; PERFECT DISCIPLINE. If you do not enforce and maintain discipline you are potential murderers. You must set the example.

5. RUMORS

Reports based on information secured through reconnaissance conducted after dark should be viewed with skepticism. The same thing applies to reports from walking wounded and stragglers. These latter seek to justify themselves by painting alarming pictures.

It is risky and usually impossible to move reserves during darkness on every call for help. Units cannot be wholly destroyed in a night attack. They must stick. Launch your counter attack after daylight and subsequent to adequate reconnaissance, and see that it is coordinated.

6. CONDITION

High physical condition is vital to victory.

There are more tired corps and division commanders than there are tired corps and divisions.

Fatigue makes cowards of us all. Men in condition do not tire.

7. COURAGE

DO NOT TAKE COUNSEL OF YOUR FEARS.

G.S. Patton, Jr.
Lt. Gen., U.S. Army
Commanding

HEADQUARTERS
THIRD UNITED STATES ARMY
APO 403
U. S. ARMY

3 April 1944

SUBJECT: Letter of Instruction No. 2
TO: Corps, Division, and Separate Unit Commanders

I. *GENERAL*

1. This letter stresses those tactical and administrative usages which combat experience has taught myself and the officers who have served under me to consider vital.

2. You will not simply mimeograph this and call it a day. You are responsible that these usages become habitual in your command.

II. *DISCIPLINE*

1. There is only one sort of discipline; perfect discipline. Men cannot have good battle discipline and poor administrative discipline.

2. Discipline is based on pride in the profession of arms, on meticulous attention to details, and on mutual respect and confidence. Discipline must be a habit so ingrained that it is stronger than the excitement of battle or the fear of death.

3. The history of our invariably victorious armies demonstrates that we are the best soldiers in the world. This should make your men proud. This should make you proud. This should imbue your units with unconquerable self-confidence

and pride in demonstrated ability.

4. Discipline can only be obtained when all officers are so imbued with the sense of their awful obligation to their men and to their country that they cannot tolerate negligence. Officers who fail to correct errors or to praise excellence are valueless in peace and dangerous misfits in war.

5. Officers must assert themselves by example and by voice. They must be preeminent in courage, deportment, and dress.

6. One of the primary purposes of discipline is to produce alertness. A man who is so lethargic that he fails to salute will fall an easy victim to an enemy.

7. Combat experience has proven that ceremonies, such as formal guard mounts, formal retreat formations, and regular and supervised reveille formations are a great help and, in some cases, essential to prepare men and officers for battle, to give them that perfect discipline, that smartness of appearance, that alertness without which battles cannot be won.

8. In the Third Army, when troops are not in the actual combat zone nor engaged in tactical exercises, or range firing, etc., Corps and separate Division commanders will see:
a. That regular reveille formations be held, in attendance at which there will be a minimum of one officer per company or similar unit, and in addition thereto when practicable, a minimum of one field officer per regiment or separate battalion.
b. That it shall be customary for all organizations to hold formal retreat under arms. Attendance, in addition to the prescribed enlisted men, shall be all officers of company grade. In the case of regiments and separate battalions, a minimum of one field officer.
c. That in the case where music is available and it is practicable from a billeting standpoint, frequent regimental and battalion retreat parades and similar ceremonies will be held.
d. That unit and organizational guard shall be performed strictly in accordance with FM 26-5. When music is available,

formal guard mounts will be held frequently.

e. That officers in formation wear a uniform analogous to that worn by the enlisted men, and that all officers participate in all drills and marches at all times with their organizations or units. This includes marching to and from training areas and ranges.

9. Officers are always on duty and their duty extends to every individual, junior to themselves, in the U. S. Army, not only to members of their own organization.

10. Americans, with arms in their hands, are fools as well as cowards to surrender. If they fight on, they will conquer.

11. Cases of misbehavior before the enemy will be brought before General Court Martial and tried under the 75th Article of War. It has been my experience that many Courts Martial are prone to view this most heinous offense, for which the punishment of death may be inflicted, in too lenient a manner. They should realize that the lives of troops are saved by punishment of initial offenders. Cowardice is a disease and must be checked before it becomes epidemic.

III. *TACTICAL USAGES*

1. *General*

a. Combat Principles:

(1) There is no approved solution to any tactical situation.

(2) There is only one tactical principle which is not subject to change. It is, "To so use the means at hand to inflict the maximum amount of wounds, death, and destruction on the enemy in the minimum of time."

(3) In battle, casualties vary directly with the time you are exposed to effective fire. Your own fire reduces the effectiveness

and volume of the enemy's fire, while rapidity of attack shortens the time of exposure. A pint of sweat will save a gallon of blood!

(4) Battles are won by fighting the enemy. Fear is induced by inflicting death and wounds on him. Death and wounds are produced by fire. Fire from the rear is more deadly and three times more effective than fire from the front, but to get fire behind the enemy, you must hold him by frontal fire and move rapidly around his flank. Frontal attacks against prepared positions should be avoided if possible.

(5) "Catch the enemy by the nose with fire and kick him in the pants with fire emplaced through movement."

(6) Hit hard soon, that is with two battalions up in a regiment; or two divisions up in a corps, or two corps up in an army; the idea being to develop your maximum force at once before the enemy can develop his.

(7) You can never be too strong. Get every man and every gun you can secure, provided it does not unduly delay your attack. The German is the champion digger.

(8) The larger the force and the more violence you use in an attack, whether it be men, tanks, or ammunition, the smaller will be your proportional losses.

(9) Never yield ground. It is cheaper to hold what you have than to retake what you have lost. Never move troops to the rear for a rest or to reform at night, and in the daytime only where absolutely necessary. Such moves may produce a panic.

(10) Our mortars and our artillery are superb weapons when they are firing. When silent, they are junk. See that they fire!

b. Tactical Rules in Particular Subjects:

(1) Use roads to march on; fields to fight on. In France we will find roads mined or demolished in many places, certainly

when we approach the enemy. When that happens, get off the roads and keep moving. But when the roads are available for use, you save time and effort by staying on them until shot off.

(2) Troops should not deploy into line until forced to do so by enemy fire.

(3) When you are advancing in broken country against possible tank attacks and using the leap frog method described in my Sicilian Notes, be sure to keep the anti-tank guns well up.

(4) In mountain country secure the heights. This is best done by daylight reconnaissance followed by night attack of a platoon reinforced at dawn twilight.

(5) In forcing a pass secure the heights first. There are always trails leading to the rear of hills. Remember that inviting avenues of approach are invariably defended, and an advance by such lanes, without securing the heights covering them, is suicidal.

(6) The effect of mines is largely mental. Not over 10 percent of our casualties come from them. When they are encountered they must be passed through or around. There are not enough mines in the world to cover the whole country. It is cheaper to make a detour than to search; however, the engineers should start clearing the straight road while the advance elements continue via the detour. See that all types of troops have mine detectors and know how to use them. You *MUST*, repeat, *MUST* get through!

(7) Never permit a unit to dig in until the final objective is reached, then dig, wire, and mine.

(8) Slit trenches in artillery will be placed within ten yards of guns. They will not be placed under trees as these induce air bursts. Camouflage nets must be rigged so that when they catch fire they can immediately be pulled off.

(9) Take plenty of time to set up an attack. It takes at least

two hours to prepare an infantry battalion to execute a properly coordinated attack. Shoving them in too soon produces useless losses.

(10) In battle, small forces (platoons, companies, and even battalions) can do one of three things; go forward, halt, or run. If they halt or run, they will be an even easier target. Therefore, they must go forward. When caught under fire, particularly of artillery, advance out of it; never retreat from it. Artillery very seldom shortens its range.

(11) Security detachments must get out farther, and must stay out at night. One radio car well off the road, but where it can see the road, or where a member of the crew can observe the road from close quarters, can send information which will be vital.

(12) We are too slow in putting out minefields and in wiring in positions for all around defense. More training should be devoted to mine laying and mine removal.

(13) A battalion of 4.2 chemical mortars, when available, should be attached to an infantry division. An infantry regiment in combat should have a 4.2 chemical company attached.

c. General Training

(1) More emphasis will be placed on the hardening of men and officers. All soldiers and officers should be able to run a mile with combat pack in ten minutes and march 8 miles in two hours. When soldiers are in actual contact with the enemy, it is almost impossible to maintain physical condition, but if the physical condition is right before they gain contact, it will not fall off sufficiently during contact to be detrimental.

(2) Much time is wasted in mounting and dismounting mortars and machine guns. Standing gun drill will be practiced so that the operation will be automatic and can be accomplished in the dark. The ladder method of ranging with mortars is recommended.

(3) Our ability to fight at night, as opposed to moving into position at night for a dawn attack, is pitiably bad. We must learn to execute the attack in the dark.

(4) Sharpen axes, pickaxes, and shovels now and keep them sharp.

(5) Battles are fought by platoons and squads. Place emphasis on small unit combat instruction so that it is conducted with the same precision as close order drill. A good solution applied with vigor *NOW* is better than a perfect solution ten minutes later.

(6) In instruction from the squad to the regiment, sand tables should be used, and the officer or non-com being instructed should give the actual orders he will give in combat. Sand tables need not be complicated. A piece of ground in the lee of a building is just as good and much simpler.

(7) Officers and men must know their equipment. They must train with the equipment they intend to use in battle. Equipment must be in the best operational condition when taken to the Theater of Operations.

d. Guides for Officers

(1) Officers must possess self-confidence and the confidence of their men. Two of the best ways of producing this is meticulously conducted close order drill, conducted by officers, and platoon marches of 48 to 60 hours during which the platoon is wholly on its own.

(2) In the first actions, new troops must receive aggressive leadership by all grades, including general officers who must be seen in the front line during action.

(3) The Adjutant General or Secretary to the General Staff must keep for the immediate information of the Commanding General a list showing casualties, materiel losses, prisoners of war, captured materiel, and replacements of both men and

materiel received. Two lists are necessary. The first one based on rumor; the second one corrected by data. The first one will be found surprisingly close to the second one.

(4) Note the time of your requests for, and time of arrival of, all artillery and air support missions called for. If support fails to arrive, so note.

(5) There is a universal failure to repeat oral orders back. This failure is certain to result in grave errors.

(6) Messages and orders must use concise, military verbiage.

(7) Push wire communications to the limit. A wire phone is worth three radios for both speed and security.

(8) battalion and company commanders fail to use runners and "walki-talki" radios. They frequently fail to have runners with or near them.

(9) Military Police at road junctions must have a map or diagram showing the points to which various roads lead and the units to be found on them.

(10) Don't place large radio sets near CP's if the CP's are to be in position more than six hours. If radios must be used for longer periods, put them well away, scatter them, and use remote control.

e. Prisoners

(1) German prisoners over 40 talk more easily than the younger ones. They must be examined separately, and not returned to the cages where the young ones are. Prisoners other than Germans usually talk freely and inaccurately. They, too, should be examined out of the hearing of, and later separated from, the young Nazis.

f. Needless Firing

(1) The needless firing of artillery will be checked by the senior artillery officer.

g. Needless Requirements

(1) There is a tendency for the chain of command to overload junior officers with excessive requirements in the way of training and reports. You will alleviate this burden by eliminating non-essential demands.

2. *Infantry*

a. Infantry must move in order to close with the enemy. It must shoot in order to move. When physical targets are not visible, the fire of all infantry weapons must search the area probably occupied by the enemy. Use marching fire. It reduces the accuracy of his fire and increases our confidence. Shoot short. Ricochets make nastier sounds and wounds. To halt under fire is folly. To halt under fire and not fire back is suicide. Move forward out of fire. Officers must set the example.

b. The heavy weapons set the pace. In the battalion the heavy weapons company paces the battalion. In the regiment the cannon company paces the regiment, but it is the function of the rifles and light machine guns to see that the heavy weapons have a chance to move. In other words, the rifles and machine guns move the heavy weapons in to do the killing.

c. Mortars use great quantities of ammunition. The 81mm will fire 800 rounds and a 60mm 500 rounds in 24 hours. To provide this ammunition, transport of all kinds must be utilized, and infantry riflemen in the vicinity of the mortars should each carry one round which they can dump at a pre-designated spot on going into the fire fight. When not on the move, all mortars, machine guns, and anti-tank guns of the infantry must be emplaced to fire.

d. Anti-tank guns should be placed where they cannot see or be seen beyond their lethal anti-tank range unless they are being used in the role of light artillery.

e. Few men are killed by the bayonet; many are scared of it. Bayonets should be fixed when the fire fight starts. Bayonets must be sharpened by the individual soldier. The German hates the bayonet and is inferior to our men with it. Our men should know this.

f. The M-1 rifle is the most deadly rifle in the world. If you cannot see the enemy, you can at least shoot at the place where he is apt to be.

g. Flat trajectory fire against machine guns must be delivered near and parallel to the axis of enemy fire. This pins him down until the grenadiers with bomb and bayonet can kill him from behind.

h. Fire distribution is practically non-existent in our army, with the result that those portions of the enemy who are visible receive all the fire, while those portions who are not visible, fire on our men with perfect impunity. This defect will be corrected.

i. The infantry battalion is the smallest unit which can be sent on a separate mission. When so used, it always is desirable to reinforce it with artillery, anti-tank guns, AA guns, and if possible, tanks and engineers.

j. Armored infantry should not attack mounted; it should use its vehicles to deploy mounted and also to assemble from deployed formation.

k. Night attacks mean attacks during darkness or by moonlight. On moonless nights the attack should start two and a half hours before dawn twilight; on moonlight nights with the moon. Night attacks must be preceded by careful day reconnaissance and ample warning. Limited objectives must be sought and must be easily recognizable in the dark. Attack formation is in column or line of columns. Distances and intervals are reduced. Depth is necessary.

l. Supporting fires must be arranged first to attack the enemy after our infantry has been discovered, and second to destroy counter attacks at dawn. Assaulting columns are preceded by a security detachment, which in turn is preceded by a patrol. The security detachment and patrol are absorbed when contact is made. In addition to the assaulting columns, a reserve should be available for exploitation after daylight. Countersign and challenge and identification marks on helmet or sleeve are necessary. Land marks and compass bearings to objective are necessary. Offensive grenades should be used. When discovered, open rapid fire and make as much noise as possible, while rushing in to use the bayonet.

m. The defense will consist of mutually supporting small groups arranged in depth and completely wired in. Mines will be placed.

n. All infantry officers must be able to observe and direct artillery fire.

3. *Artillery*

a. 65 to 75 percent of all artillery targets are provided by forward observers. The same percentage of tactical information originates with these observers, but much of the information of both characters the observers get, comes from the infantry. Therefore the forward observer must be in intimate association with the infantry. He must be under the control of the artillery liaison officer with the battalion. Artillery officers with infantry do not return to their batteries at night.

b. As soon as a position is captured, the forward observer must report through the liaison officer which of the possible channels of hostile counter attack he is in a position to cover with observed fire. This information must go to the infantry battalion commander.

c. Observers must be able to operate both by day and night. Use any calibre of gun at any time to hit any target of oppor-

tunity. For this reason forward observers for large calibres must
be up.

d. Artillery observers on their own initiative will bring fire
on enemy weapons firing on our infantry. Infantry officers are
equally responsible to call for such fire.

e. Machine guns giving local protection to artillery must be
sufficiently far out to prevent small arms fire from bothering
the battery.

f. Construct dummy batteries. In choosing sites for them,
avoid places where fire directed at them will adversely affect
other arms.

g. Tank attacks can be stopped by artillery concentrations of
white phosphorus and high explosives.

h. Artillery will be implaced as far forward as possible and
will move forward at every opportunity.

4. *Armor*

a. The primary mission of armored units is the attacking of
infantry and artillery. The enemy's rear is the happy hunting
ground for armor; use every means to get it there.

b. The tactical and technical training of our armored units
is correct. Added emphasis should be put on tank crew training
with a view to hitting the enemy first.

c. Against counter attacks, the offensive use of armor striking
the flank is decisive. Hence, a deep penetration by infantry,
whose rear is protected by armor, is feasible and safe.

d. There is no such thing as "tank country" in a restrictive
sense. Some types of country are better than others, but tanks
have and can operate anywhere.

e. The integrity of armored divisions should be preserved through the use of GHQ tank battalions for special close supporting missions with infantry. On such missions the tanks should advance by bounds from cover to cover in rear of the infantry. They will only be exposed when the situation demands their intervention. In such cases they will attack in close association with the infantry.

5. *Reconnaissance*

a. Reconnaissance, particularly on the part of the infantry must be stressed, especially at night. It is necessary to secure information every night through the capture of prisoners and the observation of hostile actions. Good men must lead these patrols. Mechanized observation units should not be employed for security except in cases of dire emergency.

b. Junior officers of reconnaissance units must be very inquisitive. Their reports must be accurate and factual. Negative information is as important as positive information. Information must be transmitted in the clear by radio and at once. The location of the unit giving the information should, where possible, be in a modified code. The enemy should be located by a magnetic azimuth and range from the point of observation. All members of a reconnaissance unit should know what they are trying to do. The results of all reconnaissance obtained in front of one division must be transmitted to adjacent units.

c. Reconnaissance must not lose contact. At night, when not in contact, listening posts should be at least six miles in front of our lines. Day reconnaissance must be pushed until contact is made. The use of light tanks in night reconnaissance usually induces the enemy to fire and display his position.

IV. *ANTI-AIRCRAFT AND ANTI-TANK*

1. *Anti-Aircraft*

a. At least one, preferably self-propelled, AA weapon should be attached to each company or battery of artillery, infantry, or tanks. There should be two at headquarters from the division up. The 155 and larger guns should have at least the AA mounts per battery. Owing to our air superiority, AA should never open fire until attacked. AA is also good for anti-tank.

2. Anti-Tank

a. Towed anti-tank guns should be well to the front and located to cover likely avenues of enemy tank approach. They must be emplaced so that they cannot see or be seen beyond their lethal anti-tank range. Self-propelled anti-tank weapons should be held in reserve to intervene against enemy armored attacks. They should locate routes to and firing positions from probable sites of future activities. All anti-tank guns should be trained to fire as artillery and be provided with a large proportion of high explosive shells.

V. MAINTENANCE

1. Weapons will be kept in perfect order.

2. Preventive maintenance will be enforced. Particular attention should be given to tire pressure, lubrication, battery voltage, and water in radiators. Vehicles will be serviced and made operational before their crews rest. Vehicles will be marked in accordance with paragraph 6-14, AR 850-5.

VI. CARE OF MEN

1. Officers are responsible not only for the conduct of their men in battle, but also for their health and contentment when not fighting. An officer must be the last man to take shelter from fire, and the first to move forward. Similarly, he must be the last man to look after his own comfort at the close of a march. He must see that his men are cared for. The officer must constantly interest himself in the rations of the men. He should know his men so well that any sign of sickness or nervous strain

will be apparent to him, and he can take such action as may be necessary.

2. He must look after his men's feet, see that they have properly fitting shoes in good condition, and that their socks fit; loose or tight socks make sore feet. He must anticipate change of weather and see that proper clothing and footgear is asked for and obtained.

3. Field and evacuation hospitals must be kept as close to the front as enemy fire permits. The shorter a haul of the wounded man to the hospital the better his chances for recovery.

4. Hospitals should be placed in the open and clearly marked. Do not permit liaison planes or groups of vehicles to park near them. Such action gives the enemy an excuse for attacking.

5. The successful soldier wins his battles cheaply so far as his own casualties are concerned, but he must remember that violent attacks, although costly at the time, save lives in the end. He must remember that replacements need special attention and he must see that they get acclimatized to their new units as quickly and harmoniously as possible.

G.S. Patton, Jr.
Lt. Gen., U.S. Army
Commanding

**HEADQUARTERS
THIRD UNITED STATES ARMY
APO 403
U. S. ARMY**

20 May 1944

SUBJECT: Letter of Instruction No. 3
TO: All Corps and Division Commanders

I. *USE OF ARMORED DIVISIONS*

1. The tactics prescribed for the use of armored divisions are correct, but owing to a lack of understanding of the word "Blitz," certain things are over-emphasized, and other very much more important things do not receive sufficient emphasis.

2. To begin with, *haste* and *speed* are not synonymous. By this I mean that hasty attacks do not produce speedy successes or speedy advances because hasty attacks are not coordinated attacks. "Haste makes waste."

3. In an armored division, as in an infantry division, attacks must be coordinated; and the infantry, and the tanks, and the guns must work as a unit. Wherever possible, it is desirable that the guns operate under divisional control, and with their forward observers in tanks, immediately take under fire enemy anti-tank guns, and either reduce them or blind them with smoke or white phosphorus. Success depends upon the coordinated use of the guns and the tanks, with the guns paying particular attention to hostile artillery, and above all to anti-tank guns and observation posts.

4. The decision of whether the assault should be led by the infantry or the armored vehicles depends on circumstances. When operating against known anti-tank guns or against exten-

sive anti-tank mine fields, or where it is necessary to force a river crossing or a defile, the infantry must lead and the tanks follow as and when the situation is cleared.

5. When operating against small minefields or minefields composed of boot or other "S" type mines, or against normal infantry and artillery resistance, the tanks should lead. However, it is necessary to remember that the association between tanks and infantry in the case of armored divisions operating as such is not as intimate as that which I prescribed in "Tactical Use of Separate Tank Battalions." Still, cases will arise where tanks must act in close support with their armored infantry. Normally, the armored infantry and artillery is used either to make a hole or to open a door to permit the tank battalions to move forward. As soon as this occurs, the armored infantry and artillery must immediately follow them. All this is adequately covered in existing regulations.

6. When tanks are advancing, they *must* use their guns for what is known as reconnaissance by fire; that is, they must shoot at any terrestrial objective behind which an anti-tank gun might be concealed and take these targets under fire at a range greater than that at which an anti-tank gun is effective; in other words, at a range greater than 2,000 yards. They should fire at these targets with high explosive or with white phosphorus, because if the enemy receives such fire, he will consider himself discovered and reply at a range so great as to render him ineffective.

7. When tanks are passing or approaching hedges or walls, they should comb them with machine guns so as to remove the danger from close defense anti-tank grenades and stick bombs.

8. When tanks use smoke or white phosphorus against infantry, tanks, or anti-tank guns, they should continue to fire into the smoke with high explosive or with machine guns if they are within range in order to prevent enemy movement.

9. Armored divisions should remember that many difficult open spaces can be passed with impunity if sufficient smoke is

placed on the enemy guns and observation posts by the artillery of the division or through cooperation with the air force.

10. The quickest way to get to heaven is to advance across open ground swept by effective enemy anti-tank fire.

11. The use of indirect fire by tanks is exceptional and is to be deprecated except under circumstances where tanks cannot be used in their proper role and are simply acting as artillery.

12. Tanks should never enter villages, and under those exceptional circumstances where such an entry is demanded, they should take the place from the rear. In passing villages they should move around them at a range in excess of the effective range of the anti-tank guns which are apt to be concealed in the villages. Personally, I have seldom seen a tank struck on the front silhouette by an anti-tank gun because the Germans generally put their anti-tank guns on reverse slopes or in places where they can get flanking fire. This being known, we should act accordingly and not rush in where angels fear to tread.

13. Tanks should remember that anti-tank guns are not armored and are therefore susceptible to effective results from high explosive and white phosphorus. If, therefore, they are unable to get their artillery up to remove the anti-tank guns, they should engage these guns with high explosive at a range in excess of 2,500 yards and from defilade, or if they have good observation, by indirect fire methods, because under these circumstances the high explosive will get the guns, and the guns will not have lethal effect against the tanks.

14. When tanks are taken under surprise fire by anti-tank guns or by other tanks, they should immediately fire several rounds of white phosphorus short of the target and then maneuver to get a telling shot when the smoke clears, or when the enemy emerges from it.

15. In tank-versus-tank duels, the first round should be armor piercing. If this fails, the second round must be white phosphorus and short so as to give our tank a chance to maneuver,

because by keeping its gun laid on the smoke, it has a better chance of getting in the second telling shot than has the enemy, who when he emerges from the smoke does not know the location of our vehicle.

16. Many tanks are lost through the failure of the crews or the platoon leader to make foot reconnaissance. People get vehicle bound and never dismount. Before exposing a valuable tank and the lives of its crew to the danger of destruction by crossing an unreconnoitered skyline or on emerging from cover, a foot reconnaissance with glasses should be made. Here again we have the question of haste and speed. It may seem a waste of time to take a look, but it is certain death to get on the front slope within effective range of undiscovered anti-tank guns or lurking enemy tanks.

17. It is of the utmost importance that tank crews, particularly the commander and the gunner, be trained to get a hit with the first shot against surprise targets such as anti-tank guns or enemy tanks. This shot must be correct both for range and azimuth. Exercises to produce this can be carried out in the tank park. All that is necessary is to have a number of targets which appear successively at different ranges and in different directions. The instructor must know the range to the target so he can check the range setting on the gun. He checks the azimuth by looking through the sight. It is very important that this be practiced.

18. When light tanks are engaging heavier tanks, they must attack by a section, or preferably a platoon. If they will do this, and so operate as to close the ranges to less than 400 yards, they are invariably victorious and at small loss. This close range can be obtained either by feigned retreat and ambush or by effective use of the ground.

19. In using armored infantry we should remember that it is nothing but a form of Cavalry; that is, it uses its vehicles to deploy and to redeploy mounted, thus saving time and avoiding fatigue. It does not use its vehicles, except very rarely, for mounted charges. This function is reserved to the tanks. Fur-

ther, since armored infantry is always operating with its tank elements, it does not have to hold out an infantry reserve because tanks are available, either to exploit the success of the armored infantry or to cover mistakes. Armored infantry should make a violent attack using all its men and weapons.

20. Reconnaissance in front of an armored division is of vital importance because no arm is more susceptible to terrain than is an armored unit.

21. Obviously, due to the rapidity of motion of armored divisions, information must get back more rapidly and must be obtained at greater distances to the front than is the case with slower moving units. It is more important to get the information back fast than to get it back secretly; therefore, use clear, with a limited code for name only when this is possible.

22. Armor must disabuse its mind of the rumored efficiency of German anti-tank weapons. This statement sounds peculiar in view of what I have already said, but it is nevertheless true.

23. Whenever German anti-tank guns have gotten our tanks, it has almost always been our own fault. In spite of years of instruction, tanks will go up obvious tank lanes such as cart tracks, open river bottoms, small roads or paths, or along hedges; all of which any intelligent anti-tank gunner will have arranged to cover. Furthermore, tanks will insist, as I have already said, in crossing skylines or emerging from cover without looking, in spite of the fact that it is well known that German anti-tank guns are generally on reverse slopes or in positions to fire at right angles to the axis of advance. Again, due to maneuver experience, tanks seek visual cover afforded by bushes, failing to remember that these do not stop bullets. The only cover behind which a tank has any security is that afforded by earth defilade.

24. The German anti-tank gunner is a good shot. We are better shots. He is unprotected. We are behind inches of steel. If we will use our heads and our American ingenuity and initiative, we have nothing to fear from German anti-tank guns.

25. Armored battles against infantry and anti-tanks are short and violent. They take great strength of mind and both physical and moral courage because of this violence and the speed with which they are terminated. When once launched, tanks must close at their best speed just the same as infantry, and also just the same as infantry, they must fire while closing. *The true objective of armor is enemy infantry and artillery, and above all his supply installations and command centers*

26. Every effort must be made to attack the flank, or preferably the rear, of the enemy. In executing such an attack, we must use all the means at our command to prevent the enemy from stopping these turning movements. Whenever such a movement meets enemy opposition, it must detach a portion of its force to contain the opposition and immediately begin a second and still wider envelopment because, if we are successful in getting one company of tanks alone, or supported by armored infantry and guns, in the enemy's rear, we have won the operation. Light tanks are particularly valuable for the final envelopment in such a movement because they have great speed and endurance, and adequate firepower against the type of resistance they will find in the enemy's rear.

27. In considering operations in which tank and infantry divisions are used in conjunction, we should remember that so long as the infantry attack, be it a penetration or a flank operation, is followed by armor, an enemy counter attack against the infantry flank is not particularly dangerous, because the armored division is the most ideal weapon for counter attacking such a counter attack. Both Corps and Division Commanders must constantly keep in mind such a use of armored divisions.

28. In the unlikely event that we are, at some point of our operations, in a defensive position, armored divisions should be placed to counter attack enemy assaults. These counter attacks should be rehearsed and the lines of approach carefully reconnoitered so that when the enemy appears, he will be violently and ruthlessly destroyed. The use of armored divisions for passive defense is not desirable.

29. Owing to the length of an armored division when marching on one road, it is highly desirable that the division move forward to battle on as many roads as are available. This gives flexibility without sacrificing depth.

To summarize:

We must take great and calculated risks in the use of armor, but we must not dive off the deep end without first determining whether the swimming pool is full of water.

You must never halt because some other unit is stuck. If you push on, you will release the pressure on the adjacent unit, and it will accompany you.

Troops are never defeated by casualties but by lack of resolution—of guts. Battles are won by a few brave men who refuse to fear and who push on. It should be our ambition to be members of this heroic group.

More casualties occur among those who halt or go to the rear than among those who advance and advance firing.

Finally, all of us must have a desperate desire and determination to close with the enemy and to destroy him.

II. USE OF THE BAZOOKA

1. The purpose of the Bazooka is not to hunt tanks offensively, but to be used as the last resort in keeping tanks from over running infantry. Since the Bazooka is unarmored, and always discloses its position when fired, it must get a hit on the first shot. To insure this, the range should be held to around thirty yards. When thus used, the Bazooka will hit and penetrate any tank that I have yet seen and will probably stop it. If used at longer ranges, it will probably miss and its operators will then become targets for the tank's machine guns.

III. COMMON TACTICAL FAULTS

1. It is nearly always a mistake to occupy obvious cover. This is particularly true in sparsely wooded country, because the

woods are clearly marked on the maps in enemy possession and will almost invariably be subjects of concentration.

2. The machine guns provided for close-in protection of command posts and artillery units are for the purpose of preventing enemy small arms fire from being brought on the installation to be protected. Therefore, these machine guns must be placed so far from the object they are protecting that they will take the enemy under their fire before he is within range of the points defended. All types of soldiers must know how to fight as infantry and must so fight when necessity arises.

3. The foolish practice of advancing by rushes over ground which is completely defiladed from enemy fire will be stopped. It exhausts the men to no purpose.

4. When the fire fight starts, bayonets should be fixed. They encourage our soldiers and discourage the enemy.

5. When a platoon or any other commander moves to the front to reconnoiter during a fire fight, he must not move to the rear to disseminate the information he has acquired, but rather, the unit must come up to him. The sight of officers moving to the rear has a disturbing effect on troops and serves no useful purpose.

6. The utilization of dummy guns to draw enemy fire is very important both in the case of our artillery and in the case of our anti-tank guns. In placing these dummy guns care must be taken not to put them where fire directed on them by the enemy will interfere with the movement of our troops. See that they are used.

7. There is a great lack of understanding about the use of the 57mm anti-tank guns against tanks. These guns have a lethal range against tanks of approximately a thousand yards. Therefore, they must be emplaced in positions where they cannot see the enemy or be seen by him at ranges in excess of a thousand yards; Otherwise, they will be destroyed by shell fire before they become effective. The proper place for 57mm anti-

tank guns is on reverse slopes or in positions where they can take the enemy under fire when he crosses the skyline or emerges from cover. When the 57mm is used as accompanying artillery, and it should be so used unless enemy tanks are around, it follows the methods of the cannon company.

8. Tank destroyer units must be emplaced sufficiently forward to prevent enemy tanks from over running the infantry. There is a prevalent and erroneous idea, particularly in the case of self-propelled tank destroyer units, that they should be held in reserve far to the rear. In such a position they will be impotent to get to the front in time to stop a tank attack before it has penetrated the infantry lines.

9. We are very prone to underestimate the time necessary for a coordinated attack, and we are also prone to get our infantry under fire before arrangements for coordination have been made. Prior to the infantry attack, the only people exposed to hostile fire are the scouts, and their sole mission is to find out where the enemy is so that the coordinated attack can be intelligently prepared.

10. There is a ridiculous and widespread fear among all our troops that they will run out of ammunition, particularly small arms ammunition. In my experience this has never happened. Troops should remember that if they save ammunition, which they could have effectively expended against the enemy, for some unforeseen contingency, they will also save the lives of a number of enemy who will participate in the contingency.

11. The necessity for using all weapons to their maximum fire capacity during our attacks cannot be too strongly impressed on the soldiers. Any gun that is not firing is not doing its job. In the assault where marching fire is used by the infantry, every gun, machine gun, and mortar must fire. Actual experiments have shown that using a relatively intense marching fire in an advance of over a thousand yards, that less than 35 rounds per rifle are actually expended. This is lower than would have been the case if we would have attempted to ad-

vance by rushes and taken three or four times as long reaching the enemy.

12. At the close of a fight it is very desirable that our own dead be removed from view as rapidly as possible. After this has been accomplished, the enemy dead should be removed with the same reverence we accord our own and given a proper burial.

13. There is a regrettable tendency on the part of company officers and non-commissioned officers to accompany the firing line as if they were members of a well trained chorus, simply keeping position. This attitude of mind, and the actions resulting from it, is impossible in battle. Officers and non-commissioned officers are there for the purpose of seeing that all the weapons of their respective little commands are functioning. They cannot see this by simply accompanying the movement; they must direct it.

14. In this letter, as in those preceding it, I am not laying down inflexible rules. I am simply giving you my ideas. I must and do trust to your military experience, courage, and loyalty to make these ideas tangible. There are many ways of fighting, all of which are good if they are successful.

15. We are now entering the final stage of a great war, of a great victory! This victory can only be attained by the maximum use of all weapons, both physical and spiritual. It is the duty of all commanders to see that their men are fully aware of the many vile deeds perpetrated upon civilization by the Germans, and that they attack with the utmost determination, ferocity, and hate. I am sure that every man will do his duty, and I am therefore sure that victory is simply a question of when we find the enemy.

G.S. Patton, Jr.
Lt. Gen., U. S. Army
Commanding

**HEADQUARTERS
THIRD UNITED STATES ARMY
APO 403
U. S. ARMY**

25 September 1944

SUBJECT: Letter of instruction No. 4
TO: Corps Commanders and the Commanding General XIX Tactical Air Command

1. The acute supply situation confronting us has caused the Supreme Commander to direct that until further orders, the Third Army, with its supporting troops, and those elements of the Ninth Army placed in the line, will assume the defensive.

2. It is evident that the successful accomplishment of this mission will require particular concentration upon two points;

a. First, this change in attitude on our part must be completely concealed from the enemy, who, should he learn of it, would certainly move troops from our front to oppose other Allied Armies.

b. Second, we must be in possession of a suitable line of departure so that we can move rapidly when the Supreme Commander directs us to resume the offensive.

3. In order to carry out the requirements of Paragraph 2a, above, we will not dig in, wire, or mine; but will utilize a thin outpost zone backed at suitable places by powerful mobile reserves. We will further insure that all possible avenues of tank attack are registered in by all our batteries—Division, Corps, and Army—whose guns can bear. Under the supervision of the Army Artillery Officer these zones of concentration will be numbered from north to south and recorded on a uniform map to be distributed to the units concerned, so that fire may

instantly be opened in any zone. Further, a copy of this map will be placed in the possession of the Commanding General XIX Tactical Air Command so that he may coordinate the concentration of planes upon any critical area in the most expeditious manner. Counter attacks by our mobile reserves should be planned and executed to secure a double envelopment of the hostile effort with the purpose of not only defeating it, but destroying it.

4. To insure our possessing a suitable line of departure for the future offensive, we shall secure the dotted line shown on the attached overlay by means of limited operations in consonance with our reduced scale of supply. To provide the necessary means for such limited operations, the utmost parsimony will be used in the expenditure of gasoline and ammunition consistent with the economy of the lives of our troops.

5. Whenever circumstances admit, troops not in the immediate presence of the enemy will be billeted. As soon as the troops so billeted have rested and have been equipped, they will be given constant practice in offensive tactics.

6. The defensive instructions contained in this letter will not be circulated below the grade of General Officer.

7. In closing, I desire to again compliment all of you on the magnificent dash and skill which you have shown in the operation to date. We only await the signal to resume our career of conquest.

G.S. Patton, Jr.
Lt. Gen., U.S. Army
Commanding

DISTRIBUTION:
CG Twelfth Army Group
CG XII Corps
CG XV Corps
CG XX Corps

POEMS WRITTEN
BY PATTON

GOD OF BATTLES

From pride and foolish confidence,
From every weakling creed,
From the dread fear of fearing,
Protect us, Lord, and lead.

Great God, who, through the ages,
Has braced the bloodstained hand,
As Saturn, Jove, or Woden
Has led our Warrior band,

Again we seek thy counsel—
But not in cringing guise,
We whine not for thy mercy;
To slay, God make us wise.

For slaves who shun the issue
We do not ask thy aid.
To Thee we trust our spirits,
Our bodies, unafraid.

From doubt and fearsome bodings
Still Thou our spirits guard.
Make strong our souls to conquer.
Give us the victory, Lord.

1943

A SOLDIER'S BURIAL

Not midst the chanting of the Requiem Hymn,
Nor with the solemn ritual of prayer,
'Neath misty shadows from the oriel glass,
And dreamy perfume of the incensed air
Was he interred;

But in the subtle stillness after fight,
And in the half-light between night and day,
We dragged his body all besmeared with mud,
And dropped it, clod-like, back into the clay.

Yet who shall say that he was not content,
Or missed the prayers, or drone of chanting choir,
He who had heard all day the Battle Hymn
Sung on all sides by a thousand throats of fire?

What painted glass can lovelier shadows cast
Than those the evening skies shall ever shed,
While, mingled with their light, Red Battle's Sun
Completes in magic colors o'er our dead
The flag for which they died?

1943

MARCHING IN MEXICO

The column winds on snake-like,
Through blistering, treeless spaces;
The hovering gray-black dust clouds
Tint in ghoulish shades our faces.

The sweat of muddied bubbles
Trickles down the horses' rumps;
The saddles creak, the gunboots chafe,
The swinging holster bumps.

At last the halt is sounded.
The outpost trots away.
The lines of tattered pup-tents rise—
We've marched another day.

The rolling horses raise more dust,
While from the copper skies,
Like vultures stooping on the slain,
Come multitudes of flies.

The irate cooks their rites perform
Like pixies 'round the blaze;
The smoking greasewood stings our eyes,
Sun-scorched for countless days.

The sun dips past the western ridge,
The thin dry air grows cold.
We shiver through the freezing night,
In one thin blanket rolled.

The night wind stirs the cactus,
And shifts the sand o'er all,
The horses squeal, the sentries curse,
The lean coyotes call.

1919

THE MOON AND THE DEAD

The roar of the battle languished,
The hate from the guns was still,
While the moon rose up from a smoke cloud,
And looked at the dead on the hill.

Pale was her face with anguish,
Wet were her eyes with tears,
As she gazed on the twisted corpses,
Cut off in their earliest years.

Some were bit by the bullet,
Some were kissed by the steel,
Some were crushed by the cannon,
But all were still, how still!

The smoke wreaths hung in the hollows,
The blood stink rose in the air;
And the moon looked down in pity,
At the poor dead lying there.

Light of their childhood's wonder,
Moon of their puppy love,
Goal of their first ambition,
She watched them from above.

Yet not with regret she mourned them,
Fair slain on the field of strife,
Fools only lament the hero,
Who gives for faith his life.

She sighed for the lives extinguished,
She wept for the loves that grieve,
But she glowed with pride on seeing
That manhood still doth live.

The moon sailed on contented,
Above the heaps of slain,
For she saw that manhood liveth,
And honor breathes again.

1945

ABSOLUTE WAR

Now in war we are confronted
    with conditions which are
    strange.
If we accept them we shall never
    win.
Since by being realistic, as in
    mundane combats fistic,
We will get a bloody nose and
    that's a sin.

To avoid such fell disaster, the
    result of fighting faster,
We resort to fighting carefully and
    slow.
We fill up terrestrial spaces with
    secure expensive bases
To keep our tax rate high and
    death rate low.

But with sadness and with sorrow
    we discover to our horror
That, while we build, the enemy
    gets set.

So despite our fine intentions to
   produce extensive pensions
We haven't licked the dirty bastard
   yet.

For in war just as in loving, you
   must always keep on shoving
Or you will never get your just
   reward.
For if you're dilatory in the search
   for lust and glory
You are up shit creek and that's the
   truth, Oh! Lord.

So let us do real fighting, boring
   in and gouging, biting.
Let's take a chance now that we
   have the ball.
Let's forget those fine firm bases in
   the dreary shell-raked spaces.
Let's shoot the works and win! Yes,
   win it all!

1944

A SOLDIER'S PRAYER

God of our Father, who by land and sea has ever
Led us on to victory, please continue your inspiring
Guidance in this greatest of our conflicts.

Strengthen my soul so that the weakening instinct of
Self-preservation, which besets all of us in battle,
Shall not blind me to my duty to my own manhood, to the
Glory of my calling, and to my responsibility to my
Fellow soldiers.

Grant to our Armed Forces that disciplined valor and
Mutual confidence which insures success in war.

Let me not mourn for the men who have died fighting,
But rather let me be glad that such heroes have lived.

If it be my lot to die, let me do so with courage and honor
In a manner which will bring the greatest harm to the
Enemy, and please, oh Lord, protect and guide those I
Shall leave behind.

Give us victory, Lord.

1944

VALOR

When all hearts are opened,
And all the secrets known,
When guile and lies are banished,
And subterfuge is gone;

When God rolls up the curtain,
And hidden truths appear,
When the ghastly light of Judgement Day,
Brings past and present near. . .

Then shall we know what once we knew,
Before wealth dimmed our sight,
That of all sins, the blackest is
The pride which will not fight.

The meek and pious have a place,
And necessary are,
But valor pales their puny rays,
As does the sun a star.

What race of men since time began,
Has ever yet remained,
Who trusted not its own right hand,
Or from brave deeds refrained?

Yet spite the fact for ages known,
And by all lands displayed,
We still have those who prate of peace,
And say that war is dead.

Yes, vandals rise who seek to snatch
The laurels from the brave,
And dare defame heroic dead,
Now filling hero graves.

They speak of those whose love,
Like Christ's, exceeds the lust of life,
And murderers slain to no avail,
A useless sacrifice.

With infamy without a name,
They mock our fighting youth,
And dare decry great hearts who die,
Battling for right and truth.

Woe to the land which, heeding them,
Lets avarice gain the day,
And trusting gold its right to hold,
Lets manly might decay.

Let us, while willing yet for peace,
Still keep our valor high,
So when our time of battle comes,
We shall not fear to die.

Make love of life and ease be less,
Make love of country more:
So shall our patriotism be
More than an empty roar.

For death is nothing, comfort less,
Valor is all in all;
Base nations who depart from it
Shall sure and justly fall.

THROUGH A GLASS, DARKLY

Through the travail of the ages,
Midst the pomp and toil of war,
Have I fought and strove and perished
Countless times upon this star.

In the form of many people
In all panoplies of time
Have I seen the luring vision
Of the Victory Maid, sublime.

I have battled for fresh mammoth,
I have warred for pastures new,
I have listed to the whispers
When the race trek instinct grew.

I have known the call to battle
In each changeless changing shape,
From the high souled voice of conscience
To the beastly lust for rape.

I have sinned and I have suffered,
Played the hero and the knave;
Fought for belly, shame, or country,
And for each have found a grave.

I cannot name my battles
For the visions are not clear,
Yet, I see the twisted faces
And I feel the rending spear.

Perhaps I stabbed our Savior
In His sacred helpless side.
Yet, I've called His name in blessing
When in after times I died.

In the dimness of the shadows
Where we hairy heathens warred,
I can taste in thought the lifeblood;
We used teeth before the sword.

While in later clearer vision
I can sense the coppery sweat,
Feel the pikes grow wet and slippery
When our Phalanx, Cyrus met;

Hear the rattle of the harness
Where the Persian darts bounced clear,
See their chariots wheel in panic
From the Hoplite's leveled spear.

See the goal grow monthly longer,
Reaching for the walls of Tyre.
Hear the crash of tons of granite,
Smell the quenchless eastern fire.

Still more clearly as a Roman,
Can I see the Legion close,
As our third rank moved in forward
And the short sword found our foes.

Once again I feel the anguish
Of that blistering treeless plain
When the Parthian showered death bolts,
And our discipline was in vain.

I remember all the suffering
Of those arrows in my neck.
Yet, I stabbed a grinning savage
As I died upon my back.

Once again I smell the heat sparks
When my flemish plate gave way

And the lance ripped through my entrails
As on Crécy's field I lay.

In the windless, blinding stillness
Of the glittering tropic sea
I can see the bubbles rising
Where we set the captives free.

Midst the spume of half a tempest
I have heard the bulwarks go
When the crashing, point-blank round shot
Sent destruction to our foe.

I have fought with gun and cutlass
On the red and slippery deck
With all Hell aflame within me
And a rope around my neck.

And still later as a General
Have I galloped with Murat
When we laughed at death and numbers,
Trusting in the Emperor's Star.

Till at last our star faded,
And we shouted to our doom
Where the sunken road of Ohein
Closed us in its quivering gloom.

So but now with Tanks a'clatter
Have I waddled on the foe
Belching death at twenty paces,
By the star shell's ghastly glow.

So as through a glass, and darkly
The age-long strife I see
Where I fought in many guises,
Many names—but always me.

And I see not in my blindness
What the objects were I wrought,
But as God rules o'er our bickerings
It was through His will I fought.

So forever in the future,
Shall I battle as of yore,
Dying to be born a fighter,
But to die again, once more.

Bibliography

List of Patton's Written Works

Armored Cars with Cavalry. Cavalry Journal, 1924

Army at the National Horse Show, The. Cavalry Journal, 1923

Army Racing Records for 1913. 1913

Army War College Cross Reference Cards; Purports of
  Communications. Army War College, Cadet Notebook and
  Miscellany. USMA, 1907-08

Cavalry Work of the Punitive Expedition. Cavalry Journal, 1917

Command Post Exercise. Army War College, 1932

Comments on 'Cavalry Tanks'. Cavalry Journal, 1921

Correspondence; GSP.Jr. to General Kenyon A. Joyce. 1939-1945

Desert Training Corps, The. Cavalry Journal 1942

Defense of the Saber, A. Cavalry Journal, 1916

Diary of the Instructor in Swordsmanship. Mounted Service
  School, Fort Riley, Kansas, 1915

Effects of Weapons on War, The. Cavalry Journal/Infantry Journal,
  1930

Federal Troops in Domestic Disturbances (Bonus March). 1932

Form and Use of the Saber, The. Cavalry Journal, 1913

General Talks to His Army, A. Army War College, 1957

German Army Operations of 1914. George S. Patton, Jr. Army
  War College, 1931-32

Highlights from Patton's Own Story. Saturday Evening Post, 1947

Letters of Instruction; #1, #2, #3, #4. Third Army After-Action
  Reports, 1945

Mechanized Forces, Cavalry Journal, 1933

Mechanized Units, Army War College, 1931

Motorization and Cavalry. Cavalry Journal, 1930

Motorization and Mechanization in the Cavalry. Cavalry Journal,
  1930

Mounted Swordsmanship and Army Racing. Records for 1913, the
  Rasp

Notes on Combat; Armored Divisions. 1944

Notes on the Desirability of Universal Service. 1919

Notes on the Effects of Weapons and Means of Communications
  on Tactics. Army War College, 1934

Obligation of Being an Officer, The. 1919

Orders and Tactical Problems Issued by Cadet Patton. USMA, 1907-09

Personal Experiences in the Tank Corps. 1918

Personal Glimpses of General Pershing. 1924

Present Saber; Its Form and the Use for Which it was Designed, The. Cavalry Journal, 1917

Probable Characteristics of the Next War. Army War College, 1930

Report of Operations of the Army Polo Team of 1922. Cavalry Journal, 1923

Report on the Tank Corps (Basis for Tank Corps). 1917

Request for Transfer to Tank Service. October 3, 1917

Saber Exercise-1914. Government Printing Office, 1914

Speech to the Third Army. Hope Farm Press, 1963

Success in War. Cavalry Journal/Infantry Journal, 1930

Suggestion Memo; Cavalry School, Sabers, and Military Saddles. 1929, 1930, 1939

Tanks in Future Wars. May, 1920

Tanks, Past and Future. 1928

Training Memorandum to His Regiment. Cavalry Journal, 1940

War As I Knew It. GSP.Jr. Houghton-Mifflin, 1947

War As I Knew It (Paper). GSP.Jr. Pyramid, 1972

War As She Is. 1919

What the World War Did for Cavalry. Cavalry Journal, 1922

List of Books Consulted

A Fateful Friendship. Stephen E. Ambrose. American Heritage, 1969

Across the Face of France. James A. Huston. Purdue Univ. Studies, 1963

Algonquin Project, The. Frederick Nolan. Pyramid, 1974

America's Great. Gene Moss. Alphaventure, 1975

Annals, The (Military Govt.) American Academy of Political and Social Science, 1950

At Ease; Stories I Tell My Friends. D.D. Eisenhower. Doubleday, 1967

Battle; True Stories of Combat in WWII. Sat. Eve. Post Editors. Sat. Eve. Post.

Before the Colors Fade. Frederick Ayer, Jr. Houghton-Mifflin, 1964

Bell for Adano, A. John Hersey. Avon, 1944

Biography. Sports Quiz. S-61

Blood and Guts is Going Nuts. Christopher Leopold. Berkley Books, 1978

Blood and Guts Patton. Jack Pearl, Monarch Books, 1961

Brass Ring, The. Bill Mauldin. W.W. Norton, 1971

Brass Target. Frederick Nolan. Jove/HBJ, 1974 (Algonquin Project)

Chasing Villa. Frank Tompkins. Military Svc. Publishing Co, 1934

Combat Leaders of WWII. T.N. Dupuy. Franklin Watts, 1965

Current Biography. 1943. S-52

Deadline Delayed. Overseas Press Club of America. E.P. Dutton, 1947

Dear Fatherland, Rest Quietly. Margaret Bourke-White. Simon & Schuster, 1946

Deeper Into Movies. Pauline Kael. Little, Brown, & Co., 1973

Drive. Charles R. Codman. Little, Brown, & Co., 1957

Emperor's White Horses, The. Vernon Brown. McKay Company, 1956

Famous American Generals. Shoemaker/Paris. Thomas Crowell, 1946

Famous American Military Leaders of WWII. Army Times. Dodd, Mead & Co., 1944

Fighting Generals. Curt Anders. G.P.Putnam's Sons, 1965

Fighting Generals. Phil Hirsch. Pyramid, 1960

Figures of Light. Stanley Kauffman. Harper and Row, 1971

Film 70/71. David Denby. Simon and Schuster, 1971

Fired in Anger. Robert Elman. Doubleday and Company, 1968

General Patton, Fearless Military Leader. B.F. Finke. Sam-Har Press, 1972

General Patton, Fearless Military Leader (Paper). B.F.Finke. Sam-Har Press, 1972

General Patton, the Last Cavalier. Wm. B. Mellor. G.P.Putnam's Sons, 1971

Generals and the Admirals, The. Newsweek Editors.

George Patton: General in Spurs. Alden Hatch. Julian Messner, 1950

George Patton; General in Spurs (Paper). Alden Hatch. Modern Library Editions, 1950

Great American Cavalrymen. Army Times Editors. Dodd, Mead, & Co., 1964

G-2 Intelligence For Patton. Oscar W. Koch. Army Times/ Whitmore, 1971

Heroes and Leaders of West Point. Red Reeder. Thomas Nelson, 1970

Hitler's Last Gamble. Jacques Nobecourt. Schocken Books

I Never Left Home. Bob Hope. Simon and Schuster, 1944

In Memoriam; George S. Patton, Jr. Third Army Headquarters, 1946

Kasserine Pass. Martin Blumenson. Tower Books, 1966

Kill Patton. Charles Whiting. Ballantine, 1974

Last 100 Days, The. John Toland. Random House, 1966

Lucky Forward. Robt. S. Allen. Vanguard Press, 1947

Lucky Forward (Paper). Robert S. Allen. Manor Books, 1975

Man in a Helmet, The. James Wellard. Eyre/Spottiswoode, 1947

Many Faces of George S. Patton, Jr., The. Martin Blumenson. U.S. Air Force Academy, 1972

Masters of the Art of Command. Blumenson/Stokesbury. Houghton-Mifflin, 1975

Movies Into Films. John Simon. Dial Press, 1971

National Cyclopaedia. S-53

New York Times Film Reviews; 1913-1970. George Amberg. Quadrangle Books, 1970

Nineteen Stars. Edgar F. Puryear. Coiner Publications, 1971

Past Forgetting. Kay Summersby Morgan. Simon and Schuster, 1976

Patton and His Pistols. M.F. Perry/B.W. Parke. Stackpole, 1957

Patton and His Third Army. Brenton G. Wallace. Mil. Svc. Pub., 1951

Patton Papers, The (Vol.I). Martin Blumenson. Houghton-Mifflin, 1972

Patton Papers, The (Vol.II). Martin Blumenson. Houghton-Mifflin, 1974

Patton's Best. Frankel/Smith. Hawthorne Books, 1978

Patton's Principles. Porter B. Williamson. Management/Systems Consultants, 1979

Patton's Principles (Paper). Porter B. Williamson. Management/Systems Consultants, 1979

Patton's Third Army at War. George Forty. Charles Scribner's Sons, 1978

Patton, Fighting Man. Wm. B. Mellor. G.P. Putnam's Sons, 1946

Patton, Ordeal and Triumph. Ladislas Farago. Obolensky, 1964

Patton, Ordeal and Triumph (Paper). Ladislas Farago. Dell, 1970

Patton. Charles Whiting. Ballantine, 1970

Patton. Ira Peck. Scholastic Magazines, 1970

Patton; A Study in Command. H. Essame. Charles Scribner's
   Sons, 1974
Pattons at Fort Riley, The. Henry B. Davis, Jr. Fort Riley
   Museum
Photograph listing Patton as 'Admiral Nimitz'. Window
   Dedication. S-147
Portrait of Patton. Harry H. Semmes. Appleton-Century-Crofts,
   1955
Portrait of Patton (Paper). Harry H. Semmes. Paperback Library,
   1970
Second Sight. Richard Schickel. Simon and Schuster, 1970
Tank Command, Patton's 4th Armored Division. Milton Shapiro.
   David McKay, 1979
Tanks and Armor in Modern Warfare. James Cary. Franklin
   Watts, 1966
These Are the Generals. Ted Shane. A.A. Knopf, 1943
Treasury of Great American Speeches. Charles Hurd. Hawthorn
   Books
Treasury of Great Reporting, A. Snyder/Morris. Simon and
   Schuster, 1949
United States in WWII, The. Don Lawson. Abelard/Schuman,
   1963
Voices From America's Past. Morris/Woodress. E.P. Dutton
War As I Knew It. George S. Patton, Jr. Houghton-Mifflin, 1947
War As I Knew It (Paper). George S. Patton, Jr. Bantam Books,
   1980
War As I Knew It (Paper). George S. Patton, Jr. Pyramid, 1972
War Lords, The. Michael Carver. Little, Brown, & Co., 1976
Warrior, the Story of Geo. S. Patton. Army Times Editors. G.P.
   Putnam's Sons, 1967
Wedemeyer Reports. Albert C. Wedemeyer. Holt and Company,
   1958
When the Third Cracked Europe. Paul D. Harkins. Stackpole,
   1969
Yankee G-Man. Frederick Ayer, Jr. Regnery, 1957
48 Hours to Hammelburg. Charles Whiting. Ballantine, 1970

Periodical List

America's First Cars in Combat. American Legion, 1954
Aqueduct News, The. Wartime Relics Stand Test of Time
Armor, 1952. Soldier's Reading, A. Beatrice Patton

Army. 1952. May. Comment On Night Firing. GSP(III)
Army. 1956. Nov. Armor Training at Camp Buckner. GSP(III)
Army. 1956. Nov. Eavesdropper, The. GSP(III)
Army. 1958. May. Operation Crusader. GSP(III)
Atlantic Monthly. 1945. Dec./1946. Jan. S-41
Atlantic Monthly. S-47
Auf Pattons Spuren. Jean Milmeister. Revue, 1978
Book Review. War As I Knew It. Cavalry Journal, 1947
Boss of Lucky Forward, The. George J.B. Fisher. Combat Forces
    Journal, 1951
Colliers. 1943. Jan. 13
Cosmopolitan. 1943. Nov.
Cosmopolites of the Month. Adela Rogers St. John.
    Cosmopolitan, 1943
Cowboy. Condottiere, Conquistador. Revue. Luxembourg, 1973
Flash Gordon. New Yorker, The, 1944
Fort Riley; Its Historic Past. Fort Riley, Kansas
General and the Horses, The. American Legion, 1963
General and the Movie, The. Edwin H. Randle. Army, 1971
General George Patton. George Forty. War Monthly, 1980
General Patton; Chip off the Famous Block. People, 1975
George S. Patton, Jr. CEO. Warren J. Ridge. Supervision, 1975
Highlights from General Patton's Story. George S. Patton, Jr.
    Sat. Eve. Post, 1947
Ike. T.V. Guide, 1979
Ladies Home Companion. "Fear" by Patton. S-176
Letters to the Editor (Patton's Jeep). Fourwheeler, 1979
Letters to the Editor. People, 1975
Life.
Life. 1941. Jul. S-60
Life. 1942. Nov. 30
Life. 1943. S-12
Life. 1944. Aug. 28
Life. 1945. Dec. S-78
Life. 1945. Jan. S-59
Life. 1945. Jan. 07. (Patton Cover)
Life. 1945. Jan. 15. (Patton Cover)
Life. 1946. Jan. 07
Life. 1946. Jan. 14
Life Goes to War. Time-Life Editors. Pocket Books, 1977
Look. 1943. Jun. S-58
Look. 1943. Jun. 01. (Patton Cover)

Look. 1945. Jan. S-66
Look. 1945. Jan. 23
Look. S-50
Nation. 1943. Dec. S-38
New American Mercury, 1951. Patton Speech, The.
New Republic. 1943. Dec. S-39
New Republic. 1944. May. S-40
New Yorker, The. 1944. Nov. 11
Newsweek. 1942. May. S-72
Newsweek. 1943. Dec. S-75
Newsweek. 1943. Dec. S-77
Newsweek. 1943. Jul. S-71
Newsweek. 1943. Jul. 26. (Patton Cover)
Newsweek. 1943. Mar. S-73
Newsweek. 1943. May. S-74
Newsweek. 1944. Aug. S-70
Newsweek. 1944. Aug. 28. (Patton Cover)
Newsweek. 1944. Jan. S-90
Newsweek. 1944. S-82
Newsweek. 1944. Jan. S-83
Newsweek. 1944. Sept. S-87
Newsweek. 1945. Dec. S-93
Newsweek. 1945. Dec. S-96
Newsweek. 1945. Dec. S-97
Newsweek. 1945. Jan. S-67
Newsweek. 1945. Jan. S-81
Newsweek. 1945. Jan. 08. (Patton Cover)
Newsweek. 1945. Jun. S-85
Newsweek. 1945. Oct. S-92
Newsweek. 1945. Oct. S-95
Newsweek. 1945. Sep. S-89
Newsweek. 1953. Oct. S-30
Newsweek. 1957. Sep. S-79
Newsweek. 1972. Mar. S-46
Newsweek. 1974. Oct. 7. S-127
Newsweek. 1975. Aug. GSP(III). S-139
Newsweek Clippings. S-86
Newsweek Clippings. S-88
Newsweek S-45
Newsweek Various Articles/Clippings. S-69
Newsweek Various Clippings. S-84
Notes on Tactics (Pt. I). GSP.Jr. AFV Magazine, 1978

Notes on Tactics (Pt. II). GSP.Jr. AFV Magazine, 1978
Notes on Tactics (Pt. III). GSP.Jr. AFV Magazine, 1979
Patton at the Payoff. George Creel. Colliers, 1945
Patton Country. Bill Jennings. Desert Magazine, 1977
Patton Editorial. Cavalry Journal, 1946
Patton in Mexico. Martin Blumenson. American History Illus.,
　1977
Patton Legend and Patton As Is, The. Vincent Sheean. Sat. Eve.
　Post, 1945
Patton Letters on Tank Performance. Ordnance, 1959
Patton of the Armored Force. Life. 1941
Patton Papers, The (Vol. I). Condensed Version. Book Digest,
　1975
Patton Quotations. Twenty-Five Years Ago. Armor
Patton's Bloodiest Blunder. Michael Stanley. Argosy, 1975
Patton's Premonition. American Legion, 1962
Patton's Psychology of Leadership. Harry H. Semmes. Armor,
　1955
Patton's Secret. Robert S. Allen, Army, 1971
Patton's Weihnacht. Revue. Luxembourg, 1969
Patton, The Soldier. Bell/Blumenson. Ordnance, 1959
Patton; Salute to a Rebel. Classroom Guide. Louis L. Snyder.
　20th Century-Fox, 1970
Patton; You Might As Well Die a Hero. James H. Polk, Army,
　1975
Penetrating Patton's Armor. George Winkels. High Country,
　1974
Rancho's Military Blazer. Dennis Adler. Fourwheeler, 1979
Reader's Digest. 1943. Sept.
Reader's Digest. 1943. Sept. S-22
Saturday Evening Post. 1943. Feb. 06
Saturday Evening Post. 1945. Jun. 23
Saturday Evening Post. 1947. Nov. 01
Saturday Evening Post. 1948. May. 01
Saturday Evening Post. 1976. Bi-Centennial Issue
Saturday Evening Post. S-177
Scholastic Review. 1972. Feb. S-49
T.V. Guide. 1973. Nov. S-27
Time. 1942. Feb. S-21
Time. 1942. Nov. S-17
Time. 1943. Apr. S-6
Time. 1943. Apr. S-8

Time. 1943. Apr. 12. (Patton Cover)
Time. 1943. Jan. S-10
Time. 1943. Jul. S-15
Time. 1943. Jul. 26. (Patton Cover)
Time. 1943. Mar. S-20
Time. 1944. Aug. S-24
Time. 1945. Apr. S-16
Time. 1945. Apr. 09. (Patton Cover)
Time. 1945. Dec. S-23
Time. 1945. Jun. S-14
Time. 1945. June. 18. (Pony Edition)
Time. 1945. Oct. S-26
Time. 1945. Oct. S-28
Time. 1949. Jan. S-19
Time. 1953. Oct. S-4
Time. 1970. Feb. S-54
Time. 1974. Oct. 28. S-128
Time. 1975. Aug. GSP(III). S-139
Time Capsule—1945. Time-Life Books, 1968
True Story of the Patton Prayer, The. James H. O'Neill. Review
  of the news, 1971
Two Fighting Generals. James M. Gavin. Army, 1965
Unknown. WWII's Greatest Tank Battle
We Called Him Uncle Georgie. Betty South. Quartermaster,
  1954
Whirl with Pearl, A. Jack Mitchel. Gun World, 1979.

Newspaper List

Army Navy Register. 1943-1945
Christian Science Monitor. 1943. Jan.09. S-157
Cincinnati Enquirer. 1944. Dec.29
Cincinnati Enquirer. 1945. Dec. S-183
Cincinnati Enquirer. 1945. Dec. S-185
Cincinnati Enquirer. 1945. Dec. S-190
Cincinnati Enquirer. 1945. Dec. S-192
Cincinnati Enquirer. 1945. Dec.22
Cincinnati Enquirer. Extracts of Patton and His Third Army. S-162
Cincinnati Enquirer. S-163 to S-174
Cincinnati Post. 1943. Sep. S-178
Cincinnati Post. 1945. Dec. S-188
Cincinnati Post. 1945. Dec. S-194

Cincinnati Post. S-163 to S-174
Cincinnati Times-Star. 1945. Dec. S-187
Cincinnati Times-Star. 1945. Dec. S-189
Cincinnati Times-Star. 1945. Dec. S-195
Cincinnati Times-Star. 1945. Dec.21
Cincinnati Times-Star. Advertisement for War Bonds. S-196
Cincinnati Times-Star. S-163 to S-174
Dayton Herald. 1945. Dec. S-184
Detroit News. S-163 to S-174
GSP(III). Tank Commander, Korea. S-151
I Was Paid to Kill Patton. Spotlight, The, 1979
Joanne Holbrook Weds GSP(III). S-149
Los Angeles Herald-Examiner. 1970. Jul.05
Los Angeles Times. 1945. Dec. S-137
Los Angeles Times. 1945. Dec. S-138
Los Angeles Times. Clippings. S-135
Los Angeles Times. Editorial (Death). S-136
Monteray Park Progress, San Gabriel, 1976
New York Herald Tribune. 1945. Dec.25. S-2
New York Times Magazine. 1943. Apr.4. Always Go Forward. S-122
New York Times. 1912. Jul.13. Olympics. S-119
New York Times. 1916. May.23. Kills Cardenas. S-118
New York Times. 1932. Jul.30. Bonus March. S-120
New York Times. 1943. Nov. S-13
New York Times. 1945. Dec.25. S-9
New York Times. 1964. Law Suit. S-141
New York Times. 1964. S-143
New York Times. Clippings. S-134
New York Times. Clippings. S-140
New York Times. GSP(III). S-142
New York Times. S-11
Newspaper Clippings. GSP(III). S-145
Newspaper Editorials (Pro-Patton). S-169
Parade Magazine Article. Patton Burial. S-200
Parade Magazine. 1974. S-44
Patton Clippings. Pasadena Library
Patton's Secret War Diary. San Francisco Examiner, 1952
Philadelphia Daily News. 1945. Dec. S-191
Philadelphia Daily News. S-163 to S-174
Riverside Daily Enterprise. 1968. Apr.18. S-156
San Diego Tribune-Sun. 1945. Dec.24. S-7
San Diego Tribune-Sun. 1945. Dec.25. S-5

San Diego Tribune. 1975. Aug.5. S-131
San Diego Union. 1945. Dec.25. S-3
San Diego Union. 1972. Dec.25. S-25
San Diego Union. 1973. S-44
San Diego Union. 1975. Aug.4. S-131
San Diego Union. 1976. Aug.15. Mike Province/Patton Society.
  S-151
San Diego Union. 1977. Oct. 20. GSP(III). S-197
San Francisco Chronicle. 1916. Apr.12. In Mexico. S-121
San Francisco Examiner. 1945. Dec.16
San Francisco Examiner. 1952. Jul.2. Patton's Secret Diary. S-155
San Francisco Examiner. 1945. Dec. S-193
Stars and Stripes. 1945. Dec. S-179
Stars and Stripes. 1945. Dec. S-180
Stars and Stripes. 1945. Dec. S-182
Stars and Stripes. 1945. Dec. S-182
Stars and Stripes. 1945. Dec. 182
Stars and Stripes. 1945. Sep. S-186.
Stars and Stripes. Clippings. S-175
Washington Times-Herald. S-163 to S-174
Who Killed Patton? Spotlight, The, 1979

Motion Picture List

Fighting Man, The Story of George Patton. Fox Movietone
  Newsreel. 16mm, 14 min., 1946
George Patton. Biography (ABC). 16mm, 26 min., 1965
George S. Patton, Jr. Big Picture, The. (Army). 16mm, 28 min.,
  1963
Patton and the Third Army. Twentieth Century (CBS). 16mm, 26
  min., 1960